William Shakespeare

ROMEO AND JULIET

Edited by
JOHN F. ANDREWS

Foreword by
JULIE HARRIS

EVERYMAN
J. M. DENT · LONDON
CHARLES E. TUTTLE
VERMONT

Text © 1989 by Doubleday Book & Music Clubs, Inc

Textual revisions, revisions to notes, introduction, note on
text, chronology, and all end matter © J. M. Dent 1993

First published in Everyman by J. M. Dent 1993
Published by permission of GuildAmerica Books, an imprint
of Doubleday Book and Music Clubs, Inc.

Photoset by Deltatype Ltd, Ellesmere Port, Cheshire
Printed in Great Britain by
The Guernsey Press Co. Ltd, Guernsey, C.I.
for
J. M. Dent
Orion Publishing Group
Orion House
5 Upper St Martin's Lane, London WC2H 9EA
and
Charles E. Tuttle Co.
28 South Main Street, Rutland, Vermont
05701 – USA

British Library-Cataloguing-in-Publication-Data is available
upon request

ISBN 0 460 87177 3

CONTENTS

NOTE ON AUTHOR AND EDITOR

William Shakespeare is held to have been born on St George's day, 23 April 1564. The eldest son of a prosperous glove-maker in Stratford-upon-Avon, he was probably educated at the town's grammar school.

Tradition holds that between 1585 and 1592, Shakespeare first became a schoolteacher and then set off for London. By 1595 he was a leading member of the Lord Chamberlain's Men, helping to direct their business affairs, as well as being a playwright and actor. In 1598 he became a part-owner of the company, which was the most distinguished of its age. However, he maintained his contacts with Stratford, and his family seem to have remained there.

From about 1610 he seems to have grown increasingly involved in the town's affairs, suggesting a withdrawal from London. He died on 23 April 1616, in his 53rd year, and was buried at Holy Trinity Church two days later.

John F. Andrews has recently completed a 19-volume edition, *The Guild Shakespeare*, for the Doubleday Book and Music Clubs. He is also the editor of a 3-volume reference set, *William Shakespeare: His World, His Work, His Influence*, and the former editor (1974–85) of the journal *Shakespeare Quarterly*. From 1974–84, he was Director of Academic Programs at the Folger Shakespeare Library in Washington and Chairman of the Folger Institute.

CHRONOLOGY OF SHAKESPEARE'S LIFE

---

1 It is rarely possible to be certain about the dates at which plays of this period were written. For Shakespeare's plays, this chronology follows the dates preferred by Wells and Taylor, the editors of the Oxford Shakespeare. Publication dates are given for poetry and books.

CHRONOLOGY OF HIS TIMES

Year	Literary Context	Historical Events
1565–7	Golding, Ovid's *Metamorphoses*, tr.	Elizabeth I reigning
1574	*A Mirror for Magistrates* (3rd ed.)	
1576	London's first playhouse built	
1578	John Lyly, *Euphues*	
1579	North, Plutarch's *Lives*, tr.	
	Spenser, *Shepherd's Calender*	
1587	Marlowe, *I Tamburlaine*	Mary Queen of Scots executed
	Holinshed's *Chronicles* (2nd ed.)	Defeat of Spanish Armada
1589	Kyd, *Spanish Tragedy*	Civil war in France
	Marlowe, *Jew of Malta*	
1590	Spenser, *Faerie Queene*, Bks I–III	
1591	Sidney, *Astrophel and Stella*	Proclamation against Jesuits
1592	Marlowe, *Dr Faustus* & *Edward II*	Scottish witchcraft trials
		Plague closes theatres from June
1593	Marlowe killed	
1594	Nashe, *Unfortunate Traveller*	Theatres reopen in summer
1594–6		Extreme food shortages
1595	Sidney, *Defense of Poetry*	Riots in London
1596		Calais captured by Spanish
		Cadiz expedition
1597	Bacon's *Essays*	

Year	Age	Life
1597–8		*The Merry Wives of Windsor* & *2 Henry IV*
1598	34	*Much Ado About Nothing*
1598–9		*Henry V*
1599	35	*Julius Caesar.* One of syndicate responsible for building the Globe in Southwark, where the Lord Chamberlain's Men now play
1599–1600		*As You Like It*
1600–1		*Hamlet*
1601	37	*Twelfth Night.* His father is buried in Stratford
1602	38	*Troilus and Cressida.* Invests £320 in land near Stratford[2]
1603	39	*Measure for Measure.* The Lord Chamberlain's Men become the King's Men. They play at court more than all the other companies combined
1603–4		*Othello*
c.1604	40	Shakespeare sues Philip Rogers of Stratford for debt
1604–5		*All's Well That Ends Well*
1605	14	*Timon of Athens.* Invests £440 in Stratford tithes
1605–6		*King Lear*
1606	42	*Macbeth* & *Antony and Cleopatra*
1607	43	*Pericles.* Susanna marries the physician John Hall in Stratford
1608	44	*Coriolanus.* The King's Men lease Blackfriar's, an indoor theatre. His only grandchild is born. His mother dies
1609	45	*The Winter's Tale.* 'Sonnets' and 'A Lover's Complaint' published
1610	46	*Cymbeline*
1611	47	*The Tempest*
1613	49	*Henry VIII.* Buys house in London for £140
1613–14		*The Two Noble Kinsmen*
1616	52	Judith marries Thomas Quiney, a vintner, in Stratford. On 23 April he dies, and is buried two days later
1623	59	Publication of the First Folio. His wife dies in August

2 A schoolmaster would earn around £20 a year at this time.

Year	Literary Context	Historical Events
1598	Marlowe and Chapman, *Hero and Leander* Jonson, *Every Man in his Humour*	Rebellion in Ireland
1599	Children's companies begin playing George Dekker's *Shoemaker's Holiday*	Essex fails in Ireland
1601	'War of the Theatres' Jonson, *Poetaster*	Essex rebels and is executed
1602		Tyrone defeated in Ireland
1603	Florio, Montaigne's *Essays*, tr.	Elizabeth I dies, James I accedes Raleigh found guilty of treason
1604	Marston, *The Malcontent*	Peace with Spain
1605	Bacon's *Advancement of Learning*	Gunpowder plot
1606	Jonson's *Volpone*	
1607	Tourneur, *The Revenger's Tragedy*, published	Virginia colonized Enclosure riots
1609		Oath of allegiance Truce in Netherlands
1610	Jonson, *Alchemist*	
1611	Authorised Version of the Bible Donne, *Anatomy of the World*	
1612	Webster, *White Devil*	Prince Henry dies
1613	Webster, *Duchess of Malfi*	Princess Elizabeth marries
1614	Jonson, *Bartholomew Fair*	
1616	Folio edition of Jonson's plays	

Biographical note, chronology and plot summary compiled by John Lee, University of Bristol, 1993.

FOREWORD BY JULIE HARRIS

I grew up in Michigan, and never saw a production of *Romeo and Juliet* on stage when I was young. I did see the movie starring Norma Shearer and Leslie Howard with John Barrymore as Mercutio. Those actors were not in their teens when they acted in the film, and I supposed that the roles should always be played by grown-ups. Later I saw a production of the play in England; it was in the early 1950s when I first visited London and travelled to Stratford-upon-Avon to see Shakespeare's home and the theatre where his plays are produced. Romeo was Laurence Harvey, and Zena Walker was Juliet. But for me it was still a play about older young people.

When Michael Langham asked me to play Juliet in 1960 at the Stratford Festival Theatre founded by Tyrone Guthrie in Stratford, Canada, I was terrified. Other than playing the Third Witch in the 'Scottish' play (a production of *Macbeth* starring Michael Redgrave and Flora Robson), I had no experience acting in Shakespeare's plays.

Michael Langham came to New York City where I lived, and with great sensitivity and patience he guided me through the play scene by scene. He gave me a copy of the old Italian legend of Romeo and Juliet by Luigi da Porto. The legend found its way to England *and* to Shakespeare, for *Romeo and Juliet* was based on an English reworking of da Porto's story.

No matter how frightened I was of playing Juliet, I was challenged too: by the part, by the miraculous play itself, by the genius of the poetry, and by the uniqueness of the feelings expressed by a girl not yet fourteen – and I was thirty-five years old!

With Michael leading me through the play, my understanding increased and my terrors fell away – well, a little way away. But I did wonder how I could ever play the scene in which Juliet's Nurse comes to Juliet and tells her that her kinsman Tybalt is dead. And killed by Romeo. *And* Romeo banished! Juliet must go from shock at the news of Tybalt's death, to relief that Romeo is alive, to despair at knowing that Romeo has been banished and she has lost him! All these feelings tumble out in a cascade of emotion.

After the period of rehearsals at Stratford I was prepared to play Juliet, and I longed to be able to fill every moment with truth. But I didn't really realize what strength it would take to carry those three hours. Fortunately I had so much help: Kate Reid as the Nurse, Christopher Plummer as Mercutio, Douglas Rain as Tybalt, Eric Christmas as Peter, Bruno Gerussi as my Romeo, Jack Creley as my father, and Leo Ciceri as Paris. We were all helped by a brilliant vocal coach, Iris Warren.

I will always remember that season in Canada: my mountain-climbing expedition, my ascent to Mount Everest. I hardly ever reached the summit, but when I did, Oh, Glory! And even to try was a rich experience.

I had a lovely English friend, Caroline D. Hewitt, who was the headteacher of a girl's school in New York City and a great Shakespearean scholar. When 'Miss Hew' learned I was to play Juliet that season of 1960, she told me about the great Ellen Terry's performance of Juliet long ago. In the final scene, when Juliet wakes in the tomb to find Romeo dead, she holds Romeo for the last time, kisses him, and says 'Thy lips are warm!' Miss Hew told me that when Ellen Terry spoke those words she whispered them; they went right to your heart as you realized that if Juliet had woken a few moments earlier she would have found her Romeo alive. In the old Italian legend, she *does* wake before Romeo dies – but he has already drunk the poison, and so there is between them the terror that Romeo knows that he must die and Juliet must witness her lover's death!

I wondered why Shakespeare didn't use that part of the story in his play. I spoke about it to Michael Langham when we were in rehearsal, and he decided that we would use a moment of that part of the old legend. As Romeo raised the vial of poison to his lips to drink, my fingers trembled and my arms moved ever so slightly. Bruno (Romeo) was looking away from me as he drank and didn't see that I had moved. It became an exciting moment.

Eventually, I did see two *young* actors, Leonard Whiting and Olivia Hussey, portray Romeo and Juliet in Franco Zeffirelli's film. I also saw the glorious work of the great choreographer John Cranko, when he produced *Romeo and Juliet* for the Stuttgart Ballet with Marcia Haydée and Richard Cragun – heartbreakingly beautiful that work is.

So my dream has come true. I have seen the play done perfectly and had the great good fortune myself to work with an inspired director who gave me the opportunity to play one of the greatest parts ever written.

> . . . when he [Romeo] shall die,
> Take him and cut him out in little Stars,
> And he will make the Face of Heav'n so fine
> That all the World will be in love with Night
> And pay no Worship to the garish Sun.

Has language ever been used more beautifully?

JULIE HARRIS has performed such diverse roles as Emily Dickinson in *The Belle of Amherst*, Blanche du Bois in *A Streetcar Named Desire*, and Mary Lincoln in *The Last of Mrs Lincoln*, for which she won the Tony Award in 1972. Her Shakespearean roles include Juliet in *Romeo and Juliet*, Blanche in *King John*, Ophelia in *Hamlet*, and the Third Witch in *Macbeth*.

EDITOR'S INTRODUCTION TO
Romeo and Juliet

Romeo and Juliet was the first drama in English to confer full tragic dignity on the agonies of youthful love. The lyricism that enshrines their death-marked devotion has made the lovers legendary in every language that possesses a literature.

From all indications, Shakespeare's portrayal of 'Juliet and her Romeo' moved audiences in his own theatre. Within a decade the play was being presented not only in London but on the Continent, and it has maintained a prominent position in the repertory from Shakespeare's time to our own.

Not surprisingly, it has produced many offshoots, among them evocative scene-paintings by William Blake and Henry Fuseli, soul-stirring ballets by Peter Ilich Tchaikovsky and Sergei Prokofiev, a romantic opera by Hector Berlioz, a pulsating *West Side Story* by Leonard Bernstein, Arthur Laurents, Jerome Robbins, and Stephen Sondheim, an affecting Sixties film by Franco Zeffirelli, and a sentimental novel (later made into a Seventies film) by Erich Segal.

Today *Romeo and Juliet* is a title that everyone is expected to know, or at least know about. Its central figures are household names. But distorted impressions of them, and of their 'fearful Passage', are so indelibly fixed in our collective consciousness that many of us are astonished to discover how profoundly their 'Woe' can still touch the sympathies of a modern theatregoer.

Background

Romeo and Juliet is generally thought to date from the years 1594–96. Its rich imagery and its formal verse patterns link it to a period when Shakespeare was writing and publishing his major narrative poems – *Venus and Adonis* in 1593, and *The Rape of Lucrece* in 1594 – and when he was probably composing many if not all of the *Sonnets* that first saw print in a 1609 quarto.

By the time he turned to *Romeo and Juliet*, Shakespeare had almost certainly completed four of his ten history plays: *Henry VI*, Parts 1, 2 and 3, and *Richard III*. No doubt he'd also written *King John*, and at least begun work on *Richard II*. Meanwhile he'd finished *Titus Andronicus*, the earliest of the four tragedies he based on the history and politics of ancient Rome. And he'd evidently produced three of his comedies: *The Two Gentlemen of Verona*, *The Comedy of Errors*, and *Love's Labour's Lost*.

In all likelihood he conceived of *Romeo and Juliet* and *A Midsummer Night's Dream* as a paired set. *A Midsummer Night's Dream* echoes Romeo and Juliet in numerous respects, and its treatment of 'Pyramus and Thisby' was almost certainly devised as a burlesque of his own 'Lamentable Tragedie'.

Both plays dramatize the conflict between the demands of Eros and the decrees of insensitive elders. Both compare the onset of love to a flash of lightning in the 'collied Night'. And both draw inspiration from Ovid's *Metamorphoses*, whether in the original Latin or in the 1567 translation by Arthur Golding.

Although Romeo and Juliet were fictional, with their antecedents in ancient folklore, they had been regarded as historical or quasi-historical figures since 1476, when Masuccio Salernitano (in a collection bearing the title *Cinquante Novelle*) referred to them as contemporaries.

Half a century later, in his *Istoria novellamente ritrovata di due nobili amanti* (1530), Luigi da Porto placed the tragedy in Verona during the time of Bartolommeo della Scala (the Prince Escalus of Shakespeare's play). Da Porto identified the unfortunate lovers as members of the quarrelling Montecchi and Capelletti families, and it was he who gave them the names Romeo and Giulietta. Da Porto also created several of the other characters who would eventually find their way into Shakespeare's drama, among them Marcuccio (Mercutio), Theobaldo (Tybalt), Friar Lorenzo (Friar Lawrence), and the Conti de Lodrone (the County Paris).

From da Porto the tale passed through the hands of Matteo Bandello, whose *Novelle* (1554) included both a Nurse and a young man who would evolve into the Benvolio of *Romeo and Juliet*. Pierre Boaistuau translated Bandello's narrative into French and augmented it in a number of details for the *Histoires Tragiques* (1559) of François de Belleforest. From there the story made its way to the two English versions available to Shakespeare: Arthur Brooke's *Tragical History of Romeus and Juliet* (1562) and William Painter's 'Rhomeo and Julietta' in the *Palace of Pleasure* anthology of 1567.

Although Shakespeare derived some of his material from Chaucer's *Troilus and Criseyde* (c. 1385) and from an assortment of lesser sources, his primary debt for the plot of his tragedy was to Arthur Brooke's *Romeus and Juliet*. Like Brooke, Shakespeare treated the lovers compassionately, and like Brooke he prefaced the action with a sonnet. But unlike Brooke, he avoided the kind of overt moralizing that had led the earlier author to describe the protagonists as

> thralling themselves to unhonest desire, neglecting the authority and advice of parents and friends, conferring their principal counsels with dronken gossips, and superstitious friars (the naturally fit instruments of unchastity) attempting all adventures of peril, for th' attaining of their wished lust, using aricular confession (the key of whoredome, and treason) for furtherance of ther purpose, abusing the honourable name of laweful marriage to cloak the shame of stolen contracts, finally, by all means of unhonest life, hasting to most unhappy death.

Shakespeare made scores of alterations to Brooke's narrative. For example, he reduced Juliet's age from sixteen to thirteen. He turned her Nurse into a more endearing, if still somewhat amoral, confidante for the 'young Lady'. He made the Friar a more conscientious, considerate counsellor than his predecessor in

Brooke. He compressed the time-frame of the story from several months to less than a week. He set the play in the hottest part of the summer. He emphasized the omnipresence of the feud by opening the action with a 'Mutiny' that would require the Prince's intervention. He inserted the fiery Tybalt into both the opening scene and the scene in which Romeo falls in love with Juliet. He developed Benvolio into the play's good-will ambassador, a peacemaker who can serve as foil both for the irascible Tybalt and for the volatile Mercutio. He virtually invented Mercutio, taking a character who was little more than a hint in Brooke and transforming him into one of the most vivid personalities in the history of drama. He gave much more prominence to Paris, introducing him to us as a suitor for Capulet's daughter before we even hear Juliet's name, and then keeping him before us in later scenes as an unwitting, ineffectual, and ultimately tragic rival to Romeo.

Comment on the Play

Before we see Romeo and Juliet together for the first time, we learn something about the social contexts that will constrain their freedom of movement. We observe that Romeo belongs to a hot-blooded male world that lives by the *code duello*. In this environment tempers are always near boiling point, and even placid gentlemen like the law-abiding Benvolio must be prepared to defend their 'honour', and by extension their lives, at the slightest provocation.

At the same time we note that Juliet, who is probably to be thought of as a few years younger than Romeo, has led a sheltered life under the tutelage of an earthy Nurse who functions as a buffer between the child she has reared and an older generation of Capulets whose primary objective is to use their daughter to advance the family 'Hopes'.

Fittingly, the words Romeo and Juliet employ at their initial 'Greeting' comprise a love sonnet. By now Romeo has established himself as a devotee of Petrarchan melancholy, and Juliet takes to 'the Book' with an alacrity that shows her to be comparably adept at Cupid's courtesy. After their initial exchange the lovers quickly launch into a second sonnet. But in what will turn out to be a prophetic intrusion, their dialogue is interrupted by the Nurse with a call from Juliet's mother. Meanwhile, in what will prove to be another ominous development, Tybalt has recognized Romeo's voice as that of a Mountague and has vowed revenge for what he regards as a scornful encroachment on Capulet 'Solemnity'.

In this scene Shakespeare plants the seeds of a denouement in which 'violent Delights' will bear fruit in 'violent Ends'. The quoted words are Friar Lawrence's, and he plays a role in the tragedy that is perhaps best described as equivocal. On the one hand, he speaks sincerely and eloquently for a tradition of 'Learning' and 'Philosophy' that is several times invoked to remind the protagonists that they must use their heads if they hope to foster the desires of their hearts. On the other hand, he acts in ways that encourage precisely the behaviour he warns against. In an effort to forge an 'Alliance' that will turn their 'Households' Rancour to pure Love', he agrees to marry the lovers secretly and, when things go awry, to assist them with expedients that will buy time until they can live openly as husband and wife. At the end of the play it can be said of the Friar, as of Romeo in his intervention to stop the duel between Mercutio and Tybalt, that he 'meant all for the best'. But if some of the Friar's wise 'Sentences' inform the way we view the calamities that close the tragedy, many of those same sentences seem applicable to the part 'good Counsel' has played in bringing the sad events to pass.

What most of us recall most vividly from *Romeo and Juliet* is the scene in Capulet's orchard when Romeo looks up to Juliet's window and the two lovers exchange the most poetic vows in the annals of courtship. This tableau is mirrored in a later scene when Romeo descends from their one night together and Juliet has a premonition of him standing in a grave. But it is a more public image between these two scenes that we should register as the fulcrum of the drama. This is the moment when Romeo draws his sword to repay Tybalt for the death of Mercutio.

A few minutes earlier Romeo has turned the other cheek in response to the insults of his new cousin. Now, however, with Mercutio's 'Plague' ringing in his ears, he can hear only the promptings of 'Fire' and 'Fury'. We're surely meant to identify with Romeo's plight. But as soon as he makes his fatal decision and the deed is done, we recognize, with him, that he has reacted impulsively and is now 'Fortune's Fool'.

From this point on, the course of the action is downward. Once Romeo learns that he is banished, he becomes suicidal. Meanwhile, Juliet's parents resolve to cure her supposed grief over the death of Tybalt by wedding her to Paris. Shortly thereafter the Nurse, who has been so comically loquacious and in her own way so supportive of Juliet, displays a stunning incapacity to understand her dilemma. Suddenly Juliet finds herself completely alone, and the fortitude she displays in her own crisis, both now and later in the Capulet tomb, is one of the most gripping displays of character in all of Shakespeare.

In the last words he speaks in the play Capulet refers to Romeo and Juliet as 'Poor Sacrifices of our Enmity'. Juliet's father is surely correct to acknowledge the 'damned Hate' between the feuding families as the underlying cause of 'their Children's End'. But whether he is also correct to portray Verona's pride as 'Sacrifices' in the theological sense is another question. If the Prince's final speech is to be credited, an Elizabethan audience would probably have judged the play's concluding mood as, at best, a 'glooming Peace'.

John F. Andrews, 1993

Background

THE EARLY PRINTINGS OF SHAKESPEARE'S WORKS

Many of us enjoy our first encounter with Shakespeare when we're introduced to *Julius Caesar* or *Macbeth* at school. It may therefore surprise us that neither of these tragedies could ever have been read, let alone studied, by most of the playwright's contemporaries. They began as scripts for performance and, along with seventeen other titles that never saw print during Shakespeare's lifetime, they made their inaugural appearance as 'literary' works seven years after his death, in the 1623 collection we know today as the First Folio.

The Folio contained thirty-six titles in all. Of these, half had been issued previously in the small paperbacks we now refer to as quartos.* Like several of the plays first published in the Folio, the most trustworthy of the quarto printings appear to have been set either from Shakespeare's own manuscripts or from faithful copies of them. It's not impossible that the poet himself prepared some of these works for the press, and it's intriguing to imagine him reviewing proof-pages as the words he'd written for actors to speak and embody were being transposed into the type that readers would filter through their eyes, minds, and imaginations. But, alas, there's no indisputable evidence that Shakespeare had any direct involvement with the publication of these early editions of his plays.

---

* Quartos derived their name from the four-leaf units of which these small books were comprised: large sheets of paper that had been folded twice after printing to yield four leaves, or eight pages. Folios, volumes with twice the page-size of quartos, were put together from two-leaf units: sheets that had been folded once after printing to yield four pages.

What about the scripts that achieved print for the first time in the Folio? Had the dramatist taken any steps to give the permanency of book form to those texts? We don't know. All we can say is that when he fell fatally ill in 1616, Shakespeare was denied any opportunities he might otherwise have taken to ensure that his 'insubstantial Pageants' survived the mortal who was now slipping into the 'dark Backward and Abysm of Time'.

Fortunately, two of the playwright's colleagues felt an obligation, as they put it, 'to procure his Orphans Guardians'. Sometime after his death John Heminge and Henry Condell made arrangements to preserve Shakespeare's theatrical compositions in a manner that would keep them vibrant for all time. They dedicated their endeavour to two noblemen who had helped see England's foremost acting company through some of its most trying vicissitudes. They solicited several poetic tributes for the volume, among them a now-famous eulogy by fellow writer Ben Jonson. They commissioned an engraved portrait of Shakespeare to adorn the frontispiece. And they did their utmost to display the author's dramatic works in a style that would both dignify them and make them accessible to 'the great Variety of Readers'.

As they prepared Shakespeare's plays for the compositors who would set them into stately Folio columns, Heminge and Condell (or editors designated to carry out their wishes) revised and augmented many of the entrances, exits, and other stage directions in the manuscripts. They divided most of the works into acts and scenes.* For a number of plays they appended 'Names of the Actors', or casts of characters. Meanwhile they made every effort to guarantee that the Folio printers had reliable copy-texts for each of the titles: authoritative manuscripts for the plays that had not been published previously, and good quarto printings (annotated in some instances to insert staging details, mark script changes, and add supplementary material) for the ones that had been issued prior to the Folio. For several titles they supplied texts

---

* The early quartos, reflecting the unbroken sequence that probably typified Elizabethan and Jacobean performances of the plays, had been printed without the structural demarcations usual in Renaissance editions of classical drama.

that were substantively different from, if not always demonstrably superior to, the quarto versions that preceded them.

Like even the most accurate of the printings that preceded it, the Folio collection was flawed by minor blemishes. But it more than fulfilled the purpose of its generous-minded compilers: 'to keep the memory of so worthy a Friend and Fellow alive as was our Shakespeare'. In the process it provided a publishing model that remains instructive today.

MODERN EDITIONS OF THE PLAYS AND POEMS

When we compare the First Folio and its predecessors with the usual modern edition of Shakespeare's works, we're more apt to be impressed by the differences than by the similarities. Today's texts of Renaissance drama are normally produced in conformity with twentieth-century standards of punctuation and usage; as a consequence they look more neat, clean, and, to our eyes, 'right' than do the original printings. Thanks to an editorial tradition that extends back to the early eighteenth century, most of the rough spots in the early printings of Shakespeare have long been smoothed away. Textual scholars have ferreted out redundancies and eradicated inconsistencies. They've mended what they've perceived to be errors and oversights in the playscripts, and they've systematically attended to what they've construed as misreadings by the copyists and compositors who transmitted these playscripts to posterity. They've added '[Within]' brackets and other theatrical notations. They've revised stage directions they've judged incomplete or inadequate in the initial printings. They've regularized disparities in the speech headings. They've gone back to the playwright's sources and reinstated the proper forms for many of the character and place names which a presumably hasty or inattentive author got 'wrong' as he conferred identities on his dramatis personae and stage locales. They've replaced obsolete words like *bankrout* with their modern heirs (in this case *bankrupt*). And in a multitude of other ways they've accommodated Shakespeare to the tastes, interests, and expectations of latter-day readers.

The results, on the whole, have been splendid. But interpreting the artistic designs of a complex writer is always problematical, and the task is especially challenging when that writer happens to have been a poet who felt unconstrained by many of the 'rules' that more conventional dramatists respected. The undertaking becomes further complicated when new rules, and new criteria of linguistic and social correctness, are imposed by subsequent generations of artists and critics.

To some degree in his own era, but even more in the neoclassical period (1660–1800) that came in its wake, Shakespeare's most ardent admirers thought it necessary to apologise for what Ben Jonson hinted at in his allusion to the 'small Latin, and less Greek' of an untutored prodigy. To be sure, the 'sweet Swan of Avon' sustained his popularity; in fact his reputation rose so steadily that by the end of the eighteenth century he'd eclipsed Jonson and his other peers and become the object of universal Bardolatry. But in the theatre most of his plays were being adapted in ways that were deemed advisable to tame their supposed wildness and bring them into conformity with the decorum of a society that took pride in its refinement. As one might expect, some of the attitudes that induced theatre proprietors to metamorphose an unpolished poet from the provinces into something closer to an urbane man of letters also influenced Shakespeare's editors. Persuaded that the dramatist's works were marred by crudities that needed expunging, they applied their ministrations to the canon with painstaking diligence.

Twentieth-century editors have moved away from many of the presuppositions that guided a succession of earlier improvers. But a glance at the textual apparatus accompanying virtually any modern publication of the plays and poems will show that emendations and editorial procedures deriving from such forebears as the sets published by Nicholas Rowe (1709), Alexander Pope (1723–25, 1728), Lewis Theobald (1733, 1740, 1757), Thomas Hanmer (1743–45, 1770–71), Samuel Johnson (1765), Edward Capell (1768), George Steevens (1773), and Edmond Malone (1790) retain a strong hold on today's renderings of the playwright's works. The consequence is a 'Shakespeare' who offers the tidiness we've come to expect in our libraries of treasured authors, but not necessarily the playwright a 1599 reader of the Second Quarto of *Romeo and Juliet* would still be able to recognize as a contemporary.

OLD LIGHT ON THE TOPIC

Over the last two decades we've learned from art curators that paintings by Old Masters such as Michelangelo and Rembrandt look a lot brighter when centuries of grime are removed from their surfaces – when hues that had become dulled with soot and other extraneous matter are allowed to radiate again with something approximating their pristine luminosity. We've learned from conductors like Christopher Hogwood that there are aesthetic rewards to be gained from a return to the scorings and instruments with which Renaissance and Baroque musical compositions were first presented. We've learned from twentieth-century experiments in the performance of Shakespeare's plays that an open, multi-level stage, analogous to that on which the scripts were originally enacted, does more justice to their dramaturgical techniques than does a proscenium auditorium devised for works that came later in the development of Western theatre. We've learned from archaeological excavations in London's Bankside area that the foundations of playhouses such as the Rose and the Globe look rather different from what many historians had previously expected. And we're now learning from a close scrutiny of Shakespeare's texts that they too look different, and function differently, when we accept them for what they are and resist the impulse to 'normalize' features that strike us initially as quirky, unkempt, or unsophisticated.

The Aims that Guide the Everyman Text

Like other modern editions of the dramatist's plays and poems, The Everyman Shakespeare owes an incalculable debt to the scholarship that has led to so many excellent renderings of the author's works. But in an attempt to draw fresh inspiration from the spirit that animated those remarkable achievements at the outset, the Everyman edition departs in a number of respects from the usual post-Folio approach to the presentation of Shakespeare's texts.

RESTORING SOME OF THE NUANCES OF RENAISSANCE PUNCTUATION

In its punctuation, Everyman attempts to give equal emphasis to sound and sense. In places where Renaissance practice calls for heavier punctuation than we'd normally employ – to mark the caesural pause in the middle of a line of verse, for instance – Everyman sometimes retains commas that other modern editions omit. Meanwhile, in places where current practice usually calls for the inclusion of commas – after vocatives and interjections such as 'O' and 'alas', say, or before 'Madam' or 'Sir' in phrases such as 'Ay Madam' or 'Yes Sir' – Everyman follows the original printings and omits them.

Occasionally the absence of a comma has a significant bearing on what an expression means, or can mean. At one point in *Othello*, for example, Iago tells the Moor 'Marry patience' (IV.i.90). Inserting a comma after 'Marry', as most of today's editions do, limits Iago's utterance to one that says 'Come now, have patience.' Leaving the clause as it stands in the Folio, the way the Everyman text does, permits Iago's words to have the additional, agonizingly ironic sense 'Be wed to Patience'.

The early texts generally deploy exclamation points quite sparingly, and the Everyman text follows suit. Everyman also follows the early editions, more often than not, when they use question marks in places that seem unusual by current standards: at the ends of what we'd normally treat as exclamations, for example, or at the ends of interrogative clauses in sentences that we'd ordinarily denote as questions in their entirety.

The early texts make no orthographic distinction between simple plurals and either singular or plural possessives, and there are times when the context doesn't indicate whether a word spelled *Sisters*, say, should be rendered *Sisters*, *Sisters'*, or *Sister's* in today's usage. In such situations the Everyman edition prints the word in the form modern usage prescribes for plurals.

REVIVING SOME OF THE FLEXIBILITY OF RENAISSANCE SPELLING

Spelling had not become standardized by Shakespeare's time, and that meant that many words could take a variety of forms. Like James Joyce and some of the other innovative prose and verse stylists of our own century, Shakespeare revelled in the freedom a largely unanchored language provided, and with that in mind Everyman retains original spelling forms (or adaptations of those forms that preserve their key distinctions from modern spellings) whenever there is any reason to suspect that they might have a bearing on how a word was intended to be pronounced or on what it meant, or could have meant, in the playwright's day. When there is any likelihood that multiple forms of the same word could be significant, moreover, the Everyman text mirrors the diversity to be found in the original printings.

In many cases this practice affects the personalities of Shakespeare's characters. One of the heroine's most familiar questions in *Romeo and Juliet* is 'What's in a Name?' For two and a half centuries readers – and as a consequence actors, directors, theatre audiences, and commentators – have been led to believe that Juliet was addressing this query to a Romeo named 'Montague'. In fact 'Montague' *was* the name Shakespeare found in his principle source for the play. For reasons that will become apparent to anyone who examines the tragedy in detail, however, the playwright changed his protagonist's surname to 'Mountague', a word that plays on both 'mount' and 'ague' (fever). Setting aside an editorial practice that began with Lewis Theobald in the middle of the eighteenth century, Everyman resurrects the name the dramatist himself gave Juliet's lover.

Readers of *The Merchant of Venice* in the Everyman set will be amused to learn that the character modern editions usually identify as 'Lancelot' is in reality 'Launcelet', a name that calls attention to the clown's lusty 'little lance'. Like Costard in *Love's Labour's Lost*, another stage bumpkin who was probably played by the actor Will Kemp, Launcelet is an upright 'Member of the Commonwealth'; we eventually learn that he's left a pliant wench 'with Child'.

Readers of *Hamlet* will find that 'Fortinbras' (as the name of the Prince's Norwegian opposite is rendered in the First Folio and in most modern editions) appears in the earlier, authoritative 1604 Second Quarto of the play as 'Fortinbrasse'. In the opening scene of that text a surname that meant 'strong in arms' in French is introduced to the accompaniment of puns on *brazen*, in the phrase 'brazon Cannon', and on *metal*, in the phrase 'unimprooued mettle'. In the same play readers of the Everyman text will encounter 'Ostricke', the ostrich-like courtier who invites the Prince of Denmark to participate in the fateful fencing match that draws *Hamlet* to a close. Only in its final entrance direction for the obsequious fop does the Second Quarto call this character 'Osric', the name he bears in all the Folio text's references to him and in most modern editions of Shakespeare's most popular tragedy.

Readers of the Everyman *Macbeth* will discover that the fabled 'Weird Sisters' appear only as the 'weyward' or 'weyard' Sisters. Shakespeare and his contemporaries knew that in his *Chronicles of England, Scotland, and Ireland* Raphael Holinshed had used the term 'weird sisters' to describe the witches who accost Macbeth and Banquo on the heath; but because he wished to play on *wayward*, the playwright changed their name to *weyward*. Like Samuel Johnson, who thought punning vulgar and lamented Shakespeare's proclivity to seduction by this 'fatal Cleopatra', Lewis Theobald saw no reason to retain the playwright's weyward spelling of the witches' name. He thus restored the 'correct' form from Holinshed, and editors ever since have generally done likewise.

In many instances Renaissance English had a single spelling for what we now define as two separate words. For example, *humane* combined the senses of 'human' and 'humane' in modern English. In the First Folio printing of *Macbeth* the protagonist's wife expresses a concern that her husband is 'too full o'th' Milke of humane kindnesse.' As she phrases it, *humane kindnesse* can mean several things, among them 'humankind-ness', 'human kindness', and 'humane kindness'. It is thus a reminder that to be true to his or her own 'kind' a human being must be 'kind' in the sense we now attach to 'humane'. To disregard this logic, as the protagonist and his wife will soon prove, is to disregard a principle as basic to the cosmos as the laws of gravity.

In a way that parallels *humane*, *bad* could mean either 'bad' or 'bade', *borne* either 'born' or 'borne', *ere* either 'ere' (before) or 'e'er' (ever), *least* either 'least' or 'lest', *lye* either 'lie' or 'lye', *nere* either 'ne'er' or 'near' (though the usual spellings for the latter were *neare* or *neere*), *powre* either 'pour' or 'power', *then* either 'than' or 'then', and *tide* either 'tide' or 'tied'.

There were a number of word-forms that functioned in Renaissance English as interchangeable doublets. *Travail* could mean 'travel', for example, and *travel* could mean 'travail'. By the same token, *deer* could mean *dear* and vice versa, *dew* could mean *due*, *hart* could mean *heart*, and (as we've already noted) *mettle* could mean *metal*.

A particularly interesting instance of the equivocal or double meanings some word-forms had in Shakespeare's time is *loose*, which can often become either 'loose' or 'lose' when we render it in modern English. In *The Comedy of Errors* when Antipholus of Syracuse compares himself to 'a Drop / Of Water that in the Ocean seeks another Drop' and then says he will 'loose' himself in quest of his long-lost twin, he means both (a) that he will release himself into a vast unknown, and (b) that he will lose his own identity, if necessary, to be reunited with the brother for whom he searches. On the other hand, in *Hamlet* when Polonius says he'll 'loose' his daughter to the Prince, he little suspects that by so doing he will also lose his daughter.

In some cases the playwright employs word-forms that can be translated into words we wouldn't think of as related today: *sowre*, for instance, which can mean 'sour', 'sower', or 'sore', depending on the context. In other cases he uses forms that do have modern counterparts, but not counterparts with the same potential for multiple connotation. For example, *onely* usually means 'only' in the modern sense; but occasionally Shakespeare gives it a figurative, adverbial twist that would require a nonce word such as 'one-ly' to replicate in current English.

In a few cases Shakespeare employs word-forms that have only seeming equivalents in modern usage. For example, *abhominable*, which meant 'inhuman' (derived, however incorrectly, from *ab*, 'away from', and *homine*, 'man') to the poet and his contemporaries, is not the same word as our *abominable* (ill-omened, abhorrent). In his advice to the visiting players Hamlet complains about incompetent actors who imitate 'Humanity so abhominably' as to make the characters they depict seem unrecognizable as men. Modern readers who don't realize the distinction between Shakespeare's word and our own, and who see *abominable* on the page before them, don't register the full import of the Prince's satire.

Modern English treats as single words a number of word-forms that were normally spelled as two words in Shakespeare's time. What we render as *myself*, for example, and use primarily as a reflexive or intensifying pronoun, is almost invariably spelled *my self* in Shakespeare's works; so also with *her self*, *thy self*, *your self*, and *it self* (where *it* functions as *its* does today). Often there is no discernible difference between Shakespeare's usage and our own. At other times there is, however, as we are reminded when we come across a phrase such as 'our innocent self' in *Macbeth* and think how strained it would sound in modern parlance, or as we observe when we note how naturally the self is objectified in the balanced clauses of the Balcony Scene in *Romeo and Juliet*:

> Romeo, doffe thy name,
> And for thy name, which is no part of thee
> Take all my selfe.

Yet another difference between Renaissance orthography and our own can be exemplified with words such as *today*, *tonight*, and *tomorrow*, which (unlike *yesterday*) were treated as two words in Shakespeare's time. In *Macbeth* when the Folio prints 'Duncan comes here to Night', the unattached *to* can function either as a preposition (with *Night* as its object, or in this case its destination) or as the first part of an infinitive (with *Night* operating figuratively as a verb). Consider the ambiguity a Renaissance reader would have detected in the original publication of one of the most celebrated soliloquies in all of Shakespeare:

> To morrow, and to morrow, and to morrow,
> Creeps in this petty pace from day to day,
> To the last Syllable of Recorded time:
> And all our yesterdayes, have lighted Fooles
> The way to dusty death.

Here, by implication, the route 'to morrow' is identical with 'the way to dusty death', a relationship we miss if we don't know that for Macbeth, and for the audiences who first heard these lines spoken, *to morrow* was not a single word but a potentially equivocal two-word phrase.

RECAPTURING THE ABILITY TO HEAR WITH OUR EYES

When we fail to recall that Shakespeare's scripts were designed initially to provide words for people to hear in the theatre, we sometimes overlook a fact that is fundamental to the artistic structure of a work like *Macbeth*: that the messages a sequence of sounds convey through the ear are, if anything, even more significant than the messages a sequence of letters, punctuation marks, and white spaces on a printed page transmit through the eye. A telling illustration of this point, and of the potential for ambiguous or multiple implication in any Shakespearean script, may be found in the dethronement scene of *Richard II*. When Henry Bullingbrook asks the King if he is ready to resign his crown, Richard replies 'I, no no I; for I must nothing be.' Here the punctuation in the 1608 Fourth Quarto (the earliest text to print this richly complex passage) permits each *I* to signify either 'ay' or 'I' (*I* being the usual spelling for 'ay' in Shakespeare's time).

Understanding *I* to mean 'I' permits additional play on *no*, which can be heard (at least in its first occurrence) as 'know'. Meanwhile the second and third soundings of *I*, if not the first, can also be heard as 'eye'. In the context in which this line occurs, that sense echoes a thematically pertinent passage from Matthew 18:9: 'if thine eye offend thee, pluck it out'.

But these are not all the implications *I* can have here. It can also represent the Roman numeral for '1', which will soon be reduced, as Richard notes, to 'nothing' (o), along with the speaker's title, his worldly possessions, his manhood, and eventually his life. In Shakespeare's time, to become 'nothing' was, *inter alia*, to be emasculated, to be made a 'weaker vessel' (1 Peter 3:7) with 'no thing'. As the Fool in *King Lear* reminds another monarch who has abdicated his throne, a man in want of an 'I' is impotent, 'an O without a Figure' (I.iv.207). In addition to its other dimensions, then, Richard's reply is a statement that can be formulated mathematically, and in symbols that anticipate the binary system behind today's computer technology: '1, 0, 0, 1, for 1 must 0 be.'

Modern editions usually render Richard's line 'Ay, no; no, ay; for I must nothing be'. Presenting the line in that fashion makes good sense of what Richard is saying. But as we've seen, it doesn't make total sense of it, and it doesn't call attention to Richard's paradoxes in the same way that hearing or seeing three undifferentiated *I*'s is likely to have done for Shakespeare's contemporaries. Their culture was more attuned than ours is to the oral and aural dimensions of language, and if we want to appreciate the special qualities of their dramatic art we need to train ourselves to 'hear' the word-forms we see on the page. We must learn to recognize that for many of what we tend to think of as fixed linkages between sound and meaning (the vowel 'I', say, and the word 'eye'), there were alternative linkages (such as the vowel 'I' and the words 'I' and 'Ay') that could be just as pertinent to what the playwright was communicating through the ears of his theatre patrons at a given moment. As the word *audience* itself may help us to remember, people in Shakespeare's time normally spoke of 'hearing' rather than 'seeing' a play.

In its text of *Richard II*, the Everyman edition reproduces the title character's line as it appears in the early printings of the tragedy. Ideally the orthographic oddity of the repeated *I*'s will encourage today's readers to ponder Richard's utterance, and the play it epitomizes, as a characteristically Shakespearean enigma.

OTHER ASPECTS OF THE EVERYMAN TEXT

Now for a few words about other features of the Everyman text.

One of the first things readers will notice about this edition is its bountiful use of capitalized words. In this practice as in others, the Everyman exemplar is the First Folio, and especially the works in the Folio sections billed as 'Histories' and 'Tragedies'.* Everyman makes no attempt to adhere to the Folio printings with literal exactitude. In some instances the Folio capitalizes words that the Everyman text of the same passage lowercases; in other instances Everyman capitalizes words not uppercased in the Folio. The objective is merely to suggest something of the flavour, and what appears to have been the rationale, of Renaissance capitalization, in the hope that today's audiences will be made continually aware that the works they're contemplating derive from an earlier epoch.

Readers will also notice that instead of cluttering the text with stage directions such as '[Aside]' or '[To Rosse]', the Everyman text employs unobtrusive dashes to indicate shifts in mode of address. In an effort to keep the page relatively clear of words not supplied by the original printings, Everyman also exercises restraint in its addition of editor-generated stage directions. Where the dialogue makes it obvious that a significant action occurs, the Everyman text inserts a square-bracketed phrase such as '[Fleance escapes]'. Where what the dialogue implies is subject

---

* The quarto printings employ far fewer capital letters than does the Folio. Capitalization seems to have been regarded as a means of recognizing the status ascribed to certain words (*Noble*, for example, is almost always capitalized), titles (not only King, Queen, Duke, and Duchess, but Sir and Madam), genres (tragedies were regarded as more 'serious' than comedies in more than one sense), and forms of publication (quartos, being associated with ephemera such as 'plays', were not thought to be as 'grave' as the folios that bestowed immortality on 'works', writings that, in the words of Ben Jonson's eulogy to Shakespeare, were 'not of an age, but for all time').

to differing interpretations, however, the Everyman text provides a facing-page note to discuss the most plausible inferences.

Like other modern editions, the Everyman text combines into 'shared' verse lines (lines divided among two or more speakers) many of the part-lines to be found in the early publications of the plays. One exception to the usual modern procedure is that Everyman indents some lines that are not components of shared verses. At times, for example, the opening line of a scene stops short of the metrical norm, a pentameter (five-foot) or hexameter (six-foot) line comprised predominantly of iambic units (unstressed syllables followed by stressed ones). In such cases Everyman uses indentation as a reminder that scenes can begin as well as end in mid-line (an extension of the ancient convention that an epic commences *in media res*, 'in the midst of the action'). Everyman also uses indentation to reflect what appear to be pauses in the dialogue, either to allow other activity to transpire (as happens in *Macbeth*, II.iii.87, when a brief line 'What's the Business?' follows a Folio stage direction that reads 'Bell rings. Enter Lady') or to permit a character to hesitate for a moment of reflection (as happens a few seconds later in the same scene when Macduff responds to a demand to 'Speak, speak' with the reply 'O gentle Lady, / 'Tis not for you to hear what I can speak').

Everyman preserves many of the anomalies in the early texts. Among other things, this practice pertains to the way characters are depicted. In *A Midsummer Night's Dream*, for example, the ruler of Athens is usually identified in speech headings and stage directions as 'Theseus', but sometimes he is referred to by his title as 'Duke'. In the same play Oberon's merry sprite goes by two different names: 'Puck' and 'Robin Goodfellow'.

Readers of the Everyman edition will sometimes discover that characters they've known, or known about, for years don't appear in the original printings. When they open the pages of the Everyman *Macbeth*, for example, they'll learn that Shakespeare's audiences were unaware of any woman with the title 'Lady Macbeth'. In the only authoritative text we have of the Scottish tragedy, the protagonist's spouse goes by such names as 'Macbeth's Lady', 'Macbeth's Wife', or simply 'Lady', but at no time is she listed or mentioned as 'Lady Macbeth'. The same is true of the character usually designated 'Lady Capulet' in modern editions of *Romeo and Juliet*. 'Capulet's Wife' makes appearances as 'Mother', 'Old Lady', 'Lady', or simply 'Wife'; but she's never termed 'Lady Capulet', and her husband never treats her with the dignity such a title would connote.

Rather than 'correct' the grammar in Shakespeare's works to eliminate what modern usage would categorize as solecisms (as when Mercutio says 'my Wits faints' in *Romeo and Juliet*), the Everyman text leaves it intact. Among other things, this principle applies to instances in which archaic forms preserve idioms that differ slightly from related modern expressions (as in the clause 'you are too blame', where 'too' frequently functions as an adverb and 'blame' is used, not as a verb, but as an adjective roughly equivalent to 'blameworthy').

Finally, and most importantly, the Everyman edition leaves unchanged any reading in the original text that is not manifestly erroneous. Unlike other modern renderings of Shakespeare's works, Everyman substitutes emendations only when obvious problems can be dealt with by obvious solutions.

The Everyman *Text of* Romeo and Juliet

Romeo and Juliet was first published in 1597 in an uneven text that scholars now believe was compiled mostly if not entirely from memory.* The First Quarto of Shakespeare's romantic drama was almost certainly an unauthorized publication, and even its least imperfect scenes are riddled with error. Notwithstanding its deficiencies, however, Q1 is by no means worthless. At times it

---

* Just how pirated texts were assembled remains uncertain. One possibility is that they were produced by 'reporters' who'd taken notes as they attended performances. Another possibility, generally regarded today as more likely for most of the 'bad quartos', is that they were pieced together by actors, or former actors, who could reconstruct their own parts reasonably well but were forced to paraphrase lines they'd never had cause to master. A third possibility is that, in some cases at least, a combination of actors and reporters did the compiling.

renders the action with what looks like a fair degree of accuracy, and its unusually abundant stage directions provide indispensable evidence of what theatregoers must have seen and heard during the early years of the play's rich production history.

Happily, the First Quarto is not our only surviving witness to *Romeo and Juliet*. Within two years a Second Quarto (1599) was advertised as a 'Newly corrected, augmented, and amended' printing of this 'Most Excellent and Lamentable Tragedie'. Q2 appears to have been set either from the author's own manuscript or from a scribal copy thereof. It preserves many of the loose ends to be expected in a dramatist's unpolished 'foul papers', and it is therefore of special interest for what it discloses of Shakespeare's creative process. The only problem is that the Q2 compositors evidently found some of the playtext difficult to decipher. They seem to have misconstrued a number of words and phrases, and in a number of passages they resorted to the corrupt version of the tragedy that had been published in the First Quarto.

In due course three other quartos emerged: Q3 in 1609, Q4 around 1622, and Q5 in 1637. Each new printing derived largely from the immediately preceding text, but Q3 and Q4 also drew heavily upon Q1 to correct what their editors perceived as flaws in the Q2 printing.

From all indications the 1623 First Folio text (F1) was set from a lightly annotated copy of the 1609 Third Quarto. The Folio printers introduced a handful of new corrections and added a few stage directions. But they did little else, and they didn't divide the play into the acts and scenes to be found in many other works in the volume.

Like other modern editions, The Everyman Shakespeare relies primarily upon the Second Quarto for the text of *Romeo and Juliet*. Because Q2 is problematic in a number of passages, however, the Everyman edition also goes to the other early printings for many of its readings. With the exception of these alterations, which are found in most of today's texts, Everyman declines almost all of the emendations proposed by editors subsequent to the seventeenth century.

In three situations Everyman departs from what has become the conventional way of segmenting *Romeo and Juliet* scenically. What Everyman prints as Act I, scene iv, for example, is usually divided into two scenes, I.iv and I.v. Similarly, what Everyman prints as Act II, scene i is usually divided into two scenes, II.i and II.ii.* And what Everyman prints as Act IV, scene iii is usually divided into three scenes, IV.iii, IV.iv, and IV.v. In each of these situations the early texts indicate that the action is continuous and that the stage is never completely cleared of performers.

In a way that parallels the practice of most twentieth-century editions, the Everyman text incorporates three and a half lines that appear only in the First Quarto: I.iv.7–8 ('Nor . . . Entrance') and II.i.83 ('nor . . . Part'). The Everyman text also inserts many of Q1's stage directions; in places, moreover, it adapts Q2 stage directions to include relevant material from the corresponding stage directions in Q1. More often than is usual in modern editions, however, the Everyman text retains the stage directions, and the frequently inconsistent speech headings, of the Second Quarto.

In the instances that follow, Everyman adopts Q1, Q3, Q4, Q5, F1, or F2 (1632 Second Folio) readings in preference to those to be found in Q2. For each item the first entry, in boldface type, is the Everyman reading, followed by a parenthesis indicating the earliest edition to print the word or phrase as it appears in the Everyman text; the second entry is the rejected Q2 reading.

I.i.	28	**In Sense** (Q1) sense
	95	**Verona's** (Q3) Nerona's
	124	**Sycamour** (Q1) syramour
	150	**his** (Q3) is
	180	**create** (Q1) created
	183	**seeming** (Q1 as adapted by Q4) seeing
	192	**to too** (Q3) too too

---

* The scenes marked II.ii through II.v in the Everyman *Romeo and Juliet* thus correspond to the scenes marked II.iii through II.vi in most of the editions now on the market.

	205	**Bid a** (Q1) A **make** (Q1) makes
I.ii.	47	**one** (Q1) on
I.iii.	17	**shall** (Q1) stal
	99	**make it fly** (Q1) make fly
I.iv.	39	**done** (Q1) dum
	42	**your** (F1) you
	57	**Atomi** (Q1) ottamie
	63	**Film** (F2; Q1 prints *filmes*) Philome
	66	**Maid** (Q1) man
	74	**on** (Q1) one
	90	**Elflocks** (Q1) Elklocks
	192	**to** (Q1) too (so also in I.iv.193, 197, IV.i.100)
	210	**ready** (Q1) did ready
II.Chorus.	4	**match'd** (Q3) match
II.i.	6	S.H. MERCUTIO (Q1; in Q2 Mercutio is not designated as the speaker until the beginning of line 7)
	9	**one** (Q1) on
	10	**Dove** (Q1) day
	12	**Heir** (Q1) her
	58	**do** (Q1) to
	87	**ware** (Q1) wene
	108	**Kinsmen** (Q1) kismen (so also in II.iii.7, III.i.152, 155, 183)
	122	**prompt** (Q1) promp
	125	**wash'd** (Q1) washeth
	152	**circled** (Q1) circle
	204	**than mine** (Q4; spelled *then*) than
II.iii.	20	S.H. BENVOLIO (Q1) ROMEO
	32	**Fantasticoes** (Q1) phantacies
	44	**Petrarch** (Q1) Potrach
	204	**hear** (F1) here
II.iv.	11	**three** (Q3) there
II.v.	27	**Music's** (Q4) music

III.i	2	**Capels are** (Q1) Capels
	72	**thou** (Q1) thon
	106	**'Zounds** (Q5) Sounds
	173	**agile** (Q1) aged
	191	S.H. MOUNTAGUE (Q4) CAPULET
	195	**Hate's** (Q1) hearts
	199	**I** (Q1) It

III.ii.	47	**Death-darting** (Q3) death arting
	51	**determine of** (F1) determine
	60	**Bier** (Q4) beare
	79	**dammed** (Q4) dimme

III.iii.	61	**Men** (Q1) man
	110	**denote** (Q1) deuote
	142	**misbehav'd** (Q1) mishaved

| III.iv. | 13 | **be** (Q1) me |
| | 23 | **We'll** (Q1) Well |

III.v.	13	**exhales** (Q1) exhale
	54	S.H. JULIET (Q1) ROMEO
	83	**pardon** (Q3) padon
	107	**I beseech** (Q4) beseech
	140	**gives** (Q3) give
	172	**Gossips** (Q1) goships
	173	S.H. CAPULET (Q1; like Q1, Q2 prints *Father* here, but does not set it in the italic type customary for speech headings)
	174	NURSE (Q4; set as part of Capulet's speech in Q2)
	233)	**absolv'd** (Q1) obsolv'd

IV.i.	7	**talk'd** (Q1) talk
	78	**off** (Q1) of
	85	**in his Shroud** (Q4) in his
	98	**Breath** (Q1) breast
	110	**In** (Q3) Is
	117	**Waking** (Q3) walking

IV.iii.	49	**wake** (Q4) walk
	79	**Thou** (Q1) Twou
	137	**behold** (Q3) bedold
	186	**by my** (Q1) my my

V.i.	24 e'en (Q1: *even*) in

V.iii.	41 **Friendship** (Q3) friendshid
	189 **too** (F1) too too
	201 **slaughter'd** (Q3) slaughter
	211 **early** (Q1) earling
	301 **raise** (Q4) raie

In III.ii.76 the Everyman text endorses Lewis Theobald's decision to delete *Ravenous* from the Q2 line 'Ravenous Dove-feather'd Raven, wolvish, ravening Lamb'. *Ravenous* would break the rhetorical pattern that organizes lines 75–78, and it has every appearance of being either an authorial first thought or an erroneous insertion that Shakespeare himself would have marked for excision.

Similar reasoning has led most editors to make several other deletions. In those cases, however, it is less clear that what can be viewed as inartistic redundancies are in fact passages the playwright would have jettisoned. For that reason the Everyman text prints them. The passages in question are as follows:

II.ii.	230–34 **The . . . Wheels.** The few editors who keep these lines omit the first four lines of the following scene; they also tend to emend *flected* to *flecked* and *Friar's* to *sire's* in lines 232 and 234. Everyman retains the four lines as they appear in the Second Quarto; Everyman also preserves II.iii.1–4 as those lines appear in Q2.

III.i.	153 **O Cousin, Husband** Most editors omit *Cousin* as a word that makes this line two syllables longer than the pentameter norm. But Shakespeare may well have written the line with precisely that effect in mind: to stress the excess occasioned by the 'spill'd' grief of Capulet's Wife.

III.v.	177–78 **God's . . . Play.** Modern editors usually delete 'Hour, Tide, Time' and combine these two lines into one metrically regular pentameter. Again, the inelegant repetitiveness of the phrasing in Q2 would seem to fit

both the speaking character (an enraged Capulet) and a dramatic context in which a despotic patriarch's best-laid plans are being frustrated by his recalitrant daughter.

IV.i.   111 **Be . . . Grave** Most editors delete this line. In line 112 the Friar reiterates the information conveyed here, but again that may have been in keeping with the playwright's design.

V.iii.   102 **Why . . . believe** Modern editors normally drop 'I will believe' from this line to yield a metrically regular pentameter. But can we be sure that Shakespeare didn't intend to have Romeo pause and revise his sentence in mid-phrase, and in a line whose ungainliness mirrors the protagonist's own uncertainty?

V.iii.   108–9 **Come . . . in.** Today's editors usually delete this sentence, along with the redundant passage that follows it in Q2 and in all the other early texts: 'O true Appothocarie! / Thy drugs are quicke. Thus with a kisse I die. Depart again' (compare lines 121–22, and the first two words of line 108). It may be that Shakespeare would have scrubbed out the line the Everyman text retains here; since we cannot be certain of the playwright's intentions, however, it would seem best to preserve any material that is not duplicated elsewhere in Romeo's soliloquy.

As noted above, Everyman retains numerous Q2 readings that other twentieth-century editions alter. In the list below, the Everyman reading appears first and is set in boldface type; the reading to be found in many, if not most, modern editions follows in regular type.

Prologue.   14 **heare** here

I.i.   5 **Choler** collar
27 **I** Ay (so also in I.ii.60, 63; I.iii.44, 48, 51, 57; I.iv.126, 217, 235; II.i.132; II.iii.92, 224; III.ii.45, 48–50; III.v.140; IV.iii.186)

35 **comes of** comes two of
68 **Hartless** heartless
79 **Crowch** crutch
119 **to day** today (compare *to day*, *to morrow*, and *to night* forms in I.iv.50, II.i.129, 159, 168, 186, 195, 209; II.ii.42, 64; II.iii.2; II.iv.67; III.iv.5, 10, 11, 29; IV.i.90, 91; IV.ii.24, 35, 42, 46; IV.iii.2, 8, 22, 65; V.i.26, 34; V.iii.123, 212)
156 **same** sun
187 **Hart** heart
190 **prest** press'd
195 **Loving** lovers'
221 **make** makes

I.ii.
29 **Fennel** female
32 **one more** on more
38–39 **written.' Here it** written here. It
76 **Whither to** Whither? To

I.iii.
3 **bad** bade
22 **she marry; she;** marry,
66–67 **Hour** honour
71 **Mothers by** mothers. By
Count. count,

I.iv.
31 **cote** quote
45 **Lights, Lights** like lights *or* light lights
47 **fine** five
72 **On** O'er
strait straight (so also in I.iv.73–74)
76 **Breath** breaths
81 **he dreams** dreams he
112 **Stirrage** steerage
113 **Suit** sail
133 **about** a bout
179 **it.** it?
257 **tis** this

II.i.
10 **pronaunt** pronounce
11 **Goship** gossip

	13	**Abraham: Cupid** Abraham Cupid
		true trim
	34	**Medler** medlar
	38	**open Et-cetera** open-arse and *or* open-arse or
	62	**Eye** eyes
	124	**Pylat** pilot
	131	**Complement** compliment (so also in II.iii.22)
	143	**Coying** cunning
	162	**Sweet goodnight** sweet, good night
	188	**Right** rite (so also in III.ii.8, V.iii.20)
	205	**Romeo** Romeo's name
	209	**Neece** niesse *or* nyas
	232	**flected** fleckled
	234	**Friar's** sire's
II.ii.	2	**Checking** Check'ring
	4	**burning** fiery
	22	**sometime** sometime's
	25	**this being smelt** this, being smelt,
	93	**Hast** haste (so also in III.ii.201)
II.iii.	31	**antique** antic
	58	**Curtesy** courtesy
	90	**Cheverell** cheverel
	100	**Bable** bauble
	145	**hore** hoar (so also with *hores* in line 147)
	218	**A Mocker** Ah, mocker
		Dog dog's
II.iv.	16	**fain** feign
	24	**sower** sour (so also in III.ii.116)
	51	**a' my Back** ah, my Back
	69	**high** hie
II.v.	18	**Gossamours** gossamors
III.i.	77	**Stucatho** stoccato
	115	**soundly; to your Houses.** soundly too. Your houses!
	129	**He gan** He gone *or* Again
	131	**Fire end** fire-ey'd (compare *end* in *Macbeth*, III.iii.7)
III.ii.	9	**And by** By
	21	**I** he
	37	**A** Ah

76 **pray** pay

V.iii.   3 **young** yew (so also in V.iii.139)
         8 **some thing** something
        68 **Conjurations** conjuration
       107 **Pallat** palace *or* pallet
       192 **shrike** shriek'd
       196 **your** our
       234 **that's** that

ROMEO AND JULIET

NAMES OF THE ACTORS

ESCALUS, Prince of Verona
PARIS, a young Count, kinsman to the Prince

MOUNTAGUE, Head of the Veronese family feuding with the Capulets
MOUNTAGUE'S WIFE
ROMEO, Son of the Mountagues
BENVOLIO, Nephew to Mountague and Friend to Romeo
MERCUTIO, Kinsman to the Prince and Friend to Romeo

CAPULET, Head of the Veronese family feuding with the Mountagues
CAPULET'S WIFE
JULIET, Daughter of the Capulets
TYBALT, Nephew to Capulet's Wife
PETRUCHIO, Friend to Tybalt
COUSIN CAPULET, an old Gentleman
NURSE to Juliet

FRIAR LAWRENCE, Franciscan Confessor to Romeo and Juliet
FRIAR JOHN, another Franciscan Friar

APOTHECARY, a Druggist of Mantua
PAGE to Paris
ABRAM, Servant to Mountague
BALTHASAR, Servant to Romeo
PETER, a Capulet Servant attending on the Nurse

CLOWN
SAMPSON
GREGORY } Servingmen of the Capulet household
ANTHONY
POTPAN

MUSICIANS { Simon Catling
Hugh Rebick
James Soundpost

CHORUS

MEMBERS OF THE WATCH, CITIZENS OF VERONA, MASKERS,
    PAGES, SERVANTS

4

S.D. **Prologue** Fittingly, in a play whose atmosphere stems from the world of the love sonnet popularized by the fourteenth-century Italian poet Petrarch, this and the Chorus' other speech at the beginning of Act II are both sonnets. The verse form, however, is Shakespearean rather than Petrarchan, with three quatrains (rhyming abab cdcd efef) and a concluding couplet (gg) rather than the octave (rhyming abbaabba) and sestet (rhyming cdecde) used by Petrarch.

1 **Dignity** social standing, rank.

3 **Mutiny** insurrection against law and authority. We're given no clue about the reason for the long-standing enmity between the families.

4 **Civil Blood . . . Civil Hands** The primary meaning of *Civil* in both phrases is 'of the city' (that is, pertaining to citizen blood and citizen hands); but there is also the suggestion that hands that should be 'civil' (well-mannered, civilized) have instead become both bloody and morally stained ('unclean').

6 **Star-cross'd** thwarted by influences from 'the Stars' (a term loosely applied to both the stars and the planets, and alluding to a complex system of astrology familiar to any well-educated Elizabethan). Compare line 9, as well as I.iv.106–11, V.i.24, V.iii.111–14.

9 **Death-mark'd** both (a) designated for death (compare Exodus 11:5–7, 12:12–13), and (b) destined for death as 'an ever-fixed Mark' (Sonnet 116, line 5) or 'End' (line 11). Compare *Othello*, V.ii.261–62.

12 **Two-Hours' Traffic** Compare lines 9–13 of the Prologue to *Henry VIII*.

14 **What . . . mend** What you miss here, our dramatic efforts will try to repair (make clear to you). The Second Quarto's *heare* can mean either (a) hearing, or (b) here.

PROLOGUE

[*Enter Chorus.*]

CHORUS   Two Households both alike in Dignity,
In fair Verona, where we lay our Scene,
From auncient Grudge break to new Mutiny,
Where Civil Blood makes Civil Hands unclean;
From forth the fatal Loins of these two Foes   5
A pair of Star-cross'd Lovers take their Life,
Whose misadventur'd piteous Overthrows
Doth with their Death bury their Parents' Strife.
The fearful Passage of their Death-mark'd Love,
And the Continuance of their Parents' Rage,   10
Which but their Children's End nought could
    remove,
Is now the Two Hours' Traffic of our Stage,
The which, if you with patient Ears attend,
What heare shall miss, our Toil shall strive to
    mend.   [*Exit.*]

I.i The setting for the opening scene is a street in Verona.

1 **carry Coals** hold in our anger, submit to insults.

2 **Colliers** coal workers or coal dealers, proverbially grimy.

3 **and** if. This construction is quite frequent among lower-class characters in Shakespeare's plays.
   Choler anger.

4-5 **out of Choler** both (a) out of a situation where a display of choler would put your neck at risk, and (b) out of collar (the hangman's noose awaiting those who disturb the peace by starting duels). The First Quarto and First Folio texts both print *Collar* here.

5 **Ay** yes. For this sense (as opposed to the ejaculatory sigh, as in Romeo's 'Ay me' in line 165) the normal spelling in the early texts is *I*. Sometimes the context allows *I* to mean either 'I' or 'yes' (or both), and when there is any possibility of ambiguity the Everyman text retains the *I* spelling of the original edition, as in line 27.

6 **mov'd** prompted to angry retaliation.

9 **stir** be moved from one's 'fixed Mark' (see the note to line 9), turn coward and 'carry Coals' away. But *stir* can also refer to another way for a man 'to stand', and the following lines play on that 'Sense' (lines 28-29).

12 **move me to stand** Sampson rejects Gregory's assumption that 'to move' and 'to stand' are necessarily opposites. When he is 'mov'd' (aroused) to anger, he stands up to the Mountague men rather than running; meanwhile, he stands up *for* the Mountague maids, using his male 'weapon' to 'thrust' them (lines 19-20).

13 **take the Wall** In Shakespeare's time, when sewage ditches flowed down the middle of many streets, the pathway close to the wall was usually the cleanest place to walk; it was thus considered a sign of superiority, and frequently of social rank (or effrontery against social equals or superiors), to 'take the Wall'.

15 **shews** shows. The early texts employ both spellings for this word (compare *shrew*, which is often spelled *shrow*). Because there is sometimes play on *eschew*, the Everyman text retains the *-ew* forms that occur in the original printings.

16 **goes to the Wall** backs up to the wall, cowers.

ACT I

Scene 1

Enter Sampson and Gregory, with Swords and Bucklers, of the House of Capulet.

SAMPSON   Gregory, on my Word, we'll not carry Coals.

GREGORY   No, for then we should be Colliers.

SAMPSON   I mean, and we be in Choler we'll draw.

GREGORY   Ay, while you live, draw your Neck out of Choler.   5

SAMPSON   I strike quickly being mov'd.

GREGORY   But thou art not quickly mov'd to strike.

SAMPSON   A Dog of the House of Mountague moves me.

GREGORY   To move is to stir, and to be Valiant is to stand: therefore if thou art mov'd, thou   10 runn'st away.

SAMPSON   A Dog of that House shall move me to stand: I will take the Wall of any Man or Maid of Mountague's.

GREGORY   That shews thee a weak Slave: for the   15 weakest goes to the Wall.

17–18 **Women . . . Weaker Vessels** a proverbial expression deriving from 1 Peter 3:7 in the New Testament.

24–25 **civil with the Maids** Sampson uses the word *civil* ironically, implying that the maids whose 'heads' are cut off (that is, the maids who lose their 'Maidenheads', or virginity, to him) will derive pleasure from his 'pretty Piece of Flesh' (lines 31–32) and thus consider his tyranny 'civil'.

28 **Sense** Gregory plays on two implications of the word: (a) meaning, and (b) physical sensation. Gregory may be punning on *incense*, enflame, arouse.

34 **Poor John** dried hake, a cheap form of salted fish. Gregory's bawdy joke is probably based on two characteristics of Poor John: (a) its stiffness, and (b) its having had its roe (sperm or eggs) removed in the 'drying' or curing process. Benvolio and Mercutio engage in similar wordplay in II.iii.41–43. For similar play on flesh and fish, see *1 Henry IV*, III.ii.140–41, and *The Tempest*, III.ii.25–40.

36 **naked Weapon** This reference to an unsheathed sword provides an apt transition from talk of aggression with sexual 'tools' to action involving aggression with tools of combat. That the two kinds of 'Weapon' are associated is one of the recurring themes of this play about the relationships between love and hate, and between different manifestations of male assertiveness.

40 **marry** a mild oath, originally referring to the Virgin Mary, which had a meaning more or less equivalent to 'in faith' or 'indeed'. Shakespeare frequently embeds *marry* in phrases that hint at the matrimonial sense of the word, and Gregory's line will prove ironically pertinent to one of the central topics of *Romeo and Juliet*. Compare I.iii.61–65.

44 **as they list** as they will. *List* can also mean 'lean' or 'sway', as in *The Tempest*, III.ii.20; compare *The Winter's Tale*, IV.iv.555, and *Hamlet*, I.v.20–21.

45 **bite my Thumb** an insulting gesture made with a flick of the thumbnail against the back of the upper row of teeth.

SAMPSON 'Tis true, and therefore Women, being the
    Weaker Vessels, are ever thrust to the Wall:
    therefore I will push Mountague's Men from the
    Wall and thrust his Maids to the Wall.   20

GREGORY The Quarrel is between our Maisters, and us
    their Men.

SAMPSON 'Tis all one, I will shew my self a Tyrant:
    when I have fought with the Men, I will be civil
    with the Maids, I will cut off their Heads.   25

GREGORY The Heads of the Maids?

SAMPSON I, the Heads of the Maids, or their
    Maiden heads, take it in what Sense thou wilt.

GREGORY They must take it in Sense that feel it.

SAMPSON Me they shall feel while I am able to   30
    stand, and 'tis known I am a pretty Piece of
    Flesh.

GREGORY 'Tis well thou art not Fish: if thou hadst,
    thou hadst been Poor John. Draw thy Tool: here
    comes of the House of Mountagues.   35

Enter two other Servingmen.

SAMPSON My naked Weapon is out. Quarrel, I will
    back thee.

GREGORY How, turn thy Back and run?

SAMPSON Fear me not.

GREGORY No marry, I fear thee.   40

SAMPSON Let us take the Law of our sides, let them
    begin.

GREGORY I will frown as I pass by, and let them
    take it as they list.

SAMPSON Nay, as they dare; I will bite my Thumb at   45
    them, which is Disgrace to them if they bear it.

ABRAM Do you bite your Thumb at us, Sir?

SAMPSON I do bite my Thumb, Sir.

ABRAM Do you bite your Thumb at us, Sir?

50 **Is the Law of our side?** Are we within our legal rights?

56 **for you** ready for you, prepared to take you on. Compare III.i.86.

59 **Well, Sir** an expression equivalent to 'Fine, sir.'

65 **Washing** an alternative form for *swashing* (dashing, smashing).

67 **Put ... Swords** Benvolio (whose name, Italian for 'good will', befits his role as peacemaker) is saying 'Put away your weapons'. But his phrasing inadvertently undercuts his intent because of the way his words recall the references to standing blades in lines 9–12, 30–31, and elsewhere. Benvolio's exhortation will be echoed in III.i.87 and in IV.iii.209.

You ... do This clause alludes to one of Jesus' utterances from the Cross (see Luke 23:34). For another dramatically ironic echo of the same passage, see *Julius Caesar*, III.i.233.

68 **Hartless Hinds** literally, young or female deer ('hinds') without a 'hart' (antlered stag) to guide and protect them. Most editors print *heartless* (as the word is spelled in the 1623 First Folio printing), but the spelling in the 1599 Second Quarto more faithfully conveys Tybalt's primary accusation: that Benvolio is taking unfair advantage of the metaphorical equivalent of 'Weaker Vessels' by drawing on Capulet servants at a time when they are undefended by a Capulet master. See the note to lines 17–18.

71 **manage it** Benvolio means two things here: (a) use it, and (b) control it (employ it with restraint and sound judgement). Here *manage* plays on *man* ('Men').

SAMPSON — Is the Law of our side if I say ay?   50
GREGORY — No.
SAMPSON No Sir, I do not bite my Thumb at you,
    Sir; but I bite my Thumb, Sir.
GREGORY Do you Quarrel, Sir?
ABRAM Quarrel, Sir? No Sir.   55
SAMPSON But if you do, Sir, I am for you: I serve
    as good a Man as you.
ABRAM No better.
SAMPSON Well, Sir.

Enter Benvolio.

GREGORY Say 'better': here   60
    comes one of my Maister's Kinsmen.
SAMPSON Yes, better, Sir.
ABRAM You lie.
SAMPSON Draw if you be Men. — Gregory, remember
    thy Washing Blow.   *They fight.*   65
BENVOLIO Part, Fools.
    Put up your Swords, you know not what you do.

Enter Tybalt.

TYBALT What, art thou drawn among these Hartless
    Hinds?
    Turn thee, Benvolio: look upon thy Death.
BENVOLIO I do but keep the Peace: put up thy Sword,   70
    Or manage it to part these Men with me.
TYBALT What, drawn and talk of Peace? I hate the
    word
    As I hate Hell, all Mountagues, and thee:
    Have at thee, Coward.   *Fight.*

Enter three or four Citizens with Clubs or Partisans.

75 **Clubs, Bills, and Partisans** The citizens who intervene here are members of the Watch (the city's volunteer guard). Bills were long shafts with hooked concave blades; partisans were spears with broad double-edged blades.

S.D. **in his Gown** Capulet's dressing gown introduces an image of dignity and domesticity comically incompatible with the occasion and with the old man's impulsive determination to join the fray. Both wives emerge here as strong-willed proponents of common sense in their restraint of their husbands' childish irascibility. A 'Long Sword' was a heavy sword that required both hands to wield.

79 **Crowch** crutch (here rendered in a way that emphasizes the feebleness of the aged Capulet).

81 **flourishes** brandishes, waves flamboyantly.
in spight of me to spite or defy me.

S.D. **Escalus** This name, mentioned only here, refers to the della Scala family, one of whom ruled Verona in the fourteenth century.

85 **Neighbour-stained Steel** steel weapons stained with the blood of neighbours. The Prince calls his subjects 'Profaners' because they are desecrating what should be instruments of peace by using them against fellow citizens rather than reserving them for protection of the city against its external enemies.

88 **purple Fountains** crimson 'fountains' of blood (which is frequently referred to as 'purple' in Shakespeare's plays) rather than the beautiful water fountains (springs) for which Verona was well known. The city was famous for 'conduits', public fountains that featured sculptured figures.

89 **On pain of** on penalty of.

90 **mistempered Weapons** weapons made by tempering steel (heating and rapidly cooling the metal while beating it into the desired shape), but now profaned by intemperate (uncontrolled) violence. It takes the Prince until the end of this sentence (line 91) to quell the brawl enough to address the crowd without shouting.

91 **Sentence** The Prince means 'judgement' or 'penalty'; but *sentence* can also refer to a wise saying, as in II.ii.79.

OFFICERS   Clubs, Bills, and Partisans. Strike, beat   75
them down. Down with the Capulets, down with
the Mountagues.

Enter old Capulet in his Gown, and his Wife.

CAPULET   What Noise is this? Give me my Long Sword,
ho.
CAPULET'S WIFE   A Crowch, a Crowch, why call you
for a Sword?

Enter old Mountague, and his Wife.

CAPULET   My Sword, I say. Old Mountague is come,   80
And flourishes his Blade in spight of me.
MOUNTAGUE   Thou Villain, Capulet. – Hold me not,
Let me go.
MOUNTAGUE'S WIFE   Thou shalt not stir one Foot to
seek a Foe.

Enter Prince Escalus, with his Train.

PRINCE   Rebellious Subjects, Enemies to Peace,
Profaners of this Neighbour-stained Steel.   85
– Will they not hear? – What ho, you Men, you
Beasts,
That quench the Fire of your pernicious Rage
With purple Fountains issuing from your Veins:
On pain of Torture, from those Bloody Hands
Throw your mistempered Weapons to the Ground   90
And hear the Sentence of your moved Prince.

92 **Civil** This adjective recalls lines 24–25, as well as line 4 of the Prologue.

95 **auncient** venerable; elderly and dignified. In line 107 the word means 'of long duration' (with the suggestion that no one now alive can remember how or when it commenced). Here as elsewhere, the Everyman text preserves spellings that indicate nuances of pronunciation.

96 **grave beseeming Ornaments** ornaments suitable for persons of gravity and sobriety. The syntax in the original texts hovers between 'grave-beseeming' and 'grave, beseeming' in modern usage.

98 **cank'red** decayed, eaten away, diseased (either by a cancer or by the caterpillar that preys on rosebuds).

100 **Forfeit of the Peace** penalty for breaking the peace.

101 **For this time** for now.

105 **Free-town** an English rendering of Villafranco, the name of Capulet's castle in William Painter's *Palace of Pleasure* (1567), one of Shakespeare's sources for *Romeo and Juliet*. Here it becomes Verona's city hall.

107 **Who set . . . new abroach?** Who opened up (set flowing) this old quarrel again?

112 **prepar'd** drawn.

114 **swoong** swung.

115 **nothing hurt withal** not at all hurt thereby.
    hiss'd him in Scorn Benvolio's phrasing imitates the sound of the sword's swipe while at the same time personifying that hiss as a gust of wind ridiculing Tybalt's ineffectual blustering.

117 **on Part and Part** on one side and the other.

123 **drive** drove.

124 **Sycamour** a tree often associated with lovesick youth, probably by way of a pun on the name ('sick-amour'). Compare *Love's Labour's Lost*, V.ii.89, and *Othello*, IV.iii.39. Shakespeare's spelling of Romeo's surname may contain a related pun: *Mount* is a word for the female pudendum (the 'Mount of Venus') and for intercourse, and *ague* means 'fever'. Compare *Love's Labour's Lost*, IV.i.1–4.

– Three Civil Brawls, bred of an airy Word,
By thee, old Capulet and Mountague,
Have thrice disturb'd the Quiet of our Streets
And made Verona's auncient Citizens   95
Cast by their grave beseeming Ornaments
To wield old Partisans, in Hands as old,
Cank'red with Peace, to part your cank'red Hate.
If ever you disturb our Streets again,
Your Lives shall pay the Forfeit of the Peace.   100
– For this time all the rest depart away.
– You, Capulet, shall go along with me,
And Mountague, come you this Afternoon,
To know our farther Pleasure in this Case:
To old Free-town, our common Judgement-place.   105
– Once more, on pain of Death, all Men depart.
       Exeunt [all but the Mountagues and Benvolio.]
MOUNTAGUE   Who set this auncient Quarrel new
   abroach?
Speak, Nephew: were you by when it began?
BENVOLIO   Here were the Servants of your Adversary
   And yours, close fighting ere I did approach.   110
   I drew to part them; in the instant came
   The fiery Tybalt with his Sword prepar'd,
   Which, as he breath'd Defiance to my Ears,
   He swoong about his Head and cut the Winds,
   Who, nothing hurt withal, hiss'd him in Scorn.   115
   While we were interchanging Thrusts and Blows
   Came more and more, and fought on Part and Part,
   Till the Prince came, who parted either Part.
MOUNTAGUE'S WIFE   O where is Romeo? Saw you him
   to day?
Right glad I am he was not at this Fray.   120
BENVOLIO   Madam, an Hour before the worshipp'd Sun
   Peer'd forth the golden Window of the East,
   A troubled Mind drive me to walk abroad,
   Where underneath the Grove of Sycamour

125 **That . . . City side**   that grows to the west of the city.

127 **Towards**   here pronounced as a one-syllable word.
  ware   both 'aware' and 'wary'. Compare the Sun/Son wordplay
  in lines 121, 126, with *Hamlet*, I.ii.66–67.

128 **Covert**   cover, seclusion.

130 **most sought . . . found**   most desired to be where most people
  would not be (that is, most desired solitude). Belvolio plays on
  the idea of seeking and not finding, and he here uses *sought* in
  two senses: (a) desired, and (b) searched for.

132 **humour**   disposition, mood. Benvolio uses *humour* in its
  psychological sense (the four 'humours' believed to control
  human behaviour) as distinguished from the modern sense
  relating to wit and mirth. In line 145 'Humour' refers to a
  settled, heavy, state of melancholic depression, thought in
  Shakespeare's time to be the result of an excess of black bile
  in the body.

139 **Aurora**   Goddess of the Dawn.

141 **pens**   secludes. But Mountague's verb is a reminder that
  Romeo's condition imitates the love-melancholy that dozens
  of Renaissance poets had penned in Petrarch-inspired sonnets.
  See *The Merchant of Venice*, V.i.237, for a sense of *pen*
  (which frequently plays on 'penis') that hints at the private
  activity Mercutio alludes to in II.i.15–38 and II.iii.41–75.

144 **portendous**   portentous, ill-omened.

148 **importun'd**   pleaded with
  by any Means   using all the means at your disposal.

151 **true**   both (a) faithful, and (b) perceptive.

152 **close**   private; silent.

153 **Sounding**   both (a) having his depth gauged (a nautical term),
  and (b) sounding out (using 'Indirections' of the kind
  commended by Polonius in *Hamlet*, II.i.1–69).

154 **envious**   destructive, malicious. The 'Worm' referred to is the
  cankerworm, a type of larva feeding on the buds of flowers.
  Compare line 98. But *Worm* cal also mean what *pen* does; see
  Antony and Cleopatra, V.ii.240–79.
  Discovery   disclosure.

That westward rooteth from this City side   125
So early walking did I see your Son;
Towards him I made, but he was ware of me
And stole into the Covert of the Wood.
I measuring his Affections by my own,
Which then most sought where most might not be
    found,   130
Being one too many by my weary Self,
Pursued my Humour, not pursuing his,
And gladly shunn'd who gladly fled from me.
MOUNTAGUE   Many a Morning hath he there been seen,
With Tears augmenting the fresh Morning's Dew,   135
Adding to Clouds more Clouds with his deep Sighs.
But all so soon as the all-cheering Sun
Should in the farthest East begin to draw
The shady Curtains from Aurora's Bed,
Away from Light steals home my heavy Son   140
And private in his Chamber pens himself,
Shuts up his Windows, locks fair Day-light out,
And makes himself an artificial Night.
Black and portendous must this Humour prove
Unless good Counsel may the Cause remove.   145
BENVOLIO   My noble Uncle, do you know the Cause?
MOUNTAGUE   I neither know it nor can learn of him.
BENVOLIO   Have you importun'd him by any Means?
MOUNTAGUE   Both by my self and many other Friends.
But he his own Affection's Counsellor   150
Is to himself (I will not say how true);
But to himself so secret and so close,
So far from Sounding and Discovery,
As is the Bud bit with an envious Worm

156   **to the same** to the air. Most editors emend to 'to the sun'. But
the sense preserved in the Quarto and First Folio printings
seems quite adequate to the context. *Air* sometimes plays on
heir (as in *Macbeth*, III.v.59), and before long Romeo will be
dedicating 'his Beauty' to the heiress under discussion in the
following scene (I.ii).

162   **true Shrift** true confession. In lines 162–63, Mountague says 'I
hope you'll be so lucky by your delay as to get the true story.'
The role the Mountagues assign here to Benvolio will be
echoed in *Hamlet*, II.ii.1–39, where the King and Queen
commission two of the Prince's boyhood friends to use 'any
Means' to discover the cause of his secretive despondency.
Shrift anticipates II.iv.67.

164   **strook** a frequent Elizabethan spelling and pronunciation for
struck.

172   **in his View** both (a) in appearance, and (b) in prospect.

173   **in Proof** in reality, once experienced.

174   **whose View is muffled still** whose eyes are always covered. In
lines 175–76 Romeo alludes to the traditional image of
Cupid, the God of Love, as a blindfolded boy. Compare I.iv.4
and II.iii.15–19. Throughout this dialogue, Romeo personifies
Love, speaking of an abstraction as if it were a deity. This was
a convention of what is known as Courtly Love poetry, and it
served as a convenient means of describing an emotional
condition that seemed at times to have a mind and will of its
own. By Shakespeare's day poets had developed a tradition
that permitted Love to be spoken of as if it were a religion,
with all the rituals and symbols normally associated with
Christianity. Whether such a religion was ever taken literally
is subject to debate. The lovers depicted as practising it take it
quite seriously, but the way they are portrayed suggests that
many poets, if not all, took an ironic (albeit sympathetic) view
of the state of 'being in love'.

179–   **brawling Love . . . Still waking Sleep** The oxymorons
84   (self-contradictory images) in these lines are typical
expressions of the love-sickness depicted in romantic
literature of the Renaissance. The oxymoron was an apt way
of describing a lover's 'betwixt and between' condition.

Ere he can spread his sweet Leaves to the Air   155
Or dedicate his Beauty to the same.
Could we but learn from whence his Sorrows grow,
We would as willingly give Cure as know.

Enter Romeo.

BENVOLIO   See where he comes. So please you step
   aside,
I'll know his Grievance or be much denied.   160
MOUNTAGUE   I would thou wert so happy by thy Stay
To hear true Shrift. – Come, Madam, let's away.
                                          Exeunt.
BENVOLIO   Good morrow, Cousin.
ROMEO   Is the Day so young?
BENVOLIO   But new strook nine.
ROMEO   Ay me, sad Hours seem long.
Was that my Father that went hence so fast?   165
BENVOLIO   It was; what Sadness lengthens Romeo's
   Hours?
ROMEO   Not having that which, having, makes them
   short.
BENVOLIO   In love.
ROMEO   Out.
BENVOLIO   Of love.   170
ROMEO   Out of her Favour where I am in love.
BENVOLIO   Alas that Love, so gentle in his View,
Should be so tyrannous and rough in Proof.
ROMEO   Alas that Love, whose View is muffled still,
Should without Eyes see Pathways to his Will.   175
Where shall we dine? O me! what Fray was here?
Yet tell me not, for I have heard it all.
Here's much to do with Hate, but more with Love.
Why then, O brawling Love, O loving Hate,
O any thing of Nothing first create.   180
O heavy Lightness, serious Vanity,

182 **well-seeming**   apparently seemly (shapely). This reading derives from the First Quarto. The Second Quarto reads 'welseeing', a sense that fits almost equally well.

186 **Coze**   Coz (usually spelled with a final *e* in the early texts of this play), an abbreviation for 'Cousin'.

187 **Hart**   In this exchange the primary sense is probably 'heart' (often spelled *Hart* in the early texts), but as in line 69 there may also be a pun on the sense that relates to a noble stag.

190 **prest**   oppressed, burdened. Romeo alludes to a form of torture that was used to compel a prisoner to confess. He also refers to a means of propagation whereby a branch was weighted to the ground until it put down roots and thus started a new plant.

194 **Being purg'd . . . Eyes**   Romeo is saying that if the smoke is removed ('purg'd') from the air, Love becomes an unimpeded fire, resulting in 'sparkling' (brightly burning) eyes.

195 **Being vex'd . . . Tears**   If the smoke is stirred up ('vex'd'), the eyes will overflow with tears.

196 **discreet**   intelligent, discerning; sane. Compare *Hamlet*, II.ii.212–13.

197 **choking Gall**   a cloyingly sweet ('choking') bitterness.
preserving Sweet   a salty sweetness (an allusion to the use of salt as a preservative). Both word combinations are oxymorons. The opposition between *Gall* and *Sweet* will recur in a more ominous context in I.iv.94. Compare Sonnets 5–6 and *A Midsummer Night's Dream*, I.i.74–78.

198 **Coze**   Cousin.
Soft   here, a term more or less equivalent to 'Hush'.

202 **in Sadness**   in all seriousness. In the next line, *groan* alludes to the other sense of 'sadness' (mourning or melancholy), preserved in the usual modern usage.

210 **fair Mark**   clear or easy target, but with a pun on other senses of *fair*: (a) blond, (b) attractive, and (c) just. In line 210 the Second Quarto's *Mark man* can be rendered either (a) 'Markman' (marksman), or (b) 'Mark, man'. Compare *Love's Labour's Lost*, IV.i.114–56.

Misshapen Chaos of well-seeming Forms!
Feather of Lead, bright Smoke, cold Fire, sick
  Health;
Still waking Sleep, that is not what it is.
This Love feel I, that feel no Love in this.   185
Doest thou not laugh?
BENVOLIO   No, Coze, I rather weep.
ROMEO Good Hart, at what?
BENVOLIO   At thy good Hart's Oppression.
ROMEO Why, such is Love's Transgression.
Griefs of mine own lie heavy in my Breast,
Which thou wilt propagate to have it prest   190
With more of thine. This Love that thou hast
  shown
Doth add more Grief to too much of mine own.
Love is a Smoke made with the Fume of Sighs;
Being purg'd, a Fire sparkling in Lovers' Eyes;
Being vex'd, a Sea nourish'd with Loving Tears.   195
What is it else? A Madness most discreet,
A choking Gall, and a preserving Sweet.
Farewell, my Coze.
BENVOLIO   Soft, I will go along,
And if you leave me so, you do me wrong.
ROMEO Tut, I have lost my Self, I am not here.   200
This is not Romeo, he's some other where.
BENVOLIO Tell me in Sadness, who is that you
  love?
ROMEO What, shall I groan and tell thee?
BENVOLIO   Groan? Why no;
But sadly tell me who.
ROMEO Bid a Sick Man in Sadness make his Will: 205
A Word ill urg'd to one that is so Ill.
In Sadness, Cousin, I do love a Woman.
BENVOLIO I aim'd so near when I suppos'd you lov'd.
ROMEO A right good Mark man, and she's fair I love.
BENVOLIO A right fair Mark, fair Coze, is soonest
  hit.   210

211   **Hit**   anticipates II.i.33, II.ii.41, and II.iii.62.

212   **Dian's Wit**   the cunning that protects Diana, the Goddess of Chastity, from being 'hit' by another archer's arrow. Diana was the earthly manifestation of a goddess called 'triple Hecate' in V.ii.14–17 of *A Midsummer Night's Dream*. In her role as Goddess of the Moon she was usually called Cynthia or Phoebe, and in her role as Goddess of Hades she was normally referred to as Persephone. *Wit* can also refer to the genitalia (see I.iii.42), and that sense is pertinent here.

214   **uncharm'd**   unaffected by Love's magic spell.

217   **Nor ope . . . Gold**   Romeo seems to be implying that he has tried to buy Rosaline's favours. It is more likely, however, that he is simply saying that gold is one of the things against which her chastity is proof (shielded). Shakespeare probably expected his audience to recognize an allusion to one of Jove's sexual exploits, when he disguised himself as a shower of gold to seduce the maiden Danae. *Sainct* means both (a) saint, and (b) sanctified (holy). Most editors print 'saint-seducing'.

221   **Sparing . . . Waste**   Romeo argues that in this instance thrift ('Sparing') is actually wasteful, because what is saved will be lost, resulting in a famine for future generations. Compare Sonnets 1–14, where Shakespeare addresses the same theme.

225   **Bliss . . . Despair**   Here and elsewhere Romeo uses religious terminology to compare the states of a lover to those of a soul seeking salvation. His complaint is that Rosaline's route to bliss (the blessings of Heaven) through chastity leaves her suitor in despair (without hope of redemption).

226   **forsworn to love**   renounced (sworn against) love.

232   **To call hers . . . in question more**   to bring hers to mind even more (in ways illustrated by the lines that follow).

233   **Masks**   dark shields to protect ladies' fair skin from exposure to the sun.

235   **strooken**   stricken.

ROMEO   Well, in that Hit you Miss: she'll not be
  hit
  With Cupid's Arrow. She hath Dian's Wit:
  And in strong Proof of Chastity well arm'd
  From Love's weak, childish Bow she lives
    uncharm'd.
  She will not stay the Siege of loving Terms,   215
  Nor bide th' Encounter of assailing Eyes.
  Nor ope her Lap to Sainct seducing Gold.
  O she is rich in Beauty; onely poor
  That, when she dies, with Beauty dies her Store.
BENVOLIO   Then she hath sworn that she will still   220
  live Chaste?
ROMEO   She hath, and in that Sparing make huge
  Waste:
  For Beauty, sterv'd with her Severity,
  Cuts Beauty off from all Posterity.
  She is too Fair, too Wise, wisely too Fair,
  To merit Bliss by making me Despair.   225
  She hath forsworn to love, and in that Vow
  Do I live dead that live to tell it now.
BENVOLIO   Be rul'd by me: forget to think of her.
ROMEO   O teach me how I should forget to think.
BENVOLIO   By giving Liberty unto thine Eyes: 230
  Examine other Beauties.
ROMEO   'Tis the way
  To call hers (exquisite) in question more.
  These happy Masks that kiss fair Ladies' Brows,
  Being Black, put us in mind they hide the Fair:
  He that is strooken Blind cannot forget   235

237 **passing Fair** surpassing (extraordinarily) fair (even more lovely than all that the word *fair* conveys).

238 **Note** either (a) written reminder, or (b) explanatory annotation (such as the glosses printed in the margins of large tomes in Shakespeare's time).

239 **pass'd that passing Fair** surpassed even that beauty that was beyond fair.

241 **I'll pay that Doctrine . . . Debt** Either I'll buy that doctrine from you (and replace it with the one I've been preaching), or I'll die a bankrupt debtor to you in my effort to do so.

I.ii The setting for this scene appears to be a street outside Capulet's house. The 'Clown' referred to in the opening stage direction is a serving man whose role was originally played by Will Kemp, the actor who took the roles of clownish bumpkins in the early years of Shakespeare's company. Kemp is designated by name in the stage direction following IV.iii.186.

1 **bound** under bond to keep the peace.

4 **Reckoning** reputation, standing.

6 **Suit** request. Paris, a young Count, has just initiated negotiations with Capulet for Juliet's hand in marriage. *Count* and *County* are English renderings of the Italian word *conte*, a title roughly equivalent to Earl in England (see III.iv.21).

9 **Chaunge** both (a) passage, and (b) exchange.

10 **wither in their Pride** see their glory subside with the seasons' change. *Wither* echoes *A Midsummer Night's Dream*, I.i.6, 76–78, 180.

12 **Younger than she** maids younger than she. Shakespeare frequently uses ellipses (word omissions) to compress normal syntax.

14–15 **Earth . . . Earth** Capulet says he has buried all his offspring ('Hopes') but Juliet, so she stands to inherit all his wealth. Capulet's phrasing alludes to the French term *fille de terre*, 'heiress'. These two lines differ from the rest of the surrounding verse in two ways: (a) they are 'headless' (lacking the initial unstressed syllable usual in iambic pentameter), and (b) they do not rhyme. Some editors assume that they are non-Shakespearean lines and omit them, but they are of a piece with the rest of the speech and with the play in general, and are in no way uncharacteristic of the playwright. Compare *A Midsummer Night's Dream*, I.i.216–19.

The precious Treasure of his Eyesight lost.
Shew me a Mistress that is passing Fair:
What doth her Beauty serve but as a Note
Where I may read who pass'd that passing Fair.
Farewell, thou canst not teach me to forget.   240
BENVOLIO   I'll pay that Doctrine, or else die in
    Debt.   *Exeunt.*

Scene 2

Enter Capulet, County Paris, and the Clown.

JULIET   But Mountague is bound as well as I,
    In Penalty alike; and 'tis not hard, I think,
    For Men so old as we to keep the Peace.
PARIS   Of Honourable Reckoning are you both,
    And pity 'tis you liv'd at Odds so long.   5
    But now, my Lord, what say you to my Suit?
CAPULET   But saying o'er what I have said before:
    My Child is yet a Straunger in the World;
    She hath not seen the Chaunge of fourteen Years;
    Let two more Summers wither in their Pride   10
    Ere we may think her ripe to be a Bride.
PARIS   Younger than she are happy Mothers made.
CAPULET   And too soon marr'd are those so early
    made.
    Earth hath swallowed all my Hopes but she;
    She's the hopeful Lady of my Earth.   15
    But woo her, gentle Paris, get her Heart;
    My Will to her Consent is but a Part;

18 **scope of Choice**   range of options; freedom to choose.

19 **according Voice**   voice of agreement, accord.

26 **lusty**   robust, vigorous (as distinguished from 'lustful').

29 **Fennel**   a yellow-blossomed flowering herb whose buds were thrown at the feet of brides in the marriage ceremony.

30 **Inherit**   Here the word simply means 'have', but it keeps us mindful that Capulet's inheritance is on the minds of both participants in the conversation.

32–33 **Which one more View . . . none**   This passage can be paraphrased roughly as follows: A further look at many maidens, my daughter being one, will establish which one is the fairest – although in 'Reckoning' (numerical calculations) we must bear in mind the old proverb that one is no number ('none'). Compare Sonnet 136, which plays on the same paradox. *Reckoning* echoes line 4.

34 **Sirrah**   a designation for a social inferior, here the 'Clown' of the opening stage direction.

38–45 **'Find . . . Learned**   The Servingman who speaks these lines is probably identical to Peter, the Nurse's man. Here, in a manner that resembles the Clowns in *A Midsummer Night's Dream* (see III.i.91, IV.i.207–18), he associates each workman with a tool that actually belongs to another workman on the list he has just been handed. A *Pencil* is a fine-pointed artist's brush. Like *Yard*, *pen*, and *Worm* (see the notes to I.i.141, 154) it can here refer to the 'Piece of Flesh' (I.i.31–32) an idle tradesman may 'meddle with'. Compare *Love's Labour's Lost*, V.ii.654–55, and see the note on *Medlers* at II.i.36.

46 **In good time**   Just in time! Benvolio and Romeo, two of 'the Learned' (those who can read) the Servingman needs, appear precisely when he invokes them.

47–52 **one Fire . . . will die**   All of Benvolio's prescriptions illustrate what is known as homeopathic medicine ('fighting fire with fire'); thus, for example, the solution to giddiness (dizziness) from turning is to whirl in the opposite direction, and the cure for one infection is another that will kill the first one.

And she agreed, within her scope of Choice
Lies my Consent and fair according Voice.
This Night I hold an old accustom'd Feast,   20
Whereto I have invited many a Guest
Such as I love; and you among the Store
One more, most welcome makes my Number more.
At my poor House look to behold this Night
Earth-treading Stars that make dark Heaven Light.   25
Such Comfort as do lusty Young Men feel
When well-apparell'd April on the Heel
Of limping Winter treads, even such Delight
Among fresh Fennel Buds shall you this Night
Inherit at my House. Hear all, all see,   30
And like her most whose Merit most shall be;
Which one more View of many, mine being one,
May stand in Number, though in Reckoning none.
Come go with me. – Go, Sirrah, trudge about
Through fair Verona; find those Persons out   35
Whose Names are written there, and to them say
My House and Welcome on their Pleasure stay.

Exit [*with Paris.*]

SERVINGMAN   'Find them out whose Names are
  written.'
Here it is written that the Shoemaker should
meddle with his Yard, and the Tailor with his   40
Last, the Fisher with his Pencil, and the Painter
with his Nets. But I am sent to find those
Persons whose Names are here writ, and can never
find what Names the Writing Person hath here writ.
I must to the Learned.   45

Enter Benvolio and Romeo.

In good time.
BENVOLIO   Tut, Man, one Fire burns out an other's
  Burning;

49   **holp**   helped.

53   **Plantan**   plaintain, a broad-leafed plant used to treat superficial
      cuts and scratches. Here as in *Love's Labour's Lost*,
      III.i.73–149, it is referred to as a salve for love's wounds.

56   **bound**   tied up; imprisoned. But *bound* can also mean
      'enjoined' (under a legal injunction, as in line 1) and
      'constipated' (as in *Love's Labour's Lost*, III.i.130–33, and in
      Coriolanus, III.i.52).

58   **God-den**   good evening.

59   **God gi'god-den**   God give you good e'en (evening), a greeting
      to be used any time after noon. The expression was also
      employed as a mild expletive (as at III.v.173).

60   **I**   both (a) I [can], and (b) ay. See the note to I.i.5, and compare
      line 62 and I.iii.44, 57.

61–62 **Perhaps . . . without Book**   The Servingman's meaning seems to
      be that Romeo could well have learned to 'read' (understand)
      his misery without knowing how to read (in the literal sense
      of the word). Another meaning of 'without Book'
      (memorized, so as not to require a text to refer to) occurs in
      I.iv.7.

64   **rest you merry**   fare you well. As he speaks, the Servant
      probably prepares to depart.

71   **Rosaline**   This is the same Rosaline that Romeo loves, and it is
      of some interest that she is never mentioned in I.v, the scene
      devoted to Capulet's feast. At this point we have neither seen
      nor heard explicit mention of any other Capulet female. It is
      not until I.iii.4 that we first hear Juliet's name; and it is only
      later in that scene that we infer that she has been the daughter
      referred to in I.ii.6–34.

74   **whither should they come?**   To where are they to come?

76   **Whither to Supper?**   Many editors rearrange this speech as two
      questions: 'Whither? To supper?'

79   **Maister's**   This spelling of *Master* is common in Shakespeare,
      and it reminds us that the English word derives from the Latin
      magister. See the note to I.i.95.

One Pain is less'ned by an other's Anguish:
Turn Giddy and be holp by backward Turning.
One desperate Grief cures with an other's
    Languish: 50
Take thou some New Infection to thy Eye,
And the rank Poison of the Old will die.
ROMEO   Your Plantan Leaf is excellent for that.
BENVOLIO   For what, I pray thee?
ROMEO   For your broken Shin.
BENVOLIO   Why Romeo, art thou mad?   55
ROMEO   Not mad, but bound more than a Madman is:
Shut up in Prison, kept without my Food,
Whipp'd and tormented – and God-den, good
    Fellow.
SERVINGMAN   God gi'god-den. I pray, Sir, can you read?
ROMEO   I, mine own Fortune in my Misery.   60
SERVINGMAN   Perhaps you have learned it without
    Book. But I pray, can you read any thing you see?
ROMEO   I, if I know the Letters and the Language.
SERVINGMAN   You say honestly, rest you merry.
ROMEO   Stay, Fellow, I can read.   *He reads the Letter.*   65
'Signior Martino and his Wife and Daughters;
County Anselm and his beauteous Sisters; the
Lady Widow of Utruvio, Signior Placentio and
his lovely Nieces; Mercutio and his Brother
Valentine; mine Uncle Capulet, his Wife and   70
Daughters; my fair Niece Rosaline; Livia;
Signior Valentio and his Cousin Tybalt; Lucio
and the lively Helena.'
A fair Assembly: whither should they come?
SERVINGMAN   Up.   75
ROMEO   Whither to Supper?
SERVINGMAN   To our House.
ROMEO   Whose House?
SERVINGMAN   My Maister's.

84   **crush**   a colloquial term for 'drink' or 'down'.

85   **auncient Feast**   Earlier (line 20) Capulet has described the occasion as 'an old, accustom'd Feast'. It was probably a traditional family gathering, and recognized as such throughout Verona.

87   **admired**   wondered at; here treated as a three-syllable word. Lines 85–90 echo lines 24–34.

88   **unattainted**   (a) untainted, able to perceive objectively, (b) uninfected, and (c) guiltless of any felony.

93   **these**   Romeo's eyes. Romeo probably points to them as he speaks this line.

93–94 **who, often drown'd . . . Liars**   Romeo alludes to the practice whereby suspected disbelievers who did not start to drown when dunked to test their fidelity were thereby 'proved' to be heretics; having been 'rejected' by the water, these poor souls were then burned at the stake. Romeo says that if his eyes should prove false to Rosaline, the tears in which they have 'often drown'd' should turn to fire and consume them.

94   **Transparent**   both (a) capable of being seen through (referring to the lenses of Romeo's eyes), and (b) manifest (too obvious in their guilt to avoid having their excuses seen through as lies).

96   **Match**   equal. But Romeo's phrasing is a reminder that the Sun also never 'saw her match' in another sense: couple. Compare I.i.211–19.

99– **in that Crystal Scales . . . Maid**   Benvolio compares Romeo's
100 eyes to a pair of balance scales and suggests that instead of having Rosaline 'pois'd with her Self' (line 98) on both sides of the point of balance, Romeo should weigh her opposite 'some other Maid'.

I.iii   This scene is set in one of the rooms of Capulet's house.

ROMEO   Indeed, I should have ask'd you that before.   80
SERVINGMAN   Now I'll tell you without asking: my
   Maister is the great rich Capulet; and if you be
   not of the House of Mountagues, I pray come and
   crush a cup of Wine. Rest you merry.   *Exit.*
BENVOLIO   At this same auncient Feast of Capulets   85
   Sups the fair Rosaline whom thou so loves,
   With all the admired Beauties of Verona;
   Go thither and with unattainted Eye
   Compare her Face with some that I shall show,
   And I will make thee think thy Swan a Crow.   90
ROMEO   When the devout Religion of mine Eye
   Maintains such Falsehood, then turn Tears to
     Fire;
   And these who, often drown'd, could never die,
   Transparent Heretics, be burnt for Liars.
   One Fairer than my Love? The all-seeing Sun   95
   Ne'er saw her Match since first the World begun.
BENVOLIO   Tut, you saw her Fair none else being by,
   Her Self pois'd with her Self in either Eye.
   But in that Crystal Scales let there be weigh'd
   Your Lady's Love against some other Maid   100
   That I will shew you shining at this Feast,
   And she shall scant shew well that now seems
     best.
ROMEO   I'll go along, no such Sight to be shown,
   But to rejoice in Splendour of mine own.   *Exeunt.*

Scene 3

Enter Capulet's Wife and Nurse.

WIFE   Nurse, where's my Daughter? Call
   her forth to me.

2 **Maidenhead** both (a) virginity, and (b) the female pudendum (whether or not the hymen has been penetrated). Compare I.i.23–35, and see 1 *Henry IV*, II.iv.393–96, where 'Maidenheads' appears to refer to prostitutes rather than to virgins.

3 **bad** the usual Shakespearean spelling for the past tense of *bid* (now spelled *bade*).

 Lamb ... Ladybird the Nurse's pet nicknames for Juliet. 'Lamb' is apparently derived from 'Lammastide' (1 August, a holiday to celebrate the first-fruits of summer harvest), on the eve of which Juliet was born.

9 **thou s' hear** a contraction for 'thou shalt hear'.

10 **Thou ... a pretty Age** Juliet's mother seems to mean that Juliet is approaching the age when she should think about marriage. *Pretty* recalls I.i.31–32.

12 **o' my** of my

13 **to my Teen** possibly a colloquial contraction for 'to my teeth' (to be spoken with the metrical value of two syllables, as should the phrase 'be it spoken'), which would provide a verbal link between 'fourteen' and Juliet's age. But *teen* also meant 'grief' or 'sorrow', and that is probably the Nurse's primary meaning. Lines 10–15 echo I.ii.7–11. Here and in most modern editions, the Nurse's remarks in this scene are rendered as verse; they appear as prose in the early texts.

14 **Lammastide** 1 August.

17 **Lammas Eve** 31 July. It is fitting that Juliet's birthday is at the end of July (a date Shakespeare may have chosen with her name in mind), and the association with an early harvest feast is in accord with the play's many references to her premature ripening.

 she be A similar metrical elision would be appropriate in line 36 'sh' could'. Here *she* is probably to be contracted metrically to *sh'*.

19 **of an Age** the same age.

NURSE   Now by my Maidenhead, at twelve year old
I bad her come. – What, Lamb? What, Ladybird?
– God forbid, where's this Girl? – What, Juliet?

Enter Juliet.

JULIET   How now? Who calls?
NURSE   Your Mother.   5
JULIET   Madam, I am here. What is your will?
WIFE   This is the matter. – Nurse, give
  leave a while:
  We must talk in secret. Nurse, come back again.
  I have rememb'red me: thou s' hear our Counsel.
  Thou knowest my Daughter's of a pretty Age.   10
NURSE   Faith, I can tell her Age unto an Hour.
WIFE   She's not fourteen.
NURSE   I'll lay fourteen o' my Teeth
  (And yet to my Teen, be it spoken, I have but
    four),
  She's not fourteen. How long is it now to
    Lammastide?
WIFE   A Fortnight and odd Days.   15
NURSE   Even or odd, of all Days in the Year,
  Come Lammas Eve at Night shall she be fourteen;
  Susan and she, God rest all Christian Souls,
  Were of an Age. Well, Susan is with God:
  She was too good for me. But as I said,   20
  On Lammas Eve at night shall she be fourteen,
  That shall she marry; I remember it well.
  'Tis since the Earthquake now eleven Years,
  And she was wean'd. I never shall forget it:
  Of all the Days o' the' Year, upon that Day.   25

26 **Wormwood to my Dug** The nurse had put wormwood oil (proverbially bitter) on her nipple in order to wean Juliet. Vermouth derives its name from this herb, a derivative of the plant known to botanists as *Artemesia absinthium*.

27 **under the Dove-house Wall** beside the wall of the house where the Capulets' doves were kept.

29 **Nay . . . Brain** Evidently the Nurse is pleased with her ability to recall that the Capulets were at Mantua.

32 **teachy** tetchy, irritable.

33 **trow** assure you (usually pronounced to rhyme with *snow*).

36 **stand high 'lone** stand up by herself.
Rood Cross.

38 **broke her Brow** hurt her forehead in a fall.

40 **'A** here and elsewhere, 'he'.
merry jolly (here, and frequently elsewhere, implying bawdiness). Compare *Troilus and Cressida*, I.ii.112–14.

42 **Thou . . . Wit** The Nurse refers to the kind of 'fall' a female experiences when her 'Wit' is aroused. Compare *As You Like It*, IV.i.168–87 for an erotic sense of *Wit*. *Backward* echoes I.i.36–38 and I.ii.49.

43 **by my Holydam** an oath that was commonly thought to refer to the Virgin, though it probably originated as a reference to 'halidom' (holiness), and by extension to any holy relic.

45 **Jest** Here as elsewhere, this word is spelled *ieast* in the early printings. It could have been pronounced in a way that made it indistinguishable from *yeast*, a yellow froth or sediment resulting from the fermentation of malt and used to make dough rise and expand. In this passage and in II.iii.68–71, *ieast* hints at characteristics of yeast that could be regarded as analogous to excitation, ejaculation, and impregnation (compare *yesty* in *Hamlet*, V.ii.197–204, and *Macbeth*, IV.i.52–53).
come about be fulfilled, prove prophetic.

46 **I warrant and I** I guarantee that if I.

48 **stinted** stopped.

52 **it** its. At this time *it* was still the normal form.

For I had then laid Wormwood to my Dug,
Sitting in the Sun under the Dove-house Wall.
My Lord and you were then at Mantua
(Nay, I do bear a Brain). But as I said,
When it did taste the Wormwood on the Nipple   30
Of my Dug, and felt it bitter, pretty Fool,
To see it teachy and fall out with the Dug.
'Shake,' quoth the Dovehouse. 'Twas no need, I
    trow,
To bid me trudge.
And since that time it is eleven Years,   35
For then she could stand high 'lone; nay, by the
    Rood,
She could have run and waddled all about.
For even the Day before, she broke her Brow,
And then my Husband (God be with his Soul,
'A was a merry Man) took up the Child;   40
'Yea,' quoth he, 'doest thou fall upon thy Face?
Thou wilt fall backward when thou hast more Wit,
Wilt thou not, Jule?' And by my Holydam,
The pretty Wretch left crying and said 'I'!
To see now how a Jest shall come about.   45
I warrant and I should live a thousand Years,
I never should forget it. 'Wilt thou not, Jule?'
Quoth he. And, pretty Fool, it stinted and said
    'I.'
OLD LADY   Enough of this, I pray thee hold
    thy peace.
NURSE   Yes, Madam. Yet I cannot choose but laugh,   50
To think it should leave crying and say 'I'.
And yet I warrant it had upon it Brow

53   **Cock'rel's Stone** rooster's testicle.

54   **perilous** dangerous, fearful. In all likelihood the Nurse pronounces this word in the way it was often spelled: *parlous*. As in modern British usage for words like *clerk* (pronounced 'clark'), *-er* combinations were frequently pronounced with an *r* sound in Shakespeare's time.

59   **God . . . Grace** God bless you.

67   **onely** This is the usual Shakespearean spelling for *only*; it frequently plays on *one* and means 'solely'.

67–68 **'An Hour' . . . thy Teat** Assuming that the 1599 Second Quarto reading here is correct (the 1597 First Quarto reads 'an honour', which is easier to connect with the Nurse's response to what Juliet says), Juliet's reply impresses the Nurse as one so elevated as almost to require a special explanation. It seems likely that *thy* here is addressed to Juliet's mother. If so, the Nurse is toying with the fiction that Juliet must have been nursed by Capulet's Wife, from whom alone she could have 'suck'd Wisdom' enough to say 'an Hour'.

69–71 **younger than you . . . already Mothers** The Lady's phrasing is so similar to that used earlier by Paris (I.ii.12) as to suggest that Capulet has quoted Paris' words verbatim to his wife and instructed her to speak to Juliet of Paris' suit. Compare III.iv.12–32.

71   **Count** reckoning, accounting. This word, and variations on it, often play on English derivations from the Latin word *cunnus* (female genitalia). Here it calls to mind the title of the suitor being commended to Juliet.

72   **much upon these Years** at about the same age.

76   **Man of Wax** The nurse means 'the very model of a man'.

80   **This Night . . . Feast** Just as there is no reference to Romeo's seeing Rosaline at the feast in I.iv, there is no reference to Juliet's meeting Paris there.

A Bump as big as a young Cock'rel's Stone:
A perilous Knock, and it cried bitterly.
'Yea,' quoth my Husband, 'fall'st upon thy Face?   55
Thou wilt fall backward when thou comest to Age,
Wilt thou not, Jule?' It stinted and said 'I.'
JULIET   And stint thou too, I pray thee,
    Nurse, say I.
NURSE   Peace, I have done. – God mark thee to his
    Grace,
Thou wast the prettiest Babe that e'er I nurs'd.   60
And I might live to see thee married once,
I have my Wish.
OLD LADY   Marry, that 'marry' is the very
    Theme
    I came to talk of. Tell me, daughter Juliet,
    How stands your dispositions to be married?   65
JULIET   It is an Hour that I dream not of.
NURSE   'An Hour': were not I thine onely Nurse,
    I would say thou hadst suck'd Wisdom from thy Teat.
OLD LADY   Well, think of Marriage now:
    younger than you
    Here in Verona, Ladies of esteem,   70
    Are made already Mothers by my Count.
    I was your Mother much upon these Years
    That you are now a Maid. Thus then in brief:
    The valiant Paris seeks you for his Love.
NURSE   A Man, young Lady, Lady, such a Man   75
    As all the World. Why he's a Man of Wax.
OLD LADY   Verona's Summer hath not such a
    Flower.
NURSE   Nay, he's a Flower, in faith, a very Flower.
OLD LADY   What say you, can you love the
    Gentleman?
    This Night you shall behold him at our Feast.   80
    Read o'er the Volume of young Paris' Face,
    And find Delight, writ there with Beauty's Pen;

83   **every married Lineament**   every harmonious line and feature.
       Pen (line 82) recalls I.i.141. In other contexts *Pen* is erotically
       suggestive (see *The Merchant of Venice*, V.i.237, and *All's
       Well That Ends Well*, II.i.72–78), and by the end of her
       speech Juliet's mother is suggesting that her daughter become
       the 'Gold Clasps' that lock in Paris' 'Golden Story' (line 92).

84   **how . . . Content**   how one complements another.

86   **Margeant**   margin, where notes (called 'glosses') were supplied
       to explain the text of the volume. Compare I.i.237–39.

87   **unbound**   Books were normally sold without bound covers in
       Shakespeare's time. Here *unbound* implies 'unclothed' as well
       as 'unmarried', and it recalls I.i.30–32 and I.ii.56.

89   **Fish . . . Sea**   In a variation on Juliet's mother's elaborate
       conceit about Paris as an 'unbound' volume (line 87), the
       young Count here becomes the fish who needs a sea (here
       represented by Juliet) to hold him. As his wife, Juliet will be
       able to take 'much Pride' in being the 'Fair Without' (line 90)
       that hides 'the Fair Within' (that is, Paris). The genital
       implications of *Fish* are reinforced by their echoes of
       I.i.30–35; related imagery occurs in II.iii.41–43.

92   **Gold Clasps . . . Golden Story**   Capulet's Wife says that if Paris
       is the 'fair Volume' (line 85), 'the Golden Story', Juliet will be
       the 'Gold Clasps' designed to enclose and ornament that
       volume.

95   **Women grow by Men**   The Nurse's earthy translation of her
       Lady's concluding line is a characteristic touch of homespun
       realism, the effect of which is to render all the more ludicrous
       the overwrought metaphors in Juliet's mother's speech. The
       Nurse means that women grow 'bigger' by becoming
       pregnant; that is less important to the Capulets than the
       'bigger' status they aspire to achieve through alliance with a
       count.

97   **if Looking Liking move**   if looking prompts attraction.

98   **endart mine Eye**   Juliet is likening her eye to a dart or arrow;
       compare I.i.208–17, I.iv.19. *Consent* recalls I.ii.16–19.

102   **Nurse curs'd in the Pantry**   The Servant, probably Peter, is
       complaining that the Nurse is not helping with the
       preparations.

Examine every married Lineament,
And see how one an other lends Content;
And what obscur'd in this fair Volume lies,   85
Find written in the Margeant of his Eyes.
This precious Book of Love, this unbound Lover,
To beautify him onely lacks a Cover.
The Fish lives in the Sea, and 'tis much pride
For Fair Without the Fair Within to hide: 90
That Book in many's Eyes doth share the Glory
That in Gold Clasps locks in the Golden Story.
So shall you share all that he doth possess,
By having him making your self no less.

NURSE   No less? Nay, bigger. Women grow by Men.   95
OLD LADY   Speak briefly: can you like of
     Paris' Love?
JULIET   I'll look to like, if Looking Liking move.
     But no more deep will I endart mine Eye
     Than your Consent gives strength to make it fly.

Enter Servingman.

SERVINGMAN   Madam, the Guests are come, Supper
     serv'd up, you call'd, my young Lady ask'd for, the   100
     Nurse curs'd in the Pantry, and every thing in

103   **to wait**   to be of service to the guests.

104   **straight**   immediately.

105   **stays**   awaits your arrival.

I.iv   The scene shifts to a site just outside the Capulets' house. Romeo and his friends are prepared to don their masks and enter.

1–2   **shall this Speech . . . Apology?**   Romeo refers to a formal speech to be used as a courteous explanation or 'excuse' for their presence. Such introductions were part of the traditional decorum for masquers at masked balls. From I.ii.69–70 we know that Mercutio (whom we here meet for the first time) is an invited guest. Romeo and Benvolio are gatecrashing the party.

3   **The Date . . . Prolixity**   Such wordy prologues are now considered out of date.

4   **Cupid hoodwink'd**   blindfolded God of Love. Compare I.i.175–76.

5   **Tartar's . . . Lath**   Benvolio alludes to a classical bow with a shape resembling an upper lip.

6   **Crowkeeper**   scarecrow.

7   **without-book**   memorized. Compare I.ii.61, I.iii.81–92.

9   **measure us by what they will**   size us up without our telling them what characters we are impersonating.

10   **measure them a Measure**   dance a measure with them.

11   **Give me a Torch**   Romeo wants to carry the light because he feels 'Heavy' (depressed) and is unwilling to take part in the 'Ambling' (dancing). In lines 35–39 he says that his role in the masked party will be that of an onlooking 'Graundsire' rather than a young 'Wanton'. Compare I.i.134–45.

17–18 **You are a Lover . . . Bound**   Mercutio says that Romeo should attend the Mask in his true character as a disciple of hoodwinked Cupid. *Bound* echoes I.ii.56 and I.iii.87–88.

20   **soar**   Romeo puns on *sore* (painfully, deeply) in line 19. His image hints at the story of Icarus, who soared too high and fell to his death when the Sun melted the wax that affixed his makeshift wings to his arms (compare I.iii.76).

Extremity. I must hence to wait; I beseech you
follow straight.
MOTHER   We follow thee.
                              – Juliet, the County stays.   105
NURSE   Go, Girl: seek happy Nights to happy Days.
                                        Exeunt.

Scene 4

*Enter Romeo, Mercutio, Benvolio, with five or six other
Maskers, Torchbearers.*

ROMEO   What, shall this Speech be spoke for our
   Excuse?
   Or shall we on without Apology?
BENVOLIO   The Date is out of such Prolixity:
   We'll have no Cupid hoodwink'd with a Scarf,
   Bearing a Tartar's painted Bow of Lath,   5
   Scaring the Ladies like a Crowkeeper,
   Nor no without-book Prologue, faintly spoke
   After the Prompter, for our Entrance,
   But let them measure us by what they will.
   We'll measure them a Measure and be gone.   10
ROMEO   Give me a Torch: I am not for this Ambling;
   Being but Heavy, I will bear the Light.
MERCUTIO   Nay, gentle Romeo, we must have you
   dance.
ROMEO   Not I, believe me: you have Dancing Shoes
   With Nimble Soles; I have a Soul of Lead   15
   So stakes me to the Ground I cannot move.
MERCUTIO   You are a Lover: borrow Cupid's Wings
   And soar with them above a common Bound.
ROMEO   I am too sore enpierced with his Shaft
   To soar with his light Feathers, and so bound   20

22   **Burthen** burden. Romeo plays on two senses of 'Pitch' (line 21) to yield two senses of 'Burthen': (a) a load that keeps one from bounding to the highest pitch of a flight, and (b) the bass level (the lowest notes or pitch) in a musical composition.

23   **burthen Love** Mercutio here initiates a series of exchanges with sexual innuendo. First, he suggests that Romeo 'burthen Love' or be atop the one he loves. This leads to wordplay on various terms for the male and female genitalia in lines 24–30. Compare I.iii.42.

28   **beat Love down** cause on upright 'Tool' (I.i.35) to quit stirring and standing (I.i.9–11). See the note to I.i.141.

31   **cote** quote, take note of (with play on *coat*, cover).

39   **The Game . . . I am done** This is a proverbial expression, conveying the advice to quit gambling while you're ahead. Romeo seems to be saying that because he feels like a 'Granndsire', he is now 'done' with the 'Game' (a term normally associated with gambling, but here applied to dancing), even though it was 'ne'er so fair'. Compare line 3.

40   **Dun's the Mouse** Mercutio picks up Romeo's use of 'done' to cite a proverbial expression meaning 'be quiet as a mouse', thus casting Romeo momentarily in the role of a grave old Constable. In lines 41–43 Mercutio goes on to play on the word *Dun*, a name for a beast of burden and a word that sounds like *dung*. He thus portrays Romeo as a horse mired in 'Love'. Mercutio alludes to a Christmas game in which everyone tried to pull a horse (usually a log) out of its mired state. The Second Quarto reads *dum* (dumb, speechless) in line 39, and 'Dun's the Mouse' would also cohere with that sense.

42   **save your Reverence** begging your pardon. The expression also picks up on the implications of 'sir reverence', a euphemism for dung.

45   **Lights by Day** an expression for wasting one's resources.

46   **good Meaning** intended implication.

47   **fine Wits** proclivity to fastidious distinctions in expression. Most editors emend *fine* to *five*. The First Quarto reads *right wits*, a phrase that could refer either to (a) the five senses and the normal powers of intellect and judgement, or (b) the capacity to engage in witty banter.

I cannot bound a Pitch above dull Woe:
Under Love's heavy Burthen do I sink.
MERCUTIO   And to sink in it should you burthen
    Love:
Too great Oppression for a tender Thing.
ROMEO   Is Love a tender Thing? It is too rough,   25
    Too rude, too boist'rous, and it pricks like
    Thorn.
MERCUTIO   If Love be rough with you, be rough with
    Love:
    Prick Love for pricking, and you beat Love down.
    Give me a Case to put my Visage in,
    A Visor for a Visor: what care I   30
    What curious Eye doth cote Deformities?
    Here are the Beetle-brows shall blush for me.
BENVOLIO   Come, knock and enter; and no sooner in
    But every Man betake him to his Legs.
ROMEO   A Torch for me: let Wantons light of Heart   35
    Tickle the senseless Rushes with their Heels.
    For I am proverb'd with a Graundsire Phrase:
    I'll be a Candle-holder and look on.
    The Game was ne'er so fair, and I am done.
MERCUTIO   Tut, Dun's the Mouse: the Constable's own
    Word.   40
    If thou art Dun, we'll draw thee from the Mire
    Or, save your Reverence, Love, wherein thou
    stickest
    Up to the Ears. Come, we burn Daylight: ho.
ROMEO   Nay, that's not so.
MERCUTIO   I mean, Sir, in Delay.
    We waste our Lights in vain: Lights, Lights by
    Day.   45
    Take our good Meaning, for our Judgement sits
    Five times in that ere once in our fine Wits.

48–49 **mean well . . . no Wit** Romeo picks up on Mercutio's previous
lines, to say that though we have good intentions in attending
this Mask, we are not wise to do so. See the notes to I.i.213,
I.iii.42.

53 **Queen Mab** The name is probably meant to play on *quean*, a
word for slut, and thus to give facetious dignity to 'Mab', a
common name for a prostitute. As 'Midwife' her role is to
assist in the birth of fantasies (lines 70–103). In line 53
Mercutio is playing on the copulative sense of *lie* (line 51) to
suggest that Queen Mab had been Romeo's dream lover.
Compare lines 27–28.

55 **Agate Stone** Mercutio compares Mab to the tiny figures carved
in the agates set in seal rings.

57 **Atomi** atoms, the tiniest of creatures.

59 **long Spinners'** daddy longlegs, long-legged spiders.

61 **Traces** harness.

63 **Film** gossamer (light cobweb); spelled *Philome* in the Second
Quarto. *Collars* (line 62) recalls I.i.1–5. And *Moonshine's
Watr'y Beams* invites comparison with *A Midsummer Night's
Dream*, I.i.209–13 and III.i.203–5.

66 **Lazy Finger** probably little finger. But an old wives' tale held
that worms grew in the fingers of lazy girls. Largely for that
reason, most editors prefer the First Quarto reading, 'lazy
finger of a maid' (adopted here), to the Second Quarto
reading, 'lazy finger of a man'.

68 **joiner** cabinetmaker. Because of the squirrel's sharp teeth and
the grub's ability to bore, Mercutio assigns these creatures
their roles as 'Coachmakers'.

69 **Time out o' mind** for longer than anyone can remember.

70 **State** exalted royal dignity.

72 **strait** both (a) straight (as in I.iii.104), and (b) restrictedly.

75 **with Blisters plagues** afflicts with blisters.

ROMEO   And we mean well in going to this Mask,
  But 'tis no Wit to go.
MERCUTIO   Why, may one ask?
ROMEO   I dreamt a Dream to night.
MERCUTIO   And so did I.   50
ROMEO   Well, what was yours?
MERCUTIO   That Dreamers often lie.
ROMEO   In Bed asleep while they do dream things
  true.
MERCUTIO   O then I see Queen Mab hath been with
  you.
  She is the Fairies' Midwife, and she comes
  In Shape no bigger than an Agate Stone   55
  On the Forefinger of an Alderman,
  Drawn with a Team of little Atomi
  Over Men's Noses as they lie asleep;
  Her Wagon Spokes made of long Spinners' Legs,
  The Cover of the Wings of Grasshoppers,   60
  Her Traces of the smallest Spider Web,
  Her Collars of the Moonshine's Wat'ry Beams,
  Her Whip of Cricket's Bone, the Lash of Film,
  Her Wagoner a small grey-coated Gnat
  Not half so big as a round little Worm   65
  Prick'd from the Lazy Finger of a Maid.
  Her Chariot is an empty Hazelnut
  Made by the joiner Squirrel or old Grub,
  Time out o' mind the Fairies' Coachmakers.
  And in this State she gallops Night by Night   70
  Through Lovers' Brains, and then they dream of
    Love;
  On Courtiers' Knees, that dream on Cur'sies
    strait;
  O'er Lawyers' Fingers, who strait dream on
    Fees;
  O'er Ladies' Lips, who strait on Kisses dream,
  Which oft the angry Mab with Blisters plagues   75

76 **Sweetmeats** candies or other sweet delicacies.

78 **Suit** a request for patronage to advance his position at Court. Compare the Capulets' ambitions, as noted in I.ii.30, I.iii.95.

79 **Tithepig** a pig given to a parson as part of the tithe (tenth of one's livestock) owed by a parishioner to the Church. *Tail* puns on *tale* (the Second Quarto spelling).

80 **'a** he.

81 **Benefice** position within the Church.

84 **Breaches** penetrations of enemy defences. Compare I.i.6–36, 86–98, 107–18, 211–17; I.iii.38, 89–95.
   Ambuscados ambushes.

85 **Healths** quaffing large toasts to the health of his boon companions.
   Fadom fathoms, each equal to six feet in depth. Compare *The Tempest*, I.ii.394–400.

87 **being** here pronounced glidingly so as to constitute one syllable metrically.

89 **plats** plaits, tangles, and mats.

90 **Efflocks** clumps of hair that are matted and unkempt from lack of grooming.

91 **Which . . . bodes** Since tangled hair was thought by peasants to be the work of elves (whence the name *elflocks*), it was also assumed that elves would take revenge if their handiwork were undone.

93 **learns** teaches. Lines 92–94 anticipate II.i.33–36 and III.ii.9–13.

94 **Women of Good Carriage** Mercutio puns on three senses of *carriage*: (a) erect, dignified posture, (b) bearing a sexual partner, and (c) bearing children. Compare lines 23–28.

96 **Nothing** Romeo may be punning on a slang term for the female pudendum, based on the notion that a 'Weaker Vessel' (I.i.18) is so called because she either has 'no thing' or is limited to one that resembles an O.

Because their Breath with Sweetmeats tainted
    are.
Sometime she gallops o'er a Courtier's Nose,
And then dreams he of smelling out a Suit;
And sometime comes she with a Tithepig's Tail,
Tickling a Parson's Nose as 'a lies asleep,   80
Then he dreams of an other Benefice.
Sometime she driveth o'er a Soldier's Neck,
And then dreams he of cutting Foreign Throats,
Of Breaches, Ambuscados, Spanish Blades,
Of Healths five Fadom deep, and then anon   85
Drums in his Ear, at which he starts and wakes,
And, being thus frighted, swears a Prayer or two
And sleeps again. This is that very Mab
That plats the Manes of Horses in the Night,
And bakes the Elflocks in foul sluttish Hairs,   90
Which, once untangled, much Misfortune bodes.
This is the Hag, when Maids lie on their Backs,
That presses them and learns them first to
    bear,
Making them Women of Good Carriage: this
Is she —
ROMEO   Peace, peace, Mercutio, peace.   95
Thou talk'st of Nothing.
MERCUTIO   True: I talk of Dreams,
Which are the Children of an Idle Brain,

98   **vain Phantasy**   empty make-believe. *Fantasy* was a term for the human capacity to extrapolate from ordinary experience and conceive of imaginary realms of being. It was roughly equivalent to imagination, and it was the root word for the more common term *fancy*, which was often used as a synonym for the state of being in love. Here, as in *A Midsummer Night's Dream*, II.i.258 and V.i.5, the early texts use the spelling of *Fantasy* that derives from the word's Greek root.

102   **puffs**   an aptly chosen word that personifies the wind's gusts as the huffs of an offended suitor. Compare I.i.115–16, II.i.13.

106–13   **I fear ... Gentlemen**   Apart from the concluding sentence, which is delivered with a somewhat unconvincing bravado, this speech has a reflective quality suggestive of soliloquy. It may be that the actor playing Romeo is meant to hang back from the group for a moment and deliver the lines as if he were alone with his thoughts. Words like *Date*, *Term* and *Forfeit* compare Romeo's lifespan to a loan whose contractual term is about to expire. *Date* echoes line 3; *Forfeit* recalls I.i.101.

112   **he ... Course**   Romeo often uses navigational images (compare II.i.124–26 and V.iii.118–20); here he seems to be thinking of Love as his 'Prompter' (line 8) and 'Pilot' (II.i.124). *Stirrage*, a variation on *steerage* (the First Quarto reading), recalls I.i.9–11, 83.

S.D.   **They march about the Stage ...**   The Second Quarto stage direction suggests that the Maskers are to remain in view of the audience while the Servingmen open what is usually designated Scene v, clearing away the dishes from the feast that has just been completed. But it is equally possible that the original staging called for Romeo and his friends to exit and then re-enter when the Capulets emerge to greet them at line 132. In any event, it is obvious that the action was continuous. The setting now shifts to the interior of Capulet's house, initially to an anteroom and then to the large hall referred to in line 15 as the Great Chamber.

116   **Trencher**   wooden platter.

118   **Manners**   The Second Servingman puns on the Latin *manuarius* ('pertaining to the hand'), from which the word *manners* derives.

Begot of nothing but vain Phantasy,
Which is as thin of Substance as the Air
And more inconstant than the Wind, who woos   100
Even now the frozen Bosom of the North,
And, being anger'd, puffs away from thence,
Turning his side to the Dew-dropping South.
BENVOLIO   This Wind you talk of blows us from our
   Selves:
   Supper is done, and we shall come too late.   105
ROMEO   I fear too early: for my Mind misgives
   Some Consequence yet hanging in the Stars
   Shall bitterly begin his fearful Date
   With this Night's Revels, and expire the Term
   Of a despised Life clos'd in my Breast   110
   By some vile Forfeit of untimely Death.
   But he that hath the Stirrage of my Course
   Direct my Suit. On, lusty Gentlemen.
BENVOLIO   Strike, Drum.

They march about the Stage, and Servingmen come forth
with Napkins.

1 SERVINGMAN   Where's Potpan that he helps not to   115
   take away? He shift a Trencher, he scrape a
   Trencher?
2 SERVINGMAN   When good Manners shall lie all in
   one or two Men's Hands, and they unwash'd too,
   'tis a Foul Thing.   120

121 **Joinstools** stools made by joiners; often called jointstools.

122 **Court-Cubbert** court-cupboard, elaborate sideboard.
Plate silverware.

123 **Marchpane** marzipan, a confection made with ground
almonds, sugar, and egg-white.

124– **let . . . Nell** Now that his evening's tasks are nearly over, the
25 First Servingman prepares to do a little entertaining of his
own. *Grindstone* is a graphically apt name for the kind of
woman whose companionship he seeks after a hard day's
work. The Second Quarto does not make it clear whether
Anthony and Potpan (a) are being asked for along with Susan
Grindstone and Nell, (b) are being addressed (having already
entered along with the first two servingmen), or (c) are being
greeted as late arrivals.

126 **I** both (a) I [am here], and (b) ay. Compare I.ii.60.

130– **the . . . all** may the person among us who survives the rest of
31 us inherit everything we all possess.

132– **Welcome . . . play** Capulet's greeting, in its graciously
41 colloquial informality, is meant to put his new guests at ease.
Capulet speaks first to the visiting Maskers, then to the
Ladies, then to the Maskers again, and finally to the
Musicians. Here as elsewhere, dashes are used to indicate
interruptions or shifts in mode of address. In the original texts
lines 132–39 are set as verse.

133 **walk about** dance a turn, measure 'a bout'.

135 **makes dainty** coyly hesitates to join in.

138 **Visor** mask. Compare lines 29–30.

142 **A Hall, a Hall** This order is directed to the Servingmen, who
are being told to speed up their work in preparing the hall for
dancing. In line 143 the men are jocularly called 'Knaves', a
term that could mean 'serving boy'.

143 **turn . . . up** Apparently the Capulet hall is furnished with
trestle tables, which can be dismantled and stowed against a
wall.

145 **this unlook'd-for Sport** Capulet seems pleased to see that what
had been planned merely as a family gathering will now
feature 'Sport' with some 'unlook'd-for' (unexpected) visitors.
This line is addressed to one of the servants. 'Sirrah' is
normally a term for a social inferior. Compare lines 127–28.

1 SERVINGMAN   Away with the Joinstools; remove the
Court-Cubbert; look to the Plate. – Good thou,
save me a piece of Marchpane; and, as thou loves
me, let the Porter let in Susan Grindstone and
Nell. – Anthony, and Potpan.   125

3 SERVINGMAN   I Boy, ready.

1 SERVINGMAN   You are look'd for, and call'd for,
ask'd for, and sought for in the Great Chamber.

4 SERVINGMAN   We cannot be here and there too.
Cheerly, Boys, be brisk a while, and the Longer   130
Liver take all.   *Exeunt [Servingmen.]*

Enter all the Guests and Gentlewomen to the Maskers.

CAPULET   Welcome, Gentlemen. Ladies that have their
Toes unplagued with Corns will walk about with
you. – Ah, my Mistresses, which of you all will
now deny to daunce? She that makes dainty, she   135
I'll swear hath Corns. Am I come near ye now?
– Welcome, Gentlemen; I have seen the Day that I
have worn a Visor and could tell a whispering
Tale in a fair Lady's Ear, such as would please.
'Tis gone, 'tis gone, 'tis gone! You are welcome,   140
Gentlemen. – Come, Musicians, play.
                              Music plays, and they dance.
– A Hall, a Hall. – Give room and foot it, Girls.
– More Light, you Knaves, and turn the Tables up.
And quench the Fire: the Room is grown too hot.
– Ah Sirrah, this unlook'd-for Sport comes well.   145

146 **Nay sit** Apparently Cousin Capulet (evidently the 'Uncle
Capulet' of I.ii.70) is preparing to join the dancing. Or it may
be that Capulet is assuring him that he is not expected to be
able to keep up with the younger people.

149 **in a Mask** both (a) attired in a visor, and (b) participating
maskers in a masked ball.
By'r Lady in the name of the Virgin Mary.

151 **Nuptial** wedding.

152 **Pentecost** a holiday fifty days after Easter (also known as
Whitsunday).

156 **a Ward** a minor, subject to a guardian's supervision until the
age of twenty-one.

158 **I . . . Sir** It may be that the servingman Romeo addresses is not
one of the Capulets' regular servants; perhaps the demands of
this lavish feast require the addition of temporary help.

163 **shows** appears.
Dove . . . Crows This imagery recalls Benvolio's pledge in
I.ii.90 and proves him to have been a good prophet. Compare
I.i.229–42, I.ii.24–33, 85–104, and see *A Midsummer Night's
Dream*, II.ii.120.

165 **her place of Stand** where she stands.

166 **rude** both (a) low, common, and (b) bold, unmannerly.
Compare lines 118–20.

167 **Forswear** unswear, disavow. Compare I.i.226. *Beauty* recalls
I.i.219–40 and I.ii.85–90.

171 **Antic Face** a face masked with a grotesque or fantastic visor
(*Antic* is often spelled *antique* in English Renaissance texts).

172 **fleer** grin mockingly.

– Nay sit, nay sit, good Cousin Capulet:
For you and I are past our Dauncing Days.
How long is't now since last your self and I
Were in a Mask?
2 CAPULET   By'r Lady, thirty Years.
CAPULET   What Man, 'tis not so much, 'tis not so
    much.   150
  'Tis since the Nuptial of Lucentio,
  Come Pentecost as quickly as it will,
  Some five and twenty Years, and then we mask'd.
2 CAPULET   'Tis more, 'tis more. His Son is
    elder, Sir;
  His Son is thirty.
CAPULET   Will you tell me that?   155
  His Son was but a Ward two Years ago.
ROMEO   What Lady's that which doth enrich the Hand
  Of yonder Knight?
SERVINGMAN   I know not, Sir.
ROMEO   O she doth teach the Torches to burn bright.
  It seems she hangs upon the Cheek of Night   160
  As a rich Jewel in an Ethiop's Ear:
  Beauty too rich for Use, for Earth too dear.
  So shows a snowy Dove trooping with Crows
  As yonder Lady o'er her Fellows shows.
  The Measure done, I'll watch her place of Stand,   165
  And, touching hers, make blessed my rude Hand.
  Did my Heart love till now? Forswear it, Sight;
  For I ne'er saw true Beauty till this Night.
TYBALT   This by his Voice should be a Mountague.
  Fetch me my Rapier, Boy.   [*Exit Page.*]
                    – What dares the Slave   170
  Come hither cover'd with an Antic Face
  To fleer and scorn at our Solemnity?
  Now, by the Stock and Honour of my Kin,
  To strike him dead I hold it not a Sin.
CAPULET   Why how now, Kinsman? Wherefore storm
    you so?   175

177   **Spight**   defiance, insolence. Compare I.i.81.

179   **is it**   Most editors place a question mark after this phrase. But it is not clear that the full stop in the Second Quarto is incorrect; Capulet appears to be making an observation, not asking a question.

181   **'A**   he. *Bears* recalls lines 92–95.
       portly   well-comported, well-mannered.

186   **Note**   notice. Compare I.i.238.

187   **Will**   determination. Compare I.iii.6.

192   **goodman Boy**   By calling Tybalt both a goodman (that is, a yeoman, a man below the rank of gentleman) and a boy, Capulet delivers a double rebuke to the irascible young man's overweening dignity.
       Go to   no more protestations. This phrase is a common expression of impatience.

195   **make a Mutiny**   create an unruly disturbance. Compare the Prologue, line 3.

196   **You will set Cock a hoop**   Capulet is telling Tybalt that his behaviour is like that of a strutting cock (the sound of the phrase perhaps echoing that of a crowing rooster). The phrase may also refer to the wild drinking bouts that occur when the 'cock' (spigot) is removed and placed atop the 'hoop' of a barrel of alcoholic drink.
       you'll be the Man   Capulet probably means that Tybalt is acting like the Master (line 193) rather than an obedient nephew. Compare III.i.57–62, 69–70, 137–38.

197   **'tis a Shame**   Tybalt is saying that Romeo's unchallenged presence is an insult to the Capulets' honour.

199   **This Trick . . . scathe you**   Tybalt's unruly defiance may injure ('scathe') him if he doesn't mend his behaviour.

201   **Well said**   well done. *Hearts* recalls I.i.187.
       Princox   a name combining the words *prince* and *cock*, thus connoting a prancing audacity. Capulet's remarks in lines 201–3 are thrice interrupted by his shouts to the dancers and servants. Compare I.i.84–91.

204–5 **Patience . . . Greeting**   Tybalt allegorizes his conflict by depicting his 'Choler' (anger) as having been impeded 'perforce' (forcibly) by the 'Patience' (forbearance) of his uncle. *Choler* recalls I.i.1–5. *Gall* (line 207) echoes I.i.197.

TYBALT   Uncle, this is a Mountague, our Foe:
  A Villain that is hither come in Spight
  To scorn at our Solemnity this Night.
CAPULET   Young Romeo is it.
TYBALT   'Tis he, that villain Romeo.
CAPULET   Content thee, gentle Coze, let him alone.　　180
  'A bears him like a portly Gentleman;
  And to say truth, Verona brags of him
  To be a virtuous and well-govern'd Youth.
  I would not for the Wealth of all this Town
  Here in my House do him Disparagement:　　185
  Therefore be Patient, take no Note of him.
  It is my Will, the which if thou respect,
  Shew a Fair Presence and put off these Frowns,
  An ill-beseeming Semblance for a Feast.
TYBALT   It fits when such a Villain is a Guest:　　190
  I'll not endure him.
CAPULET   He shall be endur'd.
  What, goodman Boy, I say he shall, Go to:
  Am I the Master here or you? Go to,
  You'll not endure him. God shall mend my Soul,
  You'll make a Mutiny among my Guests;　　195
  You will set Cock a hoop; you'll be the Man.
TYBALT   Why, Uncle, 'tis a Shame.
CAPULET   Go to, go to,
  You are a saucy Boy. Is't so indeed?
  This Trick may chance to scathe you, I know
    what;
  You must contrary me. Marry 'tis Time:　　200
  – Well said, my Hearts. – You are a Princox, go.
  Be quiet, or – More light, more light, for
    shame.
  – I'll make you quiet. – What, cheerly, my Hearts.
TYBALT   Patience perforce, with wilful
    Choler meeting,
  Makes my Flesh tremble in their different
    Greeting.　　205

209 **holy Shrine**   Romeo probably says these words while holding
Juliet's hand. Throughout this scene he depicts himself as an
unworthy supplicant for redemption at a religious sanctuary.
Sin (line 211) echoes line 174, and anticipates lines 221–25.

215 **Palmers**   Palmers were pilgrims who had visited the Holy
Sepulchre in Jerusalem and wore palm leaves to signify their
devotion.

220 **Saints . . . sake**   Juliet seems to be saying that though saints do
not take the initiative to intervene in human affairs, they do
provide assistance when requested to do so by prayer. Here
her implication is that she will 'move not' to resist if the
'Pilgrim' takes the kiss he prays for. *Saint* echoes I.i.217.

225 **by th' Book**   by the rules, in a formulaic fashion; compare lines
208–25 with I.i.215–27. Though the idea of doing things by
the book is ridiculed elsewhere in the play, Juliet appears to
mean no criticism here. Her implication seems to be that
everything about Romeo's behaviour is in accordance with the
rituals of 'mannerly Devotion' (line 213). Appropriately, lines
208–21 take the form of a Shakespearean sonnet. Lines
222–25 constitute the first quatrain of a second sonnet –
interrupted, significantly, by the Nurse's intrusion with a
message from Juliet's mother. It could be said that these brief
exchanges capture the play in epitome. *Book* recalls I.ii.61,
I.iii.81–94, and I.iv.7.

227 **What is**   what is the name, and role, of. As Romeo and the
Nurse speak, Juliet goes to her mother.

230 **withal**   with.

231 **lay hold of**   win the hand (and inheritance) of. Lines 231–32
echo *A Midsummer Night's Dream*, V.i.179. In the process
they suggest a genital sense of *Chinks* unintended by the
Nurse but pertinent to what will transpire.

I will withdraw, but this Intrusion shall,
Now seeming Sweet, convert to bitt'rest Gall.

Exit.

ROMEO If I profane with my unworthiest Hand
This holy Shrine, the gentle Sin in this:
My Lips, two blushing Pilgrims, ready stand   210
To smooth that rough Touch with a tender Kiss.

JULIET Good Pilgrim, you do wrong your Hand too
    much,
Which mannerly Devotion shows in this,
For Saints have Hands that Pilgrims' Hands do
    touch,
And Palm to Palm is holy Palmers' Kiss.   215

ROMEO Have not Saints Lips, and holy Palmers too?

JULIET I, Pilgrim: Lips that they must use in
    Pray'r.

ROMEO O then, dear Saint, let Lips do what Hands
    do:
They pray. Grant thou, lest Faith turn to
    Despair.

JULIET Saints do not move, though grant for
    Prayers' sake.   220

ROMEO Then move not while my Prayer's effect I
    take.
Thus from my Lips by thine my Sin is purg'd.

JULIET Then have my Lips the Sin that they have
    took.

ROMEO Sin from my Lips? O Trespass sweetly urg'd:
Give me my Sin again.

JULIET   You kiss by th' Book.   225

NURSE Madam, your Mother craves a Word with you.

ROMEO What is her Mother?

NURSE   Marry, Bachelor,
Her Mother is the Lady of the House,
And a good Lady, and a wise and virtuous.
I nurs'd her Daughter that you talk withal;   230
I tell you, he that can lay hold of her

232 **Chinks** the coins, the money. Compare I.iii.93–95.

233 **dear Account** Romeo continues the monetary metaphor by
suggesting that he has just put his life in his 'Foe's Debt'. He
fears that this will prove to be a costly ('dear') transaction
('Account') for him. *Account* recalls I.iii.70–71.

234 **The Sport is at the best** It was proverbial that one should leave
gaming while ahead, an idea expressed earlier in line 39. The
'fear' Romeo expresses in the next line is that this moment at
the heights can only lead to a downward turning of Fortune's
wheel.

237 **Banquet** a light dessert of fruit, wine, and sweets. As we know
from I.iv.105, the feast itself is now over.

241 **by my Fay** by my faith. This line is evidently spoken to one of
the servants.

243 **What** who. *What* was often used to identify people in terms of
their title, rank, or function in society.

254 **Too early . . . too late** Juliet says that she saw Romeo 'too
early', when his identity was 'unknown' to her; now that she
is in love, she realizes that it is 'too late' to undo what might
not have happened had she first known him to be a
Mountague. Compare line 227.

255 **Progidious** portentously abnormal. The word *prodigy* was
often applied to deformed or freakish offspring, who were
thought to signify Heaven's displeasure. Compare lines
29–31.

256 **tis** this (here spelled in a way that conveys a dialectal form of
the pronoun.

257 **Rime** rhyme. This spelling, derived from Italian, is used in all
the original texts of the play.

258 **withal** with. When *with* ends a sentence or clause, Shakespeare
frequently lengthens it to *withal* for emphasis. Compare line
230. Since Juliet hasn't danced with Romeo, it seems clear
that her reply is meant to be misleading. Compare the subtle
indirection she employs in lines 243–49 to learn Romeo's
name without revealing any special interest in him. See the
note to I.i.153.
Anon equivalent to 'Right away!' or 'Coming!'

Shall have the Chinks.
ROMEO   Is she a Capulet?
O dear Account! My Life is my Foe's Debt.
BENVOLIO   Away, begone, the Sport is at the best.
ROMEO   I, so I fear: the more is my Unrest.   235
CAPULET   Nay, Gentlemen, prepare not to be gone:
We have a trifling, foolish Banquet towards.
                                        They whisper in his ear.
Is it e'en so? Why then I thank you all;
I thank you, honest Gentlemen; goodnight.
— More Torches here. Come on then, let's to Bed.   240
Ah Sirrah, by my Fay, it waxes late;
I'll to my Rest.
JULIET   Come hither, Nurse. What is yond Gentleman?
NURSE   The Son and Heir of old Tiberio.
JULIET   What's he that now is going out of door?   245
NURSE   Marry, that I think be young Petruchio.
JULIET   What's he that follows here that would not
   dance?
NURSE   I know not.
JULIET   Go ask his Name. If he be married,
My Grave is like to be my Wedding Bed.   250
NURSE   His Name is Romeo, and a Mountague:
The onely Son of your great Enemy.
JULIET   My onely Love sprung from my onely Hate:
Too early seen unknown, and known too late.
Prodigious Birth of Love it is to me.   255
That I must love a loathed Enemy.
NURSE   What's tis? What's tis?
JULIET   A Rime I learnt even now
Of one I danc'd withal.
One calls within   Juliet.
NURSE   Anon, anon.
— Come, let's away; the Strangers all are gone.
                                        Exeunt.

II.   Here the Chorus functions to effect a transition from the Mask
        scene inside the Capulets' house to the scenes that follow once
        Romeo, Benvolio, and Mercutio leave the party. A second role
        for the Chorus is to help the audience step outside the play for
        a brief but ostensibly more objective appraisal of what is
        happening.

1–2   **Now Old Desire . . . Heir**   From the point of view of the
        Chorus, the only significant difference between Romeo's new
        'Affection' and his old 'Desire' is that the new one is requited.
        There is nothing in the description of the two romantic states
        here to suggest that the Chorus considers what Romeo feels
        for Juliet to be superior in kind to what he felt for Rosaline.

2   **Young Affection gapes**   The image suggests a baby bird with its
        mouth eagerly open for food. *Groan'd* (line 3) recalls
        I.i.203–4. Compare *Hamlet*, III.ii.272–75. *Die* can refer to the
        consummation (the orgasm) a young man with a
        'mount-ague' devoutly seeks. See *Troilus and Cressida*,
        III.i.120–34, for a song about the kind of death love 'groans'
        to achieve. *Groans* will recur in II.ii.74, II.iii.95.

5   **again**   both (a) in reciprocation, and (b) a second time. *Match'd*
        (line 4) recalls I.ii.96.

6   **Charm of Looks**   Together with the word *bewitched* earlier in
        the line, this phrase suggests that, from the point of view of
        the Chorus, what Juliet feels is merely a superficial infatuation
        similar to Romeo's. In Shakespeare's time *Charm* (a binding
        spell) is normally a word with negative connotations.

8   **fearful Hooks**   a reference to the feud, and to the parental
        disapproval it would evoke if the two lovers were to go public
        with their relationship. The 'Hooks' image relates to 'Bait'
        earlier in the line – suggesting that the lovers are at best
        unwitting victims (like unsuspecting fish), at worst risk-taking
        fools. Compare I.iii.89–90.

9   **Access**   Here the metrical position dictates a stress on the
        second syllable.

10   **use**   are accustomed.

13   **Passion**   a term suggesting that the relationship between the
        lovers is founded not on reason but on undisciplined
        ('extreme', line 14) emotions. *Extremities* recalls I.iii.102–3.

ACT II

[*Enter Chorus.*]

CHORUS   Now Old Desire doth in his Deathbed lie,
And Young Affection gapes to be his Heir.
That Fair for which Love groan'd for and would
   die,
With tender Juliet match'd, is now not Fair.
Now Romeo is beloved, and loves again,   5
Alike bewitched by the Charm of Looks;
But to his Foe suppos'd he must complain,
And she steal Love's sweet Bait from fearful
   Hooks.
Being held a Foe, he may not have Access
To breathe such Vows as Lovers use to swear;   10
And she as much in love, her Means much less
To meet her new Beloved any where.
But Passion lends them Power, Time Means, to
   meet,

14   **Temp'ring** both (a) diluting (by mixing in new ingredients), and (b) strengthening (as in the process whereby steel is heated, beaten, and cooled to give it the requisite hardness, and resiliency). Implicit in lines 13–14 is the notion (deriving from Aristotle's *Nicomachean Ethics*) that 'Passion' is irrational behaviour that gravitates to 'Extremities' rather than finding the 'Means' (medians, midpoints) between extremes. From the perspective of the Chorus, Romeo and Juliet are courting disaster by their refusal to heed reason's cautions and proceed with cool, calm, measured moderation.

II.i   The setting for this scene is the wall surrounding the Capulets' Orchard. After line 2, Romeo stands just inside the wall, with Mercutio and Benvolio outside it, within earshot of Romeo. On the bare Elizabethan stage the wall could have been represented by something as simple as one of the pillars supporting the canopy above the main playing area.

2   **dull Earth** Romeo is referring to his body. Compare I.iv.19–22.
    Centre Romeo refers both to his heart and to Juliet, to whom he has just surrendered his heart. Compare Sonnet 146, line 1.

3   **He is wise** Mercutio seems to mean 'He's given us the slip and outfoxed us.' Mercutio assumes that Romeo has returned to his old tricks and retreated again from company. Compare I.i.121–56.

6   **I'll conjure** Mercutio pretends to summon Romeo as if he were a spirit subject to a magician's charms. In the Second Quarto this line is assigned to Benvolio; the First Quarto gives it to Mercutio, who proceeds to execute a mock conjuration.

10   **pronaunt** both (a) provide, and (b) pronounce (the word in the First Quarto, adopted in this passage by most editors).

11   **Goship** Most modern editions read *gossip*, the spelling in the First Quarto text. But the Second Quarto spelling ('goship'), which is also found in the Folio, is probably a purposeful combination of 'godship' and 'gossip', an apt way of reducing the Goddess Venus to a garrulous old woman.

12   **purblind** proverbially impaired in vision.

13   **Abraham** probably elided metrically to 'Abra'm'. Cupid is so called, perhaps, because Mercutio thinks him no more dignified than the half-naked 'Abraham-man' who was said to roam the country begging and stealing. If so, 'Abraham Cupid' is simply Mercutio's satirical name for 'naked Cupid'.

Temp'ring Extremities with extreme Sweet.   [*Exit.*]

Scene 1

Enter Romeo alone.

ROMEO   Can I go forward when my Heart is here?
Turn back, dull Earth, and find thy Centre out.

> *He retires.*

Enter Benvolio with Mercutio.

BENVOLIO   Romeo, my Cousin Romeo, Romeo.
MERCUTIO   He is wise,
And on my Life hath stol'n him home to Bed.
BENVOLIO   He ran this way and leapt this Orchard
    Wall.   5
Call, good Mercutio.
MERCUTIO   Nay, I'll conjure too.
Romeo, Humours, Madman, Passion, Lover,
Appear thou in the likeness of a Sigh;
Speak but one Rime, and I am satisfied.
Cry but 'Ay me', pronaunt but 'Love' and 'Dove',   10
Speak to my Goship Venus one fair Word,
One Nickname for her purblind Son and Heir,
Young Abraham Cupid, he that shot so true

14 **King Cophetua** an allusion to an old ballad about a king whom Cupid forced to love a beggar maiden at first sight.

16 **The Ape is dead** apparently a reference to a trained ape who would feign death until he heard a designated magic word from his master.

20 **Demesnes** domains.

24 **raise a Spirit . . . Circle** Mercutio is trying to summon up 'Old Desire' with an oblique sexual reference. Since conjurers normally invoked spirits to appear within a magic circle, Mercutio is perfectly orthodox in suggesting a 'Mistress' Circle' for Romeo's 'Spirit' to rise within. See the note to I.iv.96, and compare III.iii.84–90. Compare I.i.6–35, I.iv.22–31.

31 **humorous Night** Here *humorous* means both (a) damp, and (b) conducive to the moods of a person under sway of the humours. Compare I.i.144–45. *Consorted with* means 'companion to'; compare III.i.47–49.

34 **if . . . Mark** Compare I.i.208–14.

36 **Medlers** medlars; small, apple-like fruits, eaten only when nearly rotten, and thought to resemble the female genitalia. Medlars were proverbially associated with 'meddlers', those with a fondness for meddling around sexually. Compare I.ii.39–42.

38 **open Et-cetera** This reading, from the First Quarto, suggests that Mercutio has a more bawdy word in mind. Compare the play on O in lines 23–26.
Pop'rin Pear a fruit thought to resemble the male genitalia. *Pop'rin* plays on 'pop 'er in'.

40 **Field-bed** a portable bed used by soldiers on military campaigns.

42 **To . . . found** Benvolio's phrasing recalls I.i.129–33.

43 **He . . . Wound** As he speaks this line, Romeo emerges from where he has been listening to Mercutio and Benvolio's gibes. Almost immediately Romeo's focus shifts to a window above, where a light indicates Juliet's presence. Most editors begin a new scene ii here.
jests This word (spelled *ieasts* in the early texts) recalls I.iii.45 and anticipates II.iii.68–75.

When King Cophetua lov'd the Beggar Maid.
– He heareth not, he stirreth not, he moveth not: 15
The Ape is dead, and I must conjure him.
– I conjure thee, by Rosaline's bright Eyes,
By her high Forehead, and her scarlet Lip,
By her fine Foot, straight Leg, and quivering
    Thigh,
And the Demesnes that there adjacent lie,   20
That in thy Likeness thou appear to us.
BENVOLIO   And if he hear thee, thou wilt anger him.
MERCUTIO   This cannot anger him. 'Twould anger him
To raise a Spirit in his Mistress' Circle
Of some strange nature, letting it there stand   25
Till she had laid it and conjured it down:
That were some Spight. My Invocation
Is fair and honest: in his Mistress' Name
I conjure onely but to raise up him.
BENVOLIO   Come, he hath hid himself among these
    Trees   30
To be consorted with the humorous Night:
Blind is his Love, and best befits the Dark.
MERCUTIO   If Love be blind, Love cannot hit the
    Mark.
Now will he sit under a Medler Tree
And wish his Mistress were that kind of Fruit   35
As Maids call Medlers when they laugh alone.
– O Romeo, that she were, O that she were
An open Et-cetera, thou a Pop'rin Pear.
Romeo, goodnight; I'll to my Truckle-bed:
This Field-bed is too cold for me to sleep.   40
– Come, shall we go?
BENVOLIO   Go then, for 'tis in vain
To seek him here that means not to be found.
                                    Exit [with Mercutio.]
ROMEO   He jests at Scars that never felt a Wound.
– But soft, what Light through yonder Window
    breaks?

45–51 **It is . . . off** Romeo begins by likening Juliet to the Sun and thereby placing her above 'the envious Moon', who is jealous because 'her Maid' is 'more fair than she'. Romeo then prays that Juliet will cast off her allegiance to the Moon (that is, to Diana, Goddess of the Moon and patroness of virgins) and exchange the 'Livery' (uniform) of Diana for that of Venus (Goddess of Love).

50 **Vestal Livery** apparel of virgins dedicated to Vesta, Roman Goddess of the Hearth. Here Vesta's attributes are merged with those of Diana, Goddess of Chastity. Romeo's imagery recalls the voice of 'Old Desire' in I.i.211–28.
sick and green characteristics associated with (a) envy, and (b) lovesick maidens. Compare III.v.157.

51 **none . . . wear it** Court fools wore a motley uniform, with green as one of its dominant colours.

52–53 **It is . . . were** In the early texts these clauses are printed as a single line of sixteen syllables. It may be that the actor playing Romeo was to convey his excitement by speaking these words in a rush of ardour. Another possibility is that the actor was to pause after a second, short line to give Juliet a four-syllable moment to 'speak' silently.

58 **Having some Business** being compelled by other affairs to absent themselves for a while. *Business* anticipates II.iii.56–58, where Romeo gives it a bawdy implication.

59 **Spheres** Shakespeare refers to the already outdated Ptolemaic cosmology whereby the stars and planets were thought to revolve around the Earth in concentric crystalline spheres to the accompaniment of a celestial music too refined for mortal ears to hear. Compare *The Merchant of Venice*, V.i.55–65.

60 **they** the 'Stars' referred to in line 15. Romeo probably refers to bright planets.

It is the East, and Juliet is the Sun.   45
Arise, fair Sun, and kill the envious Moon,
Who is already sick and pale with Grief
That thou her Maid art far more fair than she.
Be not her Maid, since she is envious:
Her Vestal Livery is but sick and green,   50
And none but Fools do wear it. Cast it off.
It is my Lady, O it is my Love:
O that she knew she were.
She speaks, yet she says nothing: what of that?
Her Eye discourses; I will answer it.   55
I am too bold: 'tis not to me she speaks.
Two of the fairest Stars in all Heaven,
Having some Business, do entreat her Eyes
To twinkle in their Spheres till they return.
What if her Eyes were there, they in her Head?   60
The brightness of her Cheek would shame those
    Stars
As Day-light doth a Lamp; her Eyes in Heaven
Would through the Airy Region stream so bright
That Birds would sing and think it were not
    Night.

65   **Cheek** This word recalls I.iv.160–61. Lines 66–67 anticipate a famous description of the Queen of Egypt; see *Antony and Cleopatra*, II.ii.207–11, where Enobarbus refers to 'divers colour'd Fans whose Wind did seem / To glove the delicate Cheeks which they did cool, / And what they undid did'.

73   **puffing** both (a) swelling, and (b) blowing. Compare I.iv.102.

75   **wherefore art thou Romeo?** Juliet's question is 'why are you Romeo?' and not 'where', as is commonly thought. We should also note that in most of their occurrences, the names *Romeo* and *Juliet* are pronounced as two-syllable words (Roám-yo and Joól-yet). Curiously, in this scene in which so much is made of Romeo's name, the hero never once speaks Juliet's name to her.

81   **Thou . . . Mountague** You would be the same self if you were not a Mountague.

86   **By any other Name** This reading comes from the First Quarto; the Second Quarto (followed by the First Folio) reads 'By any other word'. That version of the line is equally acceptable. But because there are deficiencies in the Second Quarto rendering of this speech (for example, it does not supply the words 'nor any other part', which must be imported from the First Quarto), this edition departs from it in adopting the First Quarto's more familiar 'name' in Juliet's famous meditation.

88   **owes** owns.

89   **doff** do off, remove. Compare *don*, a contraction for 'do on'.

92   **Call . . . new baptiz'd** Romeo refers to the christening ceremony where infants are given their Christian names. He says that henceforth he will be called 'Love' rather than 'Romeo', and in that sense 'new baptiz'd'. The baptismal imagery also reinforces the suggestion that Romeo's new 'religion', centred on Juliet, has resulted in his being newly born. Romeo's phrasing echoes what Mercutio has said in lines 6–14.

95   **my Counsel** my private musings. The phrase 'stumblest on' is rich with implication. It reminds us that it is only by chance that Romeo is here to overhear Juliet's meditations. But it also reinforces the awkwardness of the moment, and the potential it has for injury to both parties. Compare II.ii.19–20, 94.

See how she leans her Cheek upon her Hand: 65
O that I were a Glove upon that Hand,
That I might touch that Cheek.
JULIET   Ay me.
ROMEO   She speaks.
— O speak again, bright Angel, for thou art
As glorious to this Night, being o'er my Head,
As is a winged Messenger of Heaven   70
Unto the white upturned wond'ring Eyes
Of Mortals that fall back to gaze on him
When he bestrides the lazy, puffing Clouds
And sails upon the Bosom of the Air.
JULIET   O Romeo, Romeo, wherefore art thou Romeo?   75
Deny thy Father and refuse thy Name;
Or if thou wilt not, be but sworn my Love
And I'll no longer be a Capulet.
ROMEO   Shall I hear more, or shall I speak at this?
JULIET   'Tis but thy Name that is my Enemy: 80
Thou art thy Self, though not a Mountague.
What's Mountague? It is nor Hand nor Foot,
Nor Arm nor Face, nor any other Part
Belonging to a Man. O be some other Name.
What's in a Name? That which we call a Rose   85
By any other Name would smell as sweet;
So Romeo would, were he not Romeo call'd,
Retain that dear Perfection which he owes
Without that Title. Romeo, doff thy Name,
And for thy Name, which is no part of thee,   90
Take all my Self.
ROMEO   I take thee at thy Word:
Call me but Love, and I'll be new baptiz'd;
Henceforth I never will be Romeo.
JULIET   What Man art thou that, thus bescreened
      in Night,
So stumblest on my Counsel?
ROMEO   By a Name   95

97   **Saint**   Romeo's epithet recalls I.i.217 and I.iv.208–25.

101 **uttering**   outflowing.

108 **Love's light Wings**   another allusion to traditional portrayals of
        Cupid as a winged boy. Compare I.iv.17–22.
        o'erperch   alight upon and then descend from; bound over.

109 **Stony Limits**   a reminder of the wall separating Pyramus and
        Thisbe, whose story as told by Ovid was the ultimate source
        of the Romeo and Juliet legend. Their tragedy was treated
        comically in *A Midsummer Night's Dream*, Shakespeare's
        companion piece to *Romeo and Juliet*. There, of course, the
        'Stony Limits' that separate the lovers are represented by a
        character called Wall.

111 **Stop**   hindrance, obstacle. Compare IV.i.1–3.

113 **Alack**   a mild intensifier, comparable to *alas* and generally more
        negative in implication than *indeed*.

114 **proof against**   protected from, invulnerable to.

116 **sweet**   inviting, welcoming. Romeo's imagery implicitly
        compares Juliet to a forbidden fruit, a sense that coheres with
        the orchard setting and evokes associations with the biblical
        Garden of Eden (where Adam and Eve disregard 'Stony
        Limits' and imprudently defy threats of 'Death') and with the
        classical Garden of the Hesperides (whose golden apples were
        guarded by a dragon until the adventurous Hercules slew him
        and stole them in the eleventh of his twelve labours).

118 **but**   provided that; if only. Compare lines 113–15.

120 **prorogued**   postponed, prolonged (here pronounced as a
        three-syllable word).
        wanting of   lacking; being separated from.

122 **prompt**   cue, instigate. This word recalls I.iv.4–8, 112–13 (a
        passage that also anticipates line 124).

123 **Counsel**   instruction. Compare lines 94–95.

124 **Pilot**   person responsible for a vessel's course.

I know not how to tell thee who I am.
My Name, dear Saint, is hateful to my Self
Because it is an Enemy to thee;
Had I it written, I would tear the Word.
JULIET   My Ears have yet not drunk a hundred Words   100
Of thy Tongue's uttering, yet I know the Sound.
Art thou not Romeo, and a Mountague?
ROMEO   Neither, fair Maid, if either thee dislike.
JULIET   How camest thou hither, tell me, and
   wherefore?
The Orchard Walls are high and hard to climb,   105
And the place Death, considering who thou art,
If any of my Kinsmen find thee here.
ROMEO   With Love's light Wings did I o'erperch
   these Walls:
For Stony Limits cannot hold Love out,
And what Love can do, that dares Love attempt.   110
Therefore thy Kinsmen are no Stop to me.
JULIET   If they do see thee, they will murther thee.
ROMEO   Alack, there lies more Peril in thine Eye
Than twenty of their Swords; look thou but sweet,
And I am proof against their Enmity.   115
JULIET   I would not for the World they saw thee
   here.
ROMEO   I have Night's Cloak to hide me from their
   Eyes;
And but thou love me, let them find me here.
My Life were better ended by their Hate
Than Death prorogued wanting of thy Love.   120
JULIET   By whose Direction found'st thou out this
   place?
ROMEO   By Love, that first did prompt me to
   inquire:
He lent me Counsel, and I lent him Eyes.
I am no Pilot, yet wert thou as far
As that vast Shore wash'd with the farthest Sea,   125

126 **Marchandise** merchandise, goods deriving from merchant ventures.

127 **Mask of Night** a reminder of the masking just concluded. Juliet describes herself as a masker costumed as Night. Her imagery echoes lines 94–95 and 117, and recalls I.iv.31.

130 **Fain** gladly.
dwell on Form insist on the rules of etiquette.

131 **Complement** compliance with and conformity to socially accepted rules of etiquette. Juliet is saying that she will no longer 'kiss by th' Book' (I.iv.225). Compare Miranda's 'Hence, bashful Cunning' in *The Tempest*, III.i.81.

132 **I** both (a) ay, and (b) I [do]. Compare I.ii.60, I.iv.126, 217, 235.

134 **Perjuries** falsehoods, infidelities. Compare *A Midsummer Night's Dream*, I.i.240–41.

136 **pronounce it faithfully** swear it with complete fidelity. *Pronounce* recalls line 10.

140 **fond** infatuated; foolishly unrestrained in my doting.

141 **light** wanton, frivolous. Maidens who yielded too easily were referred to as 'light'. Juliet also plays on the distinction between 'Light' and 'Dark' in lines 147–48.

143 **Cunning to be strange** skill at seeming distant, aloof.

145 **ware** both (a) aware and (b) wary. Compare I.i.128.

147 **Light Love** love lacking in the weightiness of truth and sincerity.

148 **discovered** disclosed. Compare I.i.154.

151 **th' inconstant Moon** The Moon was proverbial for inconstancy. Everything 'sublunary' (that is, below, or within, the sphere containing the Moon) was thought to be subject to change. See *A Midsummer Night's Dream*, I.i.1–6, V.i.253–54.

156 **Idolatry** It may be that Juliet speaks more than she realizes here, because in fact many members of Shakespeare's original audience would have interpreted her sentiments as verging on a kind of worship in the place of – if not indeed in opposition to – Christianity. The significance of lines 151–57 is highlighted by Juliet's echo of Matthew 5:34–37, where Jesus commands against any form of swearing.

I should adventure for such Marchandise.

JULIET   Thou knowest the Mask of Night is on my
    Face,
Else would a Maiden Blush bepaint my Cheek
For that which thou hast heard me speak to night.
Fain would I dwell on Form; fain, fain deny   130
What I have spoke; but farewell, Complement.
Doest thou love me? I know thou wilt say 'I',
And I will take thy Word. Yet if thou swear'st,
Thou mayest prove false; at Lovers' Perjuries
They say Jove laughs. O gentle Romeo,   135
If thou dost love, pronounce it faithfully.
Or if thou thinkest I am too quickly won,
I'll frown and be perverse and say thee nay
So thou wilt woo; but else not for the World.
In truth, fair Mountague, I am too fond: 140
And therefore thou mayest think my 'Haviour light,
But trust me, Gentleman, I'll prove more true
Than those that have more Cunning to be Strange.
I should have been more Strange, I must confess,
But that thou overheard'st ere I was ware   145
My True-love Passion; therefore pardon me,
And not impute this yielding to Light Love
Which the Dark Night hath so discovered.

ROMEO   Lady, by yonder blessed Moon I vow,
That tips with Silver all these Fruit-tree
    Tops –   150

JULIET   O swear not by the Moon, th' inconstant
    Moon,
That monthly changes in her circled Orb,
Lest that thy Love prove likewise variable.

ROMEO   What shall I swear by?

JULIET   Do not swear at all;
Or if thou wilt, swear by thy gracious Self,   155
Which is the God of my Idolatry,
And I'll believe thee.

159 **Contract** Juliet is thinking of the practice whereby vows exchanged in private by a man and a woman were considered binding in the eyes of the Church, tantamount to a kind of marriage, whether or not validated by a formal ceremony.

160 **unadvis'd** ill-considered.

161– **Too . . . lightens'** Compare *A Midsummer Night's Dream*,
62 I.i.141–49.

163– **This Bud . . . meet** Juliet appears ready to step back from what
64 she and Romeo have said and wait for 'Summer's ripening Breath' to determine whether a 'Bud' will in fact 'prove a beauteous Flow'r'. Instinctively she knows that 'Ripeness is all' (*King Lear*, V.ii.11).

168 **What Satisfaction . . . to night?** Juliet appears to fear that Romeo wants to consummate their 'Contract' right now. Courtly lovers in medieval and Renaissance poetry regularly complained of their need to be 'satisfied'.

173 **frank** free, generous.

175 **My Bounty** Juliet refers to her love. This expression serves to remind us that her other suitor, Paris, is at least as interested in the Capulet 'Bounty' she represents (what the Nurse has called 'the Chinks' in I.iv.232) as he is in the qualities that draw Romeo to her. A concern for that kind of bounty never enters Romeo's mind. Rosalind speaks to similar effect in *As You Like It*, IV.i.219–23. Juliet, like Romeo, is disavowing 'Limits' (line 109); compare lines 110–11, 124–26, 185–90.

179 **Anon** right away. Juliet's reply to the Nurse's call is a reminder of the interruption of the lovers' first meeting (see the note to I.iv.225), and an anticipation of similar intrusions in III.v.36 and V.i.153–70.

183 **flattering sweet** deceptively and misleadingly sweet.
substantial based on substance rather than on the 'nothing' to which Mercutio has reduced dreams in I.iv.96–103. Lines 181–83 recall the Queen Mab discussion in I.iv.48–103. They also echo *A Midsummer Night's Dream*, IV.i.190–224, V.i.1–27. *Boundless* (unbounded) echoes I.iv.17–22.

185 **bent** inclination, intention.
honourable based on a desire for legal matrimony.

188 **Right** rite; the ritual our contract gives us the right to enact.

ROMEO   If my Heart's dear Love —
JULIET   Well, do not swear. Although I joy in thee,
  I have no joy of this Contract to night:
  It is too rash, too unadvis'd, too sudden;   160
  Too like the Lightning, which doth cease to be
  Ere one can say 'It lightens'. Sweet, goodnight:
  This Bud of Love, by Summer's ripening Breath,
  May prove a beauteous Flow'r when next we meet.
  Goodnight, goodnight: as sweet Repose and Rest   165
  Come to thy Heart as that within my Breast.
ROMEO   O wilt thou leave me so unsatisfied?
JULIET   What Satisfaction canst thou have to night?
ROMEO   Th' Exchange of thy Love's faithful Vow for
  mine.
JULIET   I gave thee mine before thou didst request
  it;   170
  And yet I would it were to give again.
ROMEO   Wouldst thou withdraw it? For what purpose,
  Love?
JULIET   But to be frank and give it thee again.
  And yet I wish but for the thing I have.
  My Bounty is as boundless as the Sea,   175
  My Love as deep; the more I give to thee
  The more I have, for both are infinite.
  I hear some Noise within: Dear Love, adieu.
  — Anon, good Nurse. — Sweet Mountague, be true.
  Stay but a little; I will come again.   *Exit*.   180
ROMEO   O blessed, blessed Night. I am afeard,
  Being in Night, all this is but a Dream,
  Too flattering sweet to be substantial.
JULIET   Three Words, dear Romeo, and goodnight
  indeed.
  If that thy bent of Love be honourable,   185
  Thy purpose Marriage, send me Word to morrow,
  By one that I'll procure to come to thee,
  Where and what Time thou wilt perform the Right,

190 **my Lord** The Quarto and Folio texts do not set off 'my Lord' as a parenthetical phrase, so it may be that Juliet's meaning is 'follow thee as my Lord'. An alternative interpretation (which would be expressed by setting off 'my Lord' in parenthetical commas) is that she already regards him as her lord by virtue of the vows they have just exchanged.

193 **By and by** right away. Both the dramatic context and the metrical position of the phrase suggest that it be pronounced glidingly as if it were a single syllable.

194 **thy Strife** your efforts. Compare *Twelfth Night*, V.i.414.

197 **want** be deprived of; desire. *Want* recalls lines 118–20. Lines 198–99 invite comparison with the melancholy Jaques' description of the schoolboy in *As You Like It*, II.vii.145–47.

201 **Tassel gentle** gentle tercel, or male falcon. This noble peregrine could be called back to its master by a quiet signal similar to Juliet's 'hist' (line 159).

202 **Bondage is hoarse** Feeling constrained by her need for secrecy, Juliet metaphorically ascribes her whisper to hoarseness. *Bondage* echoes line 175.

204 **airy Tongue** a reference to Echo's ability to cast her voice into the air in reverberation. Juliet alludes to a nymph in classical mythology who fell in love with Narcissus; after she gave up her pursuit, she pined away until nothing was left of her but a lonely voice to be heard in caves. Ovid tells the story in Book III of the *Metamorphoses*. The metonymy of 'Tongue' for 'Voice' (line 200), a figure of speech whereby a part stands for the whole that comprises it, is an apt epitome of Echo's 'Bondage', her reduction from an autonomous voice to a reverberative whisper.

206–8 **It is my Soul . . . Ears** Romeo's reflection is apparently prompted by the softness of Juliet's voice, which makes it seem as if her words are an echo of his own thoughts, his own 'Soul'.

209 **Neece** The Second Quarto and First Folio reading is capable of being construed as 'niece', a word that could be applied to any young woman, regardless of relationship. But it could also mean 'Niesse'. A *niesse* (often spelled *nyas* or *eyas*) was a young hawk approaching the age when it was ready to leave the nest, an image particularly apt for the youthful Juliet. *Niesse* (here to be treated metrically as a two-syllable word) would cohere with Juliet's falcon imagery (lines 200–202).

And all my Fortunes at thy Foot I'll lay
And follow thee my Lord throughout the World.   190
[NURSE *within*]   Madam.
JULIET   I come, anon. – But if thou meanest not
   well,
  I do beseech thee –
[NURSE *within*]   Madam.
JULIET   By and by I come.
  – To cease thy Strife and leave me to my Grief.
  To morrow will I send.
ROMEO   So thrive my Soul.   195
JULIET   A thousand Times goodnight.   [*Exit above.*]
ROMEO   A thousand Times the worse to want thy Light.
  Love goes toward Love as Schoolboys from their
   Books,
  But Love from Love toward School with heavy
   Looks.

Enter Juliet again.

JULIET   Hist, Romeo, hist. – O for a Falc'ner's
   Voice,   200
  To lure this Tassel gentle back again.
  Bondage is hoarse, and may not speak aloud;
  Else would I tear the Cave where Echo lies
  And make her airy Tongue more hoarse than mine
  With repetition of my Romeo's Name.   205
ROMEO   It is my Soul that calls upon my Name.
  How silver sweet sound Lovers' Tongues by Night,
  Like softest Music to attending Ears.
JULIET   Romeo –
ROMEO   My Neece?
JULIET   What o'clock to morrow
  Shall I send to thee?
ROMEO   By the Hour of nine.   210
JULIET   I will not fail. 'Tis twenty Year till
  then.

216 **still** In this line, though not in line 214 (where it has its usual modern meaning), *still* apparently means 'always'.

stay both (a) remain, and (b) stand. *Stay* and *stand* derive from the same Latin verb, *stare*, and both words figure prominently in *Romeo and Juliet*. For previous variations on *stand*, see I.i.9–12, 30–32; I.ii.33; I.iii.65; I.iv.165; II.i.25. For previous uses of *stay*, see I.i.215; I.ii.37, 65; I.iii.105.

219 **Wanton's Bird** the pet of a pampered, at times cruel child. Compare *King Lear*, IV.i.36–37, where Gloucester says 'As Flies to Wanton Boys are we to th' Gods: / They kill us for their Sport'.

221 **Gyves** fetters, chain shackles for the legs and feet.

232 **flected** (a) bent, bowed, (b) deflected, sent reeling, and (c) dappled, spotted (as in II.ii.3).

233 **from forth** away from.

Titan's Wheels wheels of the chariot of the Sun God, and thus a metaphor for the Sun's course through the sky. The God of the Sun had various names: Helios, Phoebus, and Hyperion. Because he was a son of the Titans, the Gods who ruled the Universe before they were overthrown by Zeus and the Olympian Gods, the Sun God was often referred to simply as Titan. Lines 230–34 and the first four lines of the next scene are so similar that most editors assume them to be variant renderings of the same speech, with one passage or the other to have been marked for deletion. Some editions assign versions of the lines to Romeo, others to Friar Lawrence. Since it is possible that Shakespeare intended to include both speeches in the play, the Everyman text leaves them as they appear in the Second Quarto.

234 **ghostly** spiritual. This Anglo-Saxon sense of *ghost* is the one preserved in the name 'Holy Ghost', as the third person of the Trinity is normally called in the King James Version of the Bible published in 1611.

235 **dear Hap** precious happening. The phrase carries the sense of the expression 'great good fortune'. But *dear* can also mean 'costly'.

I have forgot why I did call thee back.

ROMEO   Let me stand here till thou remember it.

JULIET   I shall forget, to have thee still stand
    there,

Rememb'ring how I love thy Company.   215

ROMEO   And I'll still stay, to have thee still
    forget,

Forgetting any other Home but this.

JULIET   'Tis almost Morning: I would have thee gone,

And yet no farther than a Wanton's Bird,

That lets it hop a little from his Hand,   220

Like a poor Prisoner in his twisted Gyves,

And with a silken Thread plucks it back again,

So loving jealous of his Liberty.

ROMEO   I would I were thy Bird.

JULIET   Sweet, so would I;

Yet I should kill thee with much Cherishing.   225

Good night, good night: Parting is such sweet
    Sorrow

That I shall say good night till it be Morrow.

ROMEO   Sleep dwell upon thine Eyes, Peace in thy
    Breast.   [*Exit Juliet.*]

– Would I were Sleep and Peace, so sweet to rest.

The grey-ey'd Morn smiles on the frowning Night,   230

Check'ring the Eastern Clouds with streaks of Light,

And Darkness, flected like a Drunkard, reels

From forth Day's Pathway, made by Titan's Wheels.

Hence will I to my ghostly Friar's close Cell,

His Help to crave and my dear Hap to tell.   *Exit.*   235

II.ii   The setting shifts to the garden outside Friar Lawrence's 'close Cell'.

7   **Osier Cage**   wicker basket, made from branches of the osier, a type of willow.

8   **baleful**   harmful.

9   **that's**   which is. *That* is commonly used by Shakespeare to introduce a nonrestrictive (parenthetical) clause; in modern usage such clauses are normally introduced by *which* and set off with commas.

10   **Grave**   This word recalls I.i.96 and I.iv.249–50 and anticipates line 83 and III.i.104.

15   **mickle**   much, great.
     Grace   The Friar uses the term here to refer to any earthly manifestation of divine goodness.

16   **true Qualities**   In this passage (lines 11–22) the Friar is distinguishing between natural ('true') qualities and qualities resulting from abuse of those qualities.

19   **strain'd from that Fair Use**   constrained, forced away from its natural, proper use; perverted.

20   **Revolts from True Birth**   rebels against its natural state or use.
     stumbling on Abuse   This phrase could have either of two meanings: (a) finding ('stumbling on') a way to abuse its ordained use, or (b) falling ('stumbling') 'on' (as a result of) such abuse. Compare II.i.94–95.

22   **by Action dignified**   made virtuous by its action.

23   **Rind**   outer covering or layer.

25   **smelt**   both (a) smelled, and (b) smelted (melted and fused). Compare *Coriolanus*, V.i.31, and *King Lear*, IV.vi.104–5.
     cheers   brings health and pleasure to. The first 'part' is the nose; the second is the rest of the body. The Friar's phrasing recalls I.i.66, 71, 98, 117–18; I.ii.17; and II.i.82–84, 89–91.

Scene 2

Enter Friar alone, with a Basket.

FRIAR The grey-ey'd Morn smiles on the
  frowning Night,
Check'ring the Eastern Clouds with streaks of Light,
And fleckled Darkness like a Drunkard reels
From forth Day's Path, and Titan's burning Wheels:
Now ere the Sun advance his burning Eye,   5
The Day to cheer and Night's dank Dew to dry,
I must upfill this Osier Cage of ours
With baleful Weeds and precious juiced Flowers.
The Earth that's Nature's Mother is her Tomb;
What is her burying Grave, that is her Womb.   10
And from her Womb Children of divers kind
We sucking on her natural Bosom find:
Many for many Virtues excellent,
None but for some, and yet all different.
O mickle is the powerful Grace that lies   15
In Plants, Herbs, Stones, and their true
  Qualities:
For nought so Vile that on the Earth doth live,
But to the Earth some special Good doth give,
Nor ought so Good but, strain'd from that Fair
  Use,
Revolts from True Birth, stumbling on Abuse.   20
Virtue it self turns Vice being misapplied,
And Vice sometime's by Action dignified.

Enter Romeo.

Within the infant Rind of this weak Flower
Poison hath residence, and Medicine power:
For this being smelt with that part cheers
  each part,   25

26 **stays all Senses with the Heart**   suspends all senses as it stops
   the heart from beating. *Stays* recalls II.i.216.

30 **Canker**   the cankerworm, a larva that feeds on buds. Compare
   I.i.98, 154.

31 **Benedicite**   God bless you. (Here the Latin is used as a mild
   ejaculation of surprise.)

33 **argues**   provides evidence for.
   distempered Head   a disturbed head; a mind not governing
   itself properly. Compare II. Chorus, 14.

37 **unbruised**   untouched with the cares that 'stuff' the brains of
   older men and keep them from sleep.

38 **couch**   lay down, repose. Compare *The Merchant of Venice*,
   V.i.304–5.

40 **Distemp'rature**   mental or emotional disturbance resulting from
   the bodily humours' being out of 'temper' (lacking their
   proper balance or combination). *Hit* echoes I.i.207–14.

43 **Rest**   peace, contentment (with wordplay on the sense implied
   by the Friar's reference to 'Bed' in the preceding line).

49 **feasting with mine Enemy**   an allusion to Jesus' admonition to
   love rather than hate one's enemies (Matthew 5:43–44), and
   to his insistence on eating with 'publicans and sinners'
   (Matthew 9:10–15).

50 **wounded**   a reference to the commonplace that one who has
   fallen in love has been pierced by Cupid's golden arrow.
   Compare I.i.207–14 and II.ii.1. But Romeo's language in lines
   49–52 also calls attention to the Physician whose
   'Intercession' (Isaiah 53:5, 12) lies behind the Friar's ministry.

52 **holy Physic**   'Physic' was the term normally used for the
   doctor's healing powers (whence our word 'physician'); as a
   spiritual doctor, the Friar is now being asked to 'heal' Romeo
   and Juliet's 'wounds' by marrying the lovers.

54 **Intercession**   mediation; petitionary interceding on behalf of
   another person (usually one accused of an offence).
   steads   stands well; supports or aids.

55 **homely**   unadorned, plainspoken; direct.
   thy Drift   the direction (literally, the drive) of your discourse.

Being tasted, stays all Senses with the Heart.
Two such opposed Kings encamp them still
In Man as well as Herbs, Grace and Rude Will:
And where the Worser is predominant,
Full soon the Canker Death eats up that Plant.   30
ROMEO   Good morrow, Father.
FRIAR   *Benedicite.*
What early Tongue so sweet saluteth me?
Young Son, it argues a distempered Head
So soon to bid good morrow to thy Bed.
Care keeps his Watch in every Old Man's Eye,   35
And where Care lodges, Sleep will never lie;
But where unbruised Youth with unstuff'd Brain
Doth couch his Limbs, there golden Sleep doth
   reign.
Therefore thy Earliness doth me assure
Thou art uprous'd with some Distemp'rature.   40
Or if not so, then here I hit it right:
Our Romeo hath not been in Bed to night.
ROMEO   That last is true: the sweeter Rest was mine.
FRIAR   God pardon Sin, wast thou with Rosaline?
ROMEO   With Rosaline, my ghostly Father, no;   45
I have forgot that Name, and that Name's Woe.
FRIAR   That's my good Son, but where
   hast thou been then?
ROMEO   I'll tell thee ere thou ask it me again:
I have been feasting with mine Enemy,
Where on a sudden one hath wounded me   50
That's by me wounded; both our Remedies
Within thy Help and holy Physic lies.
I bear no Hatred, blessed Man: for lo,
My Intercession likewise steads my Foe.
FRIAR   Be plain, good Son, and homely in
   thy Drift: 55

56   **Shrift**   absolution, forgiveness of sins confessed. Compare
I.i.162.

60   **combin'd**   joined by 'exchange of Vow' (line 62, paraphrasing
II.i.158–59, 168–69).

63   **pass**   proceed, walk along. As Romeo speaks, he and the Friar
probably commence toward a place on the stage that signifies
the entrance to Friar Lawrence's 'Cell'.

64   **consent**   Romeo's verb recalls I.ii.16–19 and I.iii.99; in the
process it reminds us that neither Juliet nor the Friar will seek
her parents' consent for her to marry Romeo.

65   **Change**   This word often means 'exchange' in Shakespeare, and
that may well be one of the Friar's implications here, echoing
Romeo's use of the word in line 62 and suggesting that
Romeo has simply exchanged Rosaline for Juliet in his
immature affections. Compare I.ii.9. The 'Saint Francis' the
Friar invokes is the Assisi monk who founded the Franciscan
order in the early thirteenth century.

69   **Iesu Maria**   by Jesus and his mother Mary. See the note to
II.i.156.
Brine   salt water; here referring to Romeo's tears.

72   **season**   both (a) to flavour, and (b) to preserve with salt, as in
pickling. The Friar's verb is coloured by such biblical passages
as Psalm 1:3, Proverbs 15:23, Ecclesiastes 3:1, Isaiah 50:4,
and Matthew 21:41. Compare *The Merchant of Venice*,
IV.i.199–200, V.i.107–8, and *All's Well That Ends Well*,
I.i.54–55.

75   **here upon thy Cheek**   At this moment the Friar probably puts
his finger on Romeo's cheek. Compare II.i.65.

79   **Sentence**   *Sententiae* were maxims, pithy sayings to be
memorized and stored for use in dealing with life's crises as in
I.i.91. Here the Friar's 'Sentence' derives from the theological
premise that men were divinely ordained to provide spiritual
guidance for what St Peter called 'weaker vessels' (1 Peter
3:7). Compare I.i.6–20, 68.

Riddling Confession finds but riddling Shrift.
ROMEO　Then plainly know, my Heart's dear Love is
　　set
On the fair Daughter of rich Capulet;
As mine on hers, so hers is set on mine,
And all combin'd save what thou must combine　　60
By Holy Marriage. When and where and how
We met, we woo'd, and made exchange of Vow
I'll tell thee as we pass; but this I pray,
That thou consent to marry us to day.
FRIAR　Holy Saint Frauncis, what a Change
　　is here?　　65
Is Rosaline, that thou didst love so dear,
So soon forsaken? Young Men's Love then lies
Not truly in their Hearts but in their Eyes.
Iesu Maria, what a deal of Brine
Hast wash'd thy sallow Cheeks for Rosaline!　　70
How much Salt-water thrown away in waste
To season Love, that of it doth not taste.
The Sun not yet thy Sighs from Heaven clears;
Thy old Groans yet ringing in mine auncient Years;
Lo here upon thy Cheek the Stain doth sit　　75
Of an old Tear that is not wash'd off yet.
If e'er thou wast thy self, and these Woes
　　thine,
Thou and these Woes were all for Rosaline.
And art thou chang'd? Pronounce this Sentence
　　then:
Women may fall when there's no Strength in Men.　　80
ROMEO　Thou chid'st me oft for loving Rosaline.
FRIAR　For doting, not for loving, Pupil mine.
ROMEO　And bad'st me bury Love.
FRIAR　　　　　　　　　　　　Not in a Grave
To lay one in, an other out to have.
ROMEO　I pray thee chide me not; her I love now　　85
Doth Grace for Grace and Love for Love allow.

86   **Grace**   favour, gift. Compare lines 15–30.

88   **by rote**   by memory, by following a prescribed 'route' in a
        mechanical way.

90   **In one respect**   for one reason, in view of one consideration
        (*respect* stems from Latin and literally means 'look' or 'see').

91   **happy**   lucky, fortunate.

93   **stand on**   require, insist on. The expression *stand on sudden
        Hast* contains a paradox, of which Romeo may be unaware,
        in the contradictory meanings of *stand* and *haste*. The phrase
        echoes Sampson's 'shall move me to stand' (I.i.12), and
        Shakespeare probably expected some members of his audience
        to recognize in it a variation on the Latin motto *festina lente*
        ('make haste slowly'). The Friar's next line is another
        variation on the same theme, and a caution that those who
        think it possible to 'stand on sudden Hast' will soon discover
        to their grief that they 'stumble' instead. See the note to
        II.i.216.

94   **Wisely and slow**   Whether the Friar is heeding his own counsel
        at this moment is a question the audience may well be
        expected to ask. *Stumble* recalls lines 15–22. It thereby invites
        us to ponder whether what appears to be a 'Vice' (the Friar's
        decision to assist an 'Alliance' that Juliet has described as 'too
        rash, too unadvis'd, too sudden', II.i.160) will turn out to be
        'by Action dignified' (II.ii.21–22).

II.iii   The setting is a hot street at midday.

4   **pale**   probably Mercutio's way of parodying the Petrarchan
        lover's insistence that his Lady is a goddess with pure white
        skin. Characteristically, Mercutio insists on referring to the
        object of Romeo's worship as a common 'Wench'. Little does
        Mercutio know that Rosaline has now paled into
        insignificance. *Pale* recalls II.i.47 and anticipates II.iii.214–15,
        II.iv.17, and III.ii.55.

10–13 **answer**   Benvolio's first use of the word carries the implication
        that Romeo will accept the challenge and duel with Tybalt.
        Mercutio's reply allows only that Romeo will send back
        another letter in return. As the scene develops, we see that
        Mercutio's words prove prophetic, though for reasons of
        which he is unaware.

The other did not so.

FRIAR   O she knew well,
Thy Love did read by rote that could not spell.
But come, young Waverer, come go with me.
In one respect I'll thy Assistant be: 90
For this Alliance may so happy prove,
To turn your Households' Rancour to pure Love.

ROMEO   O let us hence: I stand on sudden Hast.

FRIAR   Wisely and slow: they stumble that run fast.   *Exeunt.*

Scene 3

Enter Benvolio and Mercutio.

MERCUTIO   Where the Devil should this Romeo be?
Came he not home to night?

BENVOLIO   Not to his Father's; I spoke with his Man.

MERCUTIO   Why that same pale, hard-hearted Wench,
that Rosaline, torments him so, that he will   5
sure run mad.

BENVOLIO   Tybalt, the Kinsman to old Capulet, hath
sent a Letter to his Father's House.

MERCUTIO   A Challenge, on my Life.

BENVOLIO   Romeo will answer it.   10

MERCUTIO   Any man that can write may answer a
Letter.

BENVOLIO   Nay, he will answer the Letter's Maister
how he dares, being dared.

MERCUTIO   Alas, poor Romeo: he is already dead,   15
stabb'd with a white Wench's black Eye, run
through the Ear with a Love Song, the very Pin

18-19 blind Bow-Boy's Butt-shaft a dismissive reference to Cupid and his arrow. The *butt* was the target, and in the white circle or 'prick' at its centre was a *pin* (line 17) or wooden peg. A butt-shaft then, was an unbarbed arrow aimed at the black pin in the centre of a white target. Romeo's 'Heart' mirrors the 'white Wench's black Eye' that has 'stabb'd' it. *Man* anticipates III.i.57–62.

21 Prince of Cats Tybalt (spelled variously) was the name of the Prince of Cats in *Reynard the Fox*, a popular fable.

21-22 he's ... Complements He complies with all the rules of etiquette in the use of the rapier. *Complements* recalls II.i.131.

23 Pricksong Mercutio refers here to printed music, which one followed with strict adherence to the notes (or 'pricks') on the page. He also alludes to another meaning of 'pricksong' as the descant or counterpoint augmenting a plainsong or simple melody. In addition, he plays on at least three other meanings of the word *prick*: (a) a verb, to puncture, (b) a noun referring to the white centre (the clout) of a target, and (c) a noun referring to the male member. Compare I.iv.27–28.

24 Minim Rests pauses equal to the shortest notes in music.

27 House probably a reference to a 'school' or college of fencing.

28 Cause reason (case) for either (a) challenging a man by declaring him guilty of a crime that merits the death penalty, or (b) defending one's own honour.
Passado forward thrust or 'pass' with the sword, as distinguished from the 'Punto Reverso' (lines 28–29) or back-handed thrust.

29 Hay 'Thou hast it!' (from Italian *hai*), marking a hit.

31-40 The ... Bones Pretending to address Benvolio as a fellow old-timer (compare I.iv.35–39, 145–47), Mercutio parodies the new fangled affectations of those who seek to follow the latest fashions. *Form* is a word for *Bench*. And *Bones* probably alludes to the 'Bone-ache' symptomatic of syphilis.

43 fishified a coinage alluding to Romeo's loss of his 'Roe' (here, the sperm of a male herring, as well as the eggs of a female herring, and the female deer a hart would miss). Mercutio assumes that when Romeo gave him and Benvolio 'the Slip' (line 54) the previous night, he found a way to release his sexual tension.

of his Heart cleft with the blind Bow-Boy's
Butt-shaft. And is he a man to encounter Tybalt?
BENVOLIO   Why what is Tybalt?   20
MERCUTIO   More than Prince of Cats. O he's the
courageous Captain of Complements. He fights as
you sing Pricksong: keeps Time, Distance, and
Proportion. He rests his Minim Rests: one, two,
and the third in your Bosom. The very Butcher of   25
a Silk Button: a Duellist, Duellist. A Gentleman
of the very First House, of the First and Second
Cause. Ah the Immortal Passado, the Punto
Reverso, the Hay.
BENVOLIO   The what?   30
MERCUTIO   The Pox of such antique lisping,
affecting Fantasticoes, these new Tuners of
Accent. 'By Jesu, a very good Blade, a very tall
Man, a very good Whore.' Why, is not this a
lamentable thing, Graundsir, that we should be   35
thus afflicted with these straunge Flies: these
Fashion-mongers, these Pardon-me's, who stand so
much on the new Form that they cannot sit at
ease on the old Bench? O their Bones, their
Bones.   40

Enter Romeo.

BENVOLIO   Here comes Romeo, here comes Romeo.
MERCUTIO   Without his Roe, like a dried Herring. O
Flesh, Flesh, how art thou fishified? Now is he

44   **flowed in**   Mercutio continues the fish and water imagery, but he now relates it to 'Numbers', or the syllable counts used in Renaissance metrical analyses of poetry. By 'flow'd in' he probably also means the expression of passion, both poetic and erotic. Compare I.i.33–34 and I.iii.89–95.

46–48 **Dido . . . Harlots**   Mercutio reduces each heroine to a form of lowborn wench: a dowdy, a gipsy, a hilding, and a harlot.

47   **Gipsy**   This word derived from 'Egyptian', and its association with Cleopatra identified it with lust (see *Antony and Cleopatra*, I.i.9–10).

50   **French Slop**   This term often referred to a pair of baggy pants, and thus probably had a meaning similar to 'baggage' (whore). But *slop* also meant 'dung', and may have been used to refer to semen as well.

51   **Counterfeit**   If the first syllable of *Counterfeit* is here meant to allude to the female genitalia (see the note to I.iii.71), the word as a whole probably refers to that which 'fits' such a receptacle or 'Case' (line 57, echoing I.iv.24–30).

54   **Slip**   A slip was a counterfeit coin, but it was also a term for the male member and for the fluid by which it was said to 'conceive' (line 55). See *Measure for Measure*, III.i.138–40 and V.i.465.

58   **strain**   both (a) stretch, and (b) constrain (force, compel). Romeo and Mercutio are joking about the kind of 'curtsy' a man performs when his 'Business' is 'great'. Compare II.ii.19–20. The alterations in shape and texture that Romeo describes echo Mercutio's remark about 'Deformities' (I.iv.29–31), a word that may also allude to what Iago calls 'making the Beast with two Backs' (*Othello*, I.i.115–16).

63   **curteous**   Here the Shakespearean spelling plays on *cur* and on the 'base Spaniel Fawning' of 'low-crook'd Curtsies' (*Julius Caesar*, III.i.43). *Hit* recalls I.i.210–11.

72–73 **O single-sol'd Jest . . . Singleness**   This jest seems to be based on the fact that, among their other implications, both *sole* and *single* mean 'standing alone'. Mercutio and Romeo are probably thinking of the upright figure of the number 1. And in the word 'Sole' (line 70, where its primary meaning has to do with a 'Pump', or light slip-on shoe) they are probably also alluding once more to a type of fish and its roe. See the notes on *Jest* (*Ieast*) at I.iii.45, II.i.43.

for the Numbers that Petrarch flowed in. Laura
to his Lady was a Kitchen Wench (marry, she had   45
a better Love to be-rime her), Dido a Dowdy,
Cleopatra a Gipsy, Helen and Hero Hildings and
Harlots, Thisbe a grey Eye or so but not to the
purpose. – Signior Romeo, *bonjour*. There's a
French Salutation to your French Slop. You gave   50
us the Counterfeit fairly last night.

ROMEO   Good morrow to you both. What Counterfeit
did I give you?

MERCUTIO   The Slip, Sir, the Slip: can you not
conceive?   55

ROMEO   Pardon, good Mercutio, my Business was
great, and in such a Case as mine a Man may
strain Curtesy.

MERCUTIO   That's as much as to say, such a Case as
yours constrains a Man to bow in the Hams.   60

ROMEO   Meaning to Cur'sy.

MERCUTIO   Thou hast most kindly hit it.

ROMEO   A most curteous Exposition.

MERCUTIO   Nay I am the very Pink of Curtesy.

ROMEO   Pink for Flower.   65

MERCUTIO   Right.

ROMEO   Why then is my Pump well flower'd.

MERCUTIO   Sure Wit, follow me this Ieast now till
thou hast worn out thy Pump, that when the
single Sole of it is worn, the Ieast may remain   70
after the wearing, solely singular.

ROMEO   O single-sol'd Jest, solely singular for the
Singleness.

74-75 **my Wits faints**   Mercutio is saying that his 'Wits' cannot 'stand up' to Romeo's. See the note to I.iii.42, and compare I.iv.46-49.

76   **Swits and Spurs**   Romeo pretends that he and Mercutio are in a wild horse race, one in which the lead rider sets the pace and course; *swits* are 'switches', and Romeo's meaning is 'keep it up'.

77   **cry 'a Match'**   declare a victory.

78   **Wild-Goose chase**   a hunting game; here a hunt for pleasure. *Goose* can mean (a) fool, and (b) whore.

81   **for the Goose**   to chase a loose woman willing to be caught.

84   **bite thee by the Ear**   a phrase usually associated with the friendly nuzzling one horse gives to another.

85   **good Goose**   simpleton, perhaps with the suggestion that it takes a goose (that is, a wanton) to chase one.

90   **Cheverell**   kid leather known for its ability to stretch, in this case from 1 inch to 45 (an ell). Mercutio uses the term to continue the innuendo on that which is expandable or stretchable (as in 'my Business was great', lines 56-57, and 'strain Curtsey', line 58), here the 'Wit' of either gender.

92   **I**   This word can mean either 'I' or 'Ay' here.

98-   **drivelling Love . . . Hole**   Love is depicted here as a drooling
100   idiot (a 'Natural') sporting a long stick with a 'Bable' (an inflated bladder) dangling from its end. Court jesters were also called 'naturals', and their baubles were topped with coxcombs. Mercutio's image reduces 'Love' to a drooling personification of obsessive lust and its paraphernalia. *Bable* (bauble) plays on *babble*. Here *Hole* refers to a 'Weaker Vessel' (see I.i.17-20). But Mercutio's words will eventually prove pertinent to a more permanent 'Hole'; compare II.ii.9-10. Also see *A Midsummer Night's Dream*, V.i.203-8.

102   **Tale**   a pun on *tail* (*penis* in Latin), a word that usually referred to the male member but could also refer to the female genitalia.

103   **against the Hair**   normally an expression for the friction caused by rubbing an animal or a person the wrong way. Here Mercutio uses *against* in an erotic sense, and he probably also intends a pun on *Hair* similar to that in line 140.

MERCUTIO   Come between us, good Benvolio: my Wits
faints.   75

ROMEO   Swits and Spurs, Swits and Spurs, or I'll
cry a Match.

MERCUTIO   Nay, if our Wits run the Wild-Goose Chase,
I am done: for thou hast more of the Wild-Goose
in one of thy Wits than I am sure I have in my   80
whole five. Was I with you there for the Goose?

ROMEO   Thou wast never with me for any thing when
thou wast not there for the Goose.

MERCUTIO   I will bite thee by the Ear for that Jest.

ROMEO   Nay, good Goose, bite not.   85

MERCUTIO   Thy Wit is a very bitter Sweeting, it is
a most sharp Sauce.

ROMEO   And is it not then well serv'd in to a sweet
Goose?

MERCUTIO   O here's a Wit of Cheverell, that   90
stretches from an inch narrow to an Ell broad!

ROMEO   I stretch it out for that word 'Broad',
which, added to the Goose, proves thee far and
wide a Broad Goose.

MERCUTIO   Why is not this better now than groaning   95
for Love? Now art thou Sociable, now art thou
Romeo: now art thou what thou art, by Art as
well as by Nature. For this drivelling Love is
like a great Natural that runs lolling up and
down to hide his Bable in a Hole.   100

BENVOLIO   Stop there, stop there.

MERCUTIO   Thou desirest me to stop in my Tale
against the Hair.

ROMEO   Thou wouldst else have made thy Tale large.

MERCUTIO   O thou art deceiv'd, I would have made it   105
short: for I was come to the whole depth of my

107 **occupy the Argument** dwell on the theme, but with 'Argument' here used to refer to a genital 'case'. Compare *Troilus and Cressida*, IV.v.26–29.

109 **goodly Gear** a reference to the elaborate get-up of the Nurse, whose efforts to dress smartly subject her to ridicule. *Gear* can also refer to the genitalia, and to the provisions made for their pleasure. See *Troilus and Cressida*, I.i.6, III.ii.221–22.
A Sail Some of the hats women wore actually resembled sailing ships. Here *Sail* may involve wordplay on *sale*, with the implication that the Nurse and Peter are a bawd and her pimp. Compare *Counsellors* ('coun-sellers') *Measure for Measure*, I.ii.110. *Shirt* and *Smock* mean male and female.

117 **God ye good-den** God give you good e'en (evening). Mercutio is reminding the Nurse that it is no longer morning.

119– **bawdy Hand . . . Prick of Noon** For Mercutio, even the clock
20 is engaged in wanton behaviour. Here the 'Prick' is the mark engraved on the O-shaped clockface to indicate the hour of twelve. Compare lines 22–23.

123 **himself to mar** In view of Mercutio's preceding line, Romeo is probably alluding to the view that sexual licence is a form of self-abuse. *Mar* recalls I.ii.12–13, and here too it plays on *marry*.

125 **quoth 'a** said he.

130 **for fault of a Worse** Romeo is facetiously saying that owing to the 'fault' (error or misstep) of a worse man of that name (that is, Romeo's father), he is 'the Youngest of that Name'. *Fault* was also a term for female genitalia, by analogy with another sense of *fault* (crack, as in the modern use of the term for a geological fault). As such, it reinforced the notion that a woman's sexual organs involved a deficiency (literally, no 'thing'). Compare I.iv.96.

134 **some Confidence** some words in private. The Nurse probably means to say 'conference'; that appears, at least, to be Benvolio's assumption.

136 **endite** probably intended as a mock malapropism (for 'invite') in imitation of the pretentious manner in which the Nurse says she wants to speak with Romeo privately.

Tale, and meant indeed to occupy the Argument no
longer.

Enter Nurse and her Man.

ROMEO   Here's goodly Gear: a Sail, a Sail.
MERCUTIO   Two, two: a Shirt and a Smock.   110
NURSE   Peter.
PETER   Anon.
NURSE   My Fan, Peter.
MERCUTIO   Good Peter, to hide her Face: for her
  Fan's the fairer Face.   115
NURSE   God ye good-morrow, Gentlemen.
MERCUTIO   God ye good-den, fair Gentlewoman.
NURSE   Is it good-den?
MERCUTIO   'Tis no less, I tell ye, for the bawdy
  Hand of the Dial is now upon the Prick of Noon.   120
NURSE   Out upon you, what a Man are you?
ROMEO   One, Gentlewoman, that God hath made,
  himself to mar.
NURSE   By my troth, it is well said: 'for himself
  to mar', quoth 'a? Gentlemen, can any of you   125
  tell me where I may find the young Romeo?
ROMEO   I can tell you, but young Romeo will be
  older when you have found him than he was when
  you sought him. I am the Youngest of that Name,
  for fault of a Worse.   130
NURSE   You say well.
MERCUTIO   Yea, is the Worst well? Very well took,
  i'faith, wisely, wisely.
NURSE   If you be he, Sir, I desire some Confidence
  with you.   135
BENVOLIO   She will endite him to some Supper.

137 **Bawd** both (a) procurer (madam or pimp), and (b) a prostitute. But as Mercutio goes on to note, *bawd* could also mean 'hare'.
    So ho Mercutio evidently says this in such a way as to convey the huntsman's message 'Eureka!' Hence Romeo's reply in the next line.

139 **Hare** The reference is to a rabbit discovered in a hunt, but Mercutio also picks up on 'hair' as a pun on 'whore'.

140 **Lenten Pie** a reference to a pie baked before the beginning of Lent (during which time meat was forbidden) and kept despite its becoming stale and 'hoar' (white with mould). In the bawdy song that follows, Mercutio puns on 'hoar' (which could also be spelled 'hore') and 'whore'. A 'Score' (line 146) is a bill. In taverns a customer's 'score' was tabulated with carved notches on a piece of wood. By analogy, then, *score* could also refer to a woman's 'fault' (see line 130). See *2 Henry IV*, II.i.24, where the Hostess calls Falstaff 'an infinitive thing upon my Score'.

154 **Ropery** indecent jesting (from 'rope', a term for the male member).

157 **stand to** make good on, defend. The sexual sense of the phrase is also pertinent. Subsequent phrases such as 'against me' (compare lines 102–3) and 'take him down' (compare I.iv.27–28 and II.i.23–29) continue the wordplay inadvertently. *Stand* recalls II.ii.93.

158 **And 'a** if he.

162 **Flurt-gills** flirting Jills (loose women), here used in connection with 'Jacks' (line 161), wanton men.
    Skain's-mates usually explained as a reference to women who were companions to cutthroats (a skain was an Irish knife), but here more likely to refer to women who encouraged men to 'lay Knife aboard' (line 210) them.

165 **use you at his Pleasure** Peter takes the Nurse to mean 'use me sexually'. The 'Weapon' he refers to in the next line, however, is probably his sword. Compare I.i.36–37.

171 **quivers** The Nurse's phrasing in lines 170–71 recalls II.i.19–20.

MERCUTIO   A Bawd, a Bawd, a Bawd. So ho.
ROMEO   What hast thou found?
MERCUTIO   No Hare, Sir, unless a Hare, Sir, in a
Lenten Pie, that is something Stale and Hoar ere   140
it be spent.   *He walks by them and sings.*
    An old Hare hoar,
    And an old Hare hoar
    Is very good Meat in Lent;
    But a Hare that is hore   145
    Is too much for a Score,
    When it hores ere it be spent.
Romeo, will you come to your Father's? We'll to
Dinner thither.
ROMEO   I will follow you.   150
MERCUTIO   Farewell, auncient Lady; farewell
Lady, Lady, Lady.   *Exeunt Mercutio and Benvolio.*
NURSE   I pray you, Sir, what saucy Merchant was
this that was so full of his Ropery?
ROMEO   A Gentleman, Nurse, that loves to hear   155
himself talk, and will speak more in a Minute
than he will stand to in a Month.
NURSE   And 'a speak anything against me, I'll take
him down, and 'a were lustier than he is, and
twenty such Jacks. And if I cannot, I'll find   160
those that shall. Scurvy Knave, I am none of his
Flurt-gills; I am none of his Skain's-mates.
– And thou must stand by too, and suffer every
Knave to use me at his Pleasure.
PETER   I saw no Man use you at his Pleasure: if I   165
had, my Weapon should quickly have been out. I
warrant you, I dare draw as soon as an other Man if I
see occasion in a good Quarrel, and the Law on
my side.
NURSE   Now, afore God, I am so vex'd that every   170
part about me quivers. Scurvy Knave. – Pray you,
Sir, a Word. And as I told you, my young Lady

175 **lead her in a Fool's Paradise** deceive her into thinking you intend marriage when all you really want is to deflower her. Compare Juliet's own words in II.i.185–90.

179 **an ill thing** an evil deed. Again the Nurse's phrasing is unintentionally apt. See the notes to lines 130, 140.

180 **Weak Dealing** underhanded treatment of a 'Weaker Vessel' (I.i.17–18).

182– **I protest . . . Woman** The Nurse understands *protest* 'profess'
84 (vow solemnly) and assumes that this high-sounding language is Romeo's assurance that his intentions are honourable.

186 **mark me** hear me out.

191 **shrived** absolved. *Shrived* derived from *shrift*, confession. Compare II.ii.56. And for a sense of 'shrift' that is not completely irrelevant to the situation here, see *3 Henry VI*, III.ii.106, *King John*, I.i.236, *Henry VIII*, I.iv.15–18, and *Measure for Measure*, V.i.268.

193 **Go to** roughly equivalent to our 'go on' or 'come on'; an indication to say no more and put up no further protest. Compare I.iv.192.

197 **Cords . . . tackled Stair** rope ladder.

198 **Topgallant** the platform atop a ship's mast, attainable by a rope ladder. Romeo's imagery is another reminder of his mount-ague, his fever to achieve 'Paradise' (line 175) with Juliet.

199 **Convoy** means of conveyance.

200 **quit** requite, reward.

204 **secret** trustworthy to keep a secret.

205 **'Two . . . away'** The point of the proverb is that only one may keep a secret. For a variation on the saying, see *Titus Andronicus*, IV.ii.144.

bid me inquire you out. What she bid me say I
will keep to my self; but first let me tell ye,
if ye should lead her in a Fool's Paradise, as   175
they say, it were a very gross kind of Behaviour,
as they say. For the Gentlewoman is young: and
therefore if you should deal double with her,
truly it were an ill thing to be off'red to any
Gentlewoman, and very Weak Dealing.   180

ROMEO   Nurse, commend me to thy Lady and Mistress,
I protest unto thee –

NURSE   Good Heart, and i'faith I will tell her as
much: Lord, Lord, she will be a joyful Woman.

ROMEO   What wilt thou tell her, Nurse? Thou doest   185
not mark me?

NURSE   I will tell her, Sir, that you do protest,
which, as I take it, is a Gentleman-like Offer.

ROMEO   Bid her devise some means to come to Shrift
This Afternoon.
And there she shall at Friar Lawrence' Cell   190
Be shrived and married. Here is for thy Pains.

NURSE   No, truly, Sir, not a Penny.

ROMEO   Go to, I say you shall.

NURSE   This Afternoon, Sir; well, she shall be
there.

ROMEO   And stay, good Nurse, behind the Abbey Wall: 195
Within this Hour my Man shall be with thee
And bring thee Cords made like a tackled Stair,
Which to the high Topgallant of my Joy
Must be my Convoy in the secret Night.
Farewell; be trusty, and I'll quit thy Pains.   200
Farewell, commend me to thy Mistress.

NURSE   Now God in Heaven bless thee. Hark you Sir –

ROMEO   What say'st thou, my dear Nurse?

NURSE   Is your Man secret? Did you ne'er hear say
'Two may keep Counsel, putting one away'?   205

ROMEO   Warrant thee, my Man's as true as Steel.

210 **would fain lay Knife aboord** would like to win her hand. This
image picks up on Romeo's 'true as Steel' (line 206), as well
as on the nautical imagery introduced earlier, with Paris here
presented as one who would mount an attack at sea. In
Shakespeare's time a person eating at an inn brought his own
knife to the table and used it both to designate his place and
to serve himself. The literal meaning of *aboord* (aboard) is 'on
board' (on the table-top).

211 **as lieve** as lief, as willingly.

213 **properer** more handsome. Compare I.iii.75–78, III.v.214–27.

214 **Clout** either (a) the white centre of a target (see the note to line
23), or (b) cloth. The phrase *as pale as any Clout* is roughly
equivalent to 'as white as a sheet'. *Pale* recalls II.i.47.

215 **'versal World** universal world (equivalent to 'whole wide
world').
Rosemary a herb thought to foster good memory, and hence
proverbial as a symbol of remembrance (gratitude). Compare
Hamlet, IV.iii.176.

216 **a Letter** The Nurse means 'the same letter'.

218 **Dog Name** The Nurse is alluding to the commonplace notion
that the sound of the letter *R* resembles a dog's growl. She
thus thinks that Romeo is simply a 'Mocker' (making fun of
her). The Dog imagery is a reminder that the action of the
play occurs in the heat of July, the 'dog days' when the
so-called Dog Star (Sirius) rises and sets with the Sun.

220 **prettiest Sententious of it** The Nurse is trying to say that Juliet
has been composing 'sentences' (her term for them seems to
be a garbled version of the Latin word *sententiae*) or maxims
linking 'Romeo' and 'Rosemary'. Compare II.ii.79.

224 **I** both 'Ay' and 'I'. Compare line 92 and II.i.132.

226 **apace** quickly, at a fast pace.

II.iv The setting is the Capulets' orchard, where the heroine waits
impatiently for the Nurse's return.

1 **strook** struck.

4 **lame** hobbled with age. Juliet is presumably thinking about the
Nurse's sore back, about which we are soon to hear a great
deal.

NURSE   Well, Sir, my Mistress is the sweetest Lady —
  Lord, Lord, when 'twas a little prating thing. —
  O there is a Nobleman in Town, one Paris, that
  would fain lay Knife aboord; but she, good Soul,   210
  had as lieve see a Toad, a very Toad, as see him.
  I anger her sometimes, and tell her that Paris
  is the properer Man; but I'll warrant you, when
  I say so, she looks as pale as any Clout in the
  'versal World. Doth not 'Rosemary' and 'Romeo'   215
  begin both with a Letter?
ROMEO   Ay, Nurse, what of that? Both with an R.
NURSE   A Mocker, that's the Dog Name. *R* is for
  the — no, I know it begins with some other Letter,
  and she hath the prettiest Sententious of it, of   220
  you and Rosemary, that it would do you good to
  hear it.
ROMEO   Commend me to thy Lady.
NURSE   I a thousand Times. — Peter!   [*Exit Romeo.*]
PETER   Anon.   225
NURSE   Before, and apace.   *Exeunt.*

Scene 4

Enter Juliet.

JULIET   The Clock strook nine when I did send the
    Nurse;
  In half an Hour she promis'd to return.
  Perchance she cannot meet him. That's not so:
  O she is lame. Love's Heralds should be Thoughts,

5 **glides** Modern usage would call for *glide*. Elizabethan grammar permitted what we would regard as errors of agreement.

6 **low'ring** lowering (louring), frowning, lurking threateningly (until their shadows are driven back by the ascending sunbeams).

7 **nimble pinion'd** nimble, winged (a pinion is the end joint of a bird's wing).
draw Love pull the chariot of Venus, the Goddess of Love.

9 **highmost Hill** meridian; the zenith of the Sun's course through the sky. This image echoes II.iii.197–99 and anticipates lines 69–79.

14 **bandy** toss or bounce (as a tennis ball).

16 **fain . . . dead** both (a) wish they were dead and (b) pretend to be dead. Compare II.i.130, II.iii.210–11, III.ii.109, and *A Midsummer Night's Dream*, I.i.31. *Pale* recalls II.i.47 and II.iii.214. *Heavy* and *Lead* recall I.i.140, 181–83, 189; I.iv.11–16, 22.

22 **News** This word was usually treated as plural in Shakespeare's time; it was understood to mean 'new things'.

24 **sower** sour. But the usual Shakespearean spelling, here retained, permits wordplay on *sow*, a verb the Elizabethans associated with such biblical passages as Matthew 6:26, 37, John 4:36, and especially Galatians 6:7 ('whatsoever a man soweth, that shall he also reap').

25 **give me leave** allow me to rest.

26 **Jaunce** a jolting jaunt.

Which ten times faster glides than the Sun's
   Beams,   5
Driving back Shadows over low'ring Hills.
Therefore do nimble pinion'd Doves draw Love,
And therefore hath the Wind swift Cupid Wings.
Now is the Sun upon the highmost Hill
Of this Day's Journey, and from nine till twelve   10
Is three long Hours. Yet she is not come.
Had she Affections and warm youthful Blood,
She would be as swift in motion as a Ball:
My Words would bandy her to my sweet Love
And his to me.   15
But Old Folks, many fain as they were dead:
Unwieldy, slow; heavy and pale as Lead.

Enter Nurse [with Peter].

O God, she comes. — O honey Nurse, what News?
Hast thou met with him? Send thy Man away.
NURSE   Peter, stay at the Gate.   20
JULIET   Now, good sweet Nurse, O Lord, why lookest
   thou sad?
   Though News be sad, yet tell them merrily.
   If good, thou shamest the Music of sweet News
   By playing it to me with so sower a Face.
NURSE   I am a-weary; give me leave a while.   25
   Fie, how my Bones ache, what a Jaunce have I!
JULIET   I would thou hadst my Bones and I thy News:
   Nay come, I pray thee, speak, good, good Nurse,
   speak.
NURSE   Iesu, what Haste, can you not stay a while?
   Do you not see that I am out of Breath?   30
JULIET   How art thou out of Breath when thou hast
   Breath
   To say to me that thou art out of Breath?
   The Excuse that thou doest make in this Delay

34   **Tale** This word echoes the bawdy puns in II.iii.102–8; it also recalls I.iv.79, and I.iv.137–40.

36   **stay the Circumstance** wait till later to hear the details. *Stay* echoes lines 20 and 29, and recalls II.ii.26 and II.iii.195. *Satisfied* (line 37) recalls II.i.167–71.

38   **simple** foolish, naïve.

40–45   **Though . . . Lamb** Despite her best efforts, the Nurse cannot maintain her pretence that Romeo is a bad choice for Juliet. Compare the description of Paris in I.iii.74–95.

42   **Body** This word is spelling *baudie* in the First Quarto, and the phrase that follows suggests that the Nurse is punning on a word that referred to things too indecent 'to be talk'd on'.

44   **Flower of Courtesy** The Nurse's image is an amusing echo of II.iii.64–67, where Romeo and Mercutio jest about the kind of curtsy that makes a 'pump' bloom and deflowers a maiden.

45   **Go . . . serve God** The Nurse is implying that Juliet should forget about Romeo and serve God patiently until a better man is provided. As with the non sequiturs in lines 38–43, she is playfully torturing Juliet by prolonging her desire to be 'satisfied' (line 37).

51   **a' t'other side** on the other side. The anxious Juliet is now rubbing the Nurse's back.

52   **Beshrew** curse.

55   **Sweet . . . Love?** Although this line has the requisite number of syllables (ten) for iambic pentameter, it is in fact a dramatic breach of the metrical norm, with long-vowelled spondees (two equally stressed syllables) in the first two feet and a trochee (a stressed syllable followed by an unstressed) in the third, leaving iambs (feet comprised of an unstressed syllable followed by a stressed) in the fourth and fifth feet only: 'Swéet, swéet, / sweét Núrse, / téll mě, / whăt sáys / mў Lóve?'

58   **warrant** am sure.

63   **hot** both (a) eager, and (b) passionate. The Nurse, of course, has used delaying tactics as a kind of foreplay, knowingly and somewhat voyeuristically working Juliet up to a frenzy of excitement. Like a 'Bawd' (II.iii.137), a Pandarus, she derives vicarious pleasure from Juliet's arousal (line 76).
        Marry come up, I trow an expression of disapproval, roughly similar to 'Come on now!' *I trow* means 'I declare'.

Is longer than the Tale thou doest excuse.
Is thy News good or bad? Answer to that: 35
Say either, and I'll stay the Circumstance.
Let me be satisfied: is't good or bad?

NURSE   Well, you have made a simple Choice: you
know not how to choose a Man. Romeo, no not he.
Though his Face be better than any Man's, yet   40
his Leg excels all Men's; and for a Hand and a
Foot and a Body, though they be not to be talk'd
on, yet they are past compare. He is not the
Flower of Courtesy, but I'll warrant him as
gentle as a Lamb. Go thy ways, Wench; serve God.   45
What, have you din'd at home?

JULIET   No, no. But all this did I know before.
What says he of our Marriage, what of that?

NURSE   Lord, how my Head aches, what a Head have I!
It beats as it would fall in twenty pieces.   50
My Back: a' t'other side. Ah, my Back, my Back.
Beshrew your Heart for sending me about
To catch my death with jauncing up and down.

JULIET   I'faith, I am sorry that thou art not well.
Sweet, sweet, sweet Nurse, tell me, what says my
    Love?   55

NURSE   Your Love says, like an honest Gentleman,
An' a courteous, and a kind, and a handsome,
And I warrant a virtuous – Where is your
    Mother?

JULIET   Where is my Mother? Why, she is within.
Where should she be? How oddly thou repliest: 60
'Your Love says, like an honest Gentleman,
"Where is your Mother?"'

NURSE   O God's Lady, dear,
Are you so hot? Marry come up, I trow.

64 **Poultice** a hot, moist paste, usually of mustard, to be applied to an aching muscle or an inflammation.

66 **Coil** turmoil.

67 **Shrift** confession. Compare I.i.161–62, II.ii.56, and II.iii.188–91.

69 **high** hie, hasten (as in lines 73, 79). Here the Second Quarto spelling is a reminder of the emotional high the anticipation of 'High Fortune' (line 79) has prompted in Juliet. Compare the wordplay on *high* and *hie* in *Macbeth*, I.v.22, 27. *High* recalls Romeo's reference to 'the high Top gallant of my Joy' (II.iii.198).

72 **in Scarlet straight** scarlet immediately (blushing with shame over your uncontrolled eroticism).

75 **Bird's Nest** This anatomically suggestive metaphor is the Nurse's variation on Romeo's 'high Topgallant' (II.iii.198), and it also provides an amusing echo of the falcon imagery employed by Romeo and Juliet at the conclusion of the Balcony Scene (II.i.200–202, 209).

76 **Drudge** slavish servant, one whose work is burdensome drudgery. *Delight* plays on *Daylight* to reinforce the rhyming *Night* in line 77.

77 **bear the Burthen** This phrase recalls I.iv.19–28, 92–94.

II.v This scene is set in Friar Lawrence's cell.

2 **After-hours** the future. Sadly 'After-hours' will begin to 'chide' the parties to this 'Holy Act' almost as soon as Romeo leaves the Friar's cell. Here *That* means 'so that'.

4 **countervail** prevail against, undo.
   exchange compare II.i.168–69, II.ii.62. *Joy* echoes II.iii.198.

6 **close** join, seal in marriage. Compare II.i.234–35.

7 **Love-devouring Death** This image foreshadows V.iii.45–48. Lines 9–13 echo *A Midsummer Night's Dream*, I.i.141–49.

10 **Triumph** height of victory. Compare II.iii.198, II.iv.69, 79. *Die* recalls II. Chorus 1–4.
    Powder gunpowder.

Is this the Poultice for my aching Bones?
Henceforward do your Messages your self.   65
JULIET   Here's such a Coil. Come, what says Romeo?
NURSE   Have you got leave to go to Shrift to day?
JULIET   I have.
NURSE   Then high you hence to Friar Lawrence' Cell:
There stays a Husband to make you a Wife.   70
Now comes the wanton Blood up in your Cheeks:
They'll be in Scarlet straight at any News.
Hie you to Church; I must an other way
To fetch a Ladder by the which your Love
Must climb a Bird's Nest soon when it is dark.   75
I am the Drudge, and toil in your Delight;
But you shall bear the Burthen soon at Night.
Go, I'll to Dinner; hie you to the Cell.
JULIET   Hie to High Fortune. Honest Nurse, farewell.
                                          Exeunt.

Scene 5

Enter Friar and Romeo.

FRIAR   So smile the Heavens upon this holy Act,
That After-hours with Sorrow chide us not.
ROMEO   Amen, amen. But come what Sorrow can,
It cannot countervail the exchange of Joy
That one short Minute gives me in her Sight.   5
Do thou but close our Hands with holy Words,
Then Love-devouring Death do what he dare.
It is enough I may but call her mine.
FRIAR   These violent Delights have violent Ends,
And in their Triumph die, like Fire and Powder,   10
Which as they kiss consume. The sweetest Honey
Is loathsome in his own Deliciousness

13   **confounds**   overwhelms, destroys. The Friar's point in this line is that too much of a good thing is cloying and self-defeating.

15   **Too Swift . . . Too Slow**   an allusion to Aesop's fable of the Hare and the Tortoise, and another variation on 'Make haste slowly.' (See II.ii.93–94.)

16–17 **so light a Foot . . . everlasting Flint**   The Friar's initial observation of Juliet suggests that she enters with a delicate footstep incapable of leaving an impression on even the softest surface. His reference to 'Vanity' (symbolic not only of lightness but also of that which is impermanent) would lead us to expect a spiritual appraisal from a man of his profession; however, the Friar's comments about Juliet are more poetic than moralistic. These lines (down to line 20) may be intended for delivery as an aside.

18   **Gossamours**   gossamers, delicate cobwebs. The spelling in the Quarto and Folio texts, retained here, suggests a purposeful weaving together of *gossamers* and *amour* (love). See the note to I.i.124.

19   **wanton**   sportive, luxuriant. Compare II.iv.71.

24   **Measure**   quantity. Compare I.iv.9–10, and see the note to II. Chorus. 14.

26   **blazon**   display, as on a coat of arms; celebrate.

27   **neighbour**   nearby. *Music's* echoes II.iv.23–24.

28   **Unfold**   disclose.

29   **dear**   precious, invaluable. But another sense, 'costly', will prove tragically pertinent. *Encounter* is a word Shakespeare frequently employs to describe the coming together of a man and a woman. It plays on *count* (see the notes to I.iii.71 and II.iii.51), and it thereby literalizes the 'exchange of Joy' that occurs when 'two in one' become 'incorporate' (line 37). Compare *Troilus and Cressida*, III.iii.217–22, *Much Ado About Nothing*, IV.i.92–93, *All's Well That Ends Well*, III.vii.32, *Measure for Measure*, III.i.263–64, *Merry Wives of Windsor*, III.v.74–75, and *Love's Labour's Lost*, I.i.242–46.

30   **Conceit**   understanding, the ability to conceive or think.

32   **count**   measure. Compare I.iii.71.

And in the Taste confounds the Appetite.
Therefore love moderately: long Love doth so.
Too Swift arrives as tardy as Too Slow.   15

Enter Juliet.

Here comes the Lady. O so light a Foot
Will ne'er wear out the everlasting Flint.
A Lover may bestride the Gossamours
That idles in the wanton Summer Air
And yet not fall, so light is Vanity.   20
JULIET   Good even to my ghostly Confessor.
FRIAR   Romeo shall thank thee, Daughter, for us both.
JULIET   As much to him, else is his Thanks too much.
ROMEO   Ah Juliet, if the Measure of thy Joy
Be heap'd like mine, and that thy Skill be more   25
To blazon it, then sweeten with thy Breath
This neighbour Air, and let rich Music's Tongue
Unfold the imagin'd Happiness that both
Receive in either by this dear Encounter.
JULIET   Conceit, more rich in Matter than in Words,   30
Brags of his Substance, not of Ornament;
They are but Beggars that can count their Worth,

33   **Excess**   extremity. See the note to line 14 of the Chorus to Act
      II. In this line *grown* provides an aural reminder of the *groan*
      imagery in I.i.203–4, II. Chorus. 3, II.ii.74, II.iii.95, and
      III.iii.72.

34   **sum up Sum**   sum up the total. Lines 30–34 recall II.i.175–77.

36   **by your leaves**   with your consent.
      stay alone   sleep together. *Stay* echoes II.iv.36; see the note to
      II.i.216. Here as elsewhere, *alone* plays on 'all one' (here
      meaning 'two in one', line 37); compare 'all one' in I.i.23 and
      in *Twelfth Night*, V.i.413–14. For other suggestive uses of
      alone, see *Henry VIII*, I.iv.34, *King Lear*, I.i.71–77,
      Coriolanus, I.iv.52 and II.i.34–37, *Measure for Measure*,
      II.i.36–40, *Troilus and Cressida*, I.ii.15–17, and *A
      Midsummer Night's Dream*, III.ii.119. For a use of *alone* that
      hints either at copulation or at a desire for it, see *Romeo and
      Juliet*, II.i.36.

37   **incorporate two in one**   join two into one body, an image
      deriving ultimately from Genesis 2:24, where a husband and
      his wife are described as 'one flesh'. Compare *Hamlet*,
      IV.iii.48–52.

But my true Love is grown to such Excess
I cannot sum up Sum of half my Wealth.
FRIAR   Come, come with me, and we will make short
    Work: 35
For by your leaves you shall not stay alone
Till holy Church incorporate two in one.   *Exeunt.*

III.i The setting is a street in Verona.

1 **retire** withdraw, go inside. As in the opening scene, the benign-spirited Benvolio attempts to prevent violence. See the note to I.i.67.

2 **Capels** an abbreviated version of *Capulets*, probably used here for metrical purposes. *Hot* echoes II.iv.63.

3 **scape** escape, avoid.

4 **Hot Days** Elizabethans believed that warmer climates and sultry weather fostered more passionate, violent forms of behaviour. See the note to II.iii.218. *Stirring* recalls I.i.9–11, 83, and I.iv.112.

6–7 **claps me** slaps down for me. The 'me' construction in Shakespeare is frequently used to convey familiarity or to signal that the speaker is imitating the manner of the person being 'presented' in a description. Compare the knife imagery in II.iii.209–10.

8–9 **by the operation . . . Cup** by the time the second cup has had its intoxicating effects.

9 **Drawer** tapster, waiter who serves wine and ale.

11 **Am . . . Fellow?** In this line Benvolio probably accentuates *I* with a note of incredulity. In his reply Mercutio emphasizes *Eye* (lines 22–23) in a way that appears to play on *I*.

12 **Jack** fellow. This word recalls II.iii.160.

13–14 **moved to be Moody** aroused to anger. Here *Mood* means irritable irascibility. Compare I.i.6–14.

14 **moody to be Moved** disposed to be aroused.

16 **and** if
    two such Mercutio says 'two' because he is pretending to misunderstand Benvolio's question 'And what to?' in the previous line. *Two* recalls II.v.35–37.

22 **Hazel** Mercutio's point is that Benvolio is so 'moody' that, to him, a man who cracks nuts is offending anyone whose eye colour shares the same name as one kind of nut. He is what a later age would call a hairsplitter. Mercutio's preoccupation with hair parodies Matthew 10:28–34, where Jesus assures believers that 'the very hairs of your head are all numbered' but goes on to say, with ominous pertinence to this scene that 'I came not to send peace, but a sword'. *Hair* recalls II.iii.102–8, 138–47.

ACT III

Scene 1

Enter Mercutio, Benvolio, and Men.

BENVOLIO   I pray thee, good Mercutio, let's retire.
  The Day is hot, the Chapels are abroad,
  And if we meet we shall not scape a Brawl:
  For now these Hot Days is the Mad Blood stirring.

MERCUTIO   Thou art like one of these Fellows that,   5
  when he enters the confines of a Tavern, claps
  me his Sword upon the Table and says 'God send
  me no need of thee,' and by the operation of the
  second Cup draws him on the Drawer, when indeed
  there is no need.   10

BENVOLIO   Am I like such a Fellow?

MERCUTIO   Come, come, thou art as hot a Jack in thy
  Mood as any in Italy; and as soon moved to be
  Moody, and as soon moody to be Moved.

BENVOLIO   And what to?   15

MERCUTIO   Nay, and there were two such we should
  have none shortly: for one would kill the other.
  Thou, why thou wilt quarrel with a Man that hath
  a Hair more or a Hair less in his Beard than
  thou hast. Thou wilt quarrel with a Man for   20
  cracking Nuts, having no other Reason but
  because thou hast Hazel Eyes; what Eye but such

24 **Meat** food (not limited to flesh).

25 **addle** muddled, addled; with a play on the expression 'addle-egg' or rotten egg.

30 **Doublet** a close-fitting jacket worn with a short tunic.

31 **Riband** ribbon, in this case shoe laces or bands.

34 **Fee-simple** total ownership. A fee-simple was a title to an estate in which no conditions or restrictions applied to the inheritance.

35 **for an Hour and a Quarter** for a fraction of its value, equivalent to the ratio between an hour and a quarter and a full lifetime.

36 **simple** feeble; absolutely stupid. Compare II.iv.38.

38 **Heel** Mercutio is being perversely scornful. He may also be alluding to Psalm 141:9, ('Yea, mine own familiar friend, in whom I trusted, which did eat of my bread, hath lifted up his heel against me'), a passage Elizabethans would have heard recited from the Book of Common Prayer.

48 **Consort?** Mercutio takes offence at Tybalt's use of a verb ('consortest') that tends to be derogatory, either suggesting association with lowlife ne'er-do-wells, or, as here, evoking the image of travelling musicians, the minstrels who depended for their livelihood on the patronage of courts or of privileged families like the Capulets. In either case, Mercutio assumes that Tybalt intends to insult Romeo and his friends by suggesting that their social status is lower than that of gentlemen such as himself. A *consort* was a group of minstrels. Compare II.i.31, and note the insulting treatment the Minstrels receive from Peter in IV.iii.187–231.

51 **Fiddlestick** Mercutio gestures to his sword while referring to the bow of a violin or fiddle. Compare the analogies between music-making and sword-fighting in II.iii.21–25, 32–33.

52 **'Zounds** a contraction of 'God's wounds'.

55 **reason coldly** consider calmly. Benvolio shifts the dialogue to blank verse, itself an indication of his desire to restore a degree of measured control to a situation that is rapidly getting overheated. For similar uses of *coldly* and related words, see 2 *Henry IV*, V.ii.97, *Measure for Measure*, II.ii.46, and *Hamlet*, I.ii.77, 179–80. Compare lines 130–31.

an Eye would spy out such a Quarrel? Thy Head is
as full of Quarrels as an Egg is full of Meat,
and yet thy Head hath been beaten as addle as an   25
Egg for Quarrelling. Thou hast quarrell'd with a
man for Coughing in the Street, because he hath
waken'd thy Dog that hath lain asleep in the Sun.
Didst thou not fall out with a Tailor for
wearing his new Doublet before Easter? With   30
an other for tying his new Shoes with old Riband?
And yet thou wilt tutor me from Quarrelling?

BENVOLIO   And I were so apt to quarrel as thou art,
any Man should buy the Fee-simple of my Life
for an Hour and a Quarter.   35

MERCUTIO   The Fee-simple: O simple.

Enter Tybalt, Petruchio, and Others.

BENVOLIO   By my Head, here comes the Capulets.

MERCUTIO   By my Heel, I care not.

TYBALT   Follow me close, for I will speak to them.
   – Gentlemen, good-den; a Word with one of you.   40

MERCUTIO   And but one Word with one of us? Couple
   it with something: make it a Word and a Blow.

TYBALT   You shall find me apt enough to that, Sir,
   and you will give me Occasion.

MERCUTIO   Could you not take some Occasion without   45
   giving?

TYBALT   Mercutio, thou consortest with Romeo.

MERCUTIO   Consort? What, doest thou make us
   Minstrels? And thou make Minstrels of us, look
   to hear nothing but Discords. Here's my   50
   Fiddlestick: here's that shall make you daunce.
   'Zounds, consort.

BENVOLIO   We talk here in the Public Haunt of Men.
   Either withdraw unto some Private Place,
   Or reason coldly of your Grievances,   55

58   **for . . . Pleasure** to please no one. *Pleasure* recalls I.i.104, I.ii.37, II.iii.163–69. *Man* recalls II.iii.19, and anticipates lines 59–62, 69–70, 100, 137–38.

60   **your Livery** Mercutio responds as if Tybalt had just called Romeo his servant ('my Man', line 59). A servant wore the 'Livery' or uniform of his master. Compare II.i.50–51.

61   **to Field** to the place appointed for a duel.

64   **Villain** originally a serf (villein) or 'Man' (lines 59–60); by extension, any man whose behaviour is cowardly, slavish, or unworthy of a gentleman.

66   **appertaining Rage** the anger that would normally pertain to a true gentleman's response to such a challenge. Line 68 echoes I.i.67.

69   **Boy** deliberately spoken as an insult. Compare *Coriolanus*, V.vi.100, where Aufidius calls the title character a 'Boy of Tears'.

72   **devise** figure out, appreciate. *Protest* recalls II.iii.182–88.

73   **the Reason of my Love** Romeo alone knows that he is now wed to Juliet, and that they will be 'one flesh' as soon as the marriage is consummated. *Reason* echoes line 21.

77   **Alla stucatho** Mercutio's rendering of *alla stoccata*, an Italian phrase from fencing manuals, describing what to do 'at the thrust'. Mercutio is appalled that Romeo is allowing a villain who 'fights by the Book of Arithmetic' (line 109) to dishonour him. *Stuchatho* plays on *stuck* and echoes I.iv.25–28, 41–43, and II.iii.22–25.

78   **Ratcatcher** the first of several allusions to Tybalt as the fabled King of Cats. Compare II.iii.20–29.

82   **dry-beat** thrash. *Use* means 'treat'. *Withal* (line 81) means 'with', as in I.iv.258.

84   **Pilcher** a leather outer garment; here used to personify Tybalt's sword as a coward who must be extracted by the ears. Mercutio puns on the proverb 'Pitchers have ears', which Shakespeare also quotes in *The Taming of the Shrew*, IV.iv.52, and in *Richard III*, II.iv.37.

Or else depart. Here all Eyes gaze on us.

MERCUTIO   Men's Eyes were made to look, and let
them gaze;
I will not budge for no man's Pleasure, I.

Enter Romeo.

TYBALT   Well, peace be with you, Sir; here comes my
Man.

MERCUTIO   But I'll be hang'd, Sir, if he wear your
Livery.   60
Marry, go before to Field, he'll be your
Follower:
Your worship in that sense may call him Man.

TYBALT   Romeo, the Love I bear thee can affoord
No better Term than this: thou art a Villain.

ROMEO   Tybalt, the Reason that I have to love thee   65
Doth much excuse the appertaining Rage
To such a Greeting. Villain am I none:
Therefore farewell, I see thou knowest me not.

TYBALT   Boy, this shall not excuse the Injuries
That thou hast done me: therefore turn and draw.   70

ROMEO   I do protest I never injur'd thee,
But love thee better than thou canst devise
Till thou shalt know the Reason of my Love;
And so, good Capulet, which Name I tender
As dearly as mine own, be satisfied.   75

MERCUTIO   O calm, dishonourable, vile Submission:
Alla stucatho carries it away.
— Tybalt, you Ratcatcher, will you walk?

TYBALT   What wouldst thou have with me?

MERCUTIO   Good King of Cats, nothing but one of   80
your Nine Lives, that I mean to make bold withal,
and as you shall use me hereafter, dry-beat the
rest of the eight. Will you pluck your Sword out
of his Pilcher by the Ears? Make haste, lest

87   **put . . . up**   Romeo's role as peacemaker recalls Benvolio's in
      I.i.67; again the combatants 'know not what' they 'do'.

88   **Passado**   the word for 'lunge' or 'pass' in the Italian fencing
      books. Mercutio is deriding Tybalt's emphasis on precise
      technique.

89   **beat . . . Weapons**   Romeo's phrasing recalls such previous
      passages as I.i.36–37, I.iv.27–28, and II.iii.158–60.

90   **forbear this Outrage**   halt this inflamed outburst of violence.
      Outrage will recur in V.iii.218.

92   **Bandying**   exchanging blows. Compare II.iv.14–15.

S.D. **Tybalt . . . flies**   This stage direction derives from the First
      Quarto. The Second Quarto simply prints '*Away Tybalt.*'
      Most editors read that phrase as dialogue and assign it to the
      'Petruchio' who entered with Tybalt after line 36.

95   **sped**   sent away; probably an ironic reference to 'Godspeed'
      (farewell).

97   **a Scratch**   another reference to Tybalt as a cat.

104   **Grave Man**   Even in the throes of death, Mercutio engages in
      wordplay, here suggesting that his 'gravity' will be that of the
      earth itself as he lies in his grave. Compare II.ii.10.

104–5 **pepper'd . . . for this World**   dealt a death blow.

105   **A . . . Houses**   may both your households be afflicted with the
      plague. The effect of Mercutio's curse will be reported in
      V.ii.1–20. The catalogue of creatures in line 106 anticipates
      King Lear, V.iii.303–4.

114   **Worm's-meat**   a decomposing corpse being eaten by
      earthworms. Compare *Hamlet*, IV.iii.16–32. This image will
      be echoed in V.iii.110–11.

116   **near Ally**   close relative.

mine be about your Ears ere it be out.   85

TYBALT   I am for you.

ROMEO   Gentle Mercutio, put thy Rapier up.

MERCUTIO   Come, Sir, your Passado.

ROMEO   Draw, Benvolio, beat down their Weapons.
  – Gentlemen, for Shame, forbear this Outrage.   90
  Tybalt, Mercutio: the Prince expressly hath
  Forbid this Bandying in Verona Streets.
  Hold, Tybalt, good Mercutio.

  Tybalt, under Romeo's arm, thrusts Mercutio in and flies.

MERCUTIO   I am hurt. A Plague a' both Houses: I am
  sped. Is he gone and hath nothing?   95

BENVOLIO   What, art thou hurt?

MERCUTIO   Ay, ay, a Scratch, a Scratch. Marry, 'tis
  enough. Where is my Page? – Go, Villain, fetch a
  Surgeon.   [*Exit Page.*]

ROMEO   Courage, Man: the Hurt cannot be much.   100

MERCUTIO   No, 'tis not so deep as a Well, nor so
  wide as a Church Door, but 'tis enough, 'twill
  serve. Ask for me to morrow, and you shall find
  me a Grave Man. I am pepper'd, I warrant, for
  this World. A Plague a' both your Houses.   105
  'Zounds, a Dog, a Rat, a Mouse, a Cat, to
  scratch a Man to death. A Braggart, a Rogue, a
  Villain, that fights by the Book of Arithmetic.
  Why the Devil came you between us? I was hurt
  under your Arm.   110

ROMEO   I thought all for the best.

MERCUTIO   Help me into some House, Benvolio, or I
  shall faint. A Plague a' both your Houses. They
  have made Worm's-meat of me. I have it, and
  soundly; to your Houses.   115

                              Exit [*with Benvolio.*]

ROMEO   This Gentleman, the Prince's near Ally,
  My very Friend, hath got this mortal Hurt
  In my behalf, my Reputation stain'd

122 **Temper** When steel was 'tempered' (by a combination of heating and rapid cooling), it was made stronger; in lines 122–23 Romeo is saying that by exercising a different kind of 'temper' (self-control, restraint in the face of Tybalt's challenge to his honour), he has allowed his love of Juliet to make 'Valour's Steel' soft and 'Effeminate' (weak). Whether or not this is a true appraisal of how he responded to Tybalt's remarks, it reflects the way Romeo evaluates his earlier behaviour now that he has Mercutio's 'Plague' ringing in his ears. Compare II.ii.33, 40, III.iii.114, and III.v.98 for other references to temper. And see the notes on effeminacy at I.i.12–20, 68; II.ii.79; II.iii.41–43, 130, 177–80.

124 **aspir'd the Clouds** risen to the Heavens. See the note to II.iii.198.

126 **moe** more. Shakespeare probably uses *moe* here to rhyme with *woe*, which occupies the same position metrically in the next line.
depend hang over, overshadow, darken; impend. Compare *Troilus and Cressida*, II.iii.20–23.

129 **Triumph** This word echoes II.v.9–11; in the process it recalls II.v.6–8.

130 **Away to Heaven** It was characteristic of revengers in tragedies of the Renaissance to recognize that personal vengeance was expressly forbidden by both Church and State, in keeping with the teachings in Romans 12:17–13:6.
respective Lenity heedful mildness, leniency, deliberation. See the note to II.ii.90.

131 **Conduct** guide. Compare I.iv.112–13, and see the note to III.ii.5–6.

138 **Thou ... here** Tybalt repeats the insults he has hurled in lines 47–52, 59–70. Compare lines 57–62, 69–70, 138–39 with I.iv.196.

139 **This** Romeo refers to his drawn sword as he speaks this word.

142 **amaz'd** bewildered, as if lost in a maze.
doom thee death condemn you to death.

With Tybalt's Slaunder: Tybalt, that an Hour
Hath been my Cousin. — O sweet Juliet,   120
Thy Beauty hath made me Effeminate,
And in my Temper soft'ned Valour's Steel.

Enter Benvolio.

BENVOLIO   O Romeo, Romeo, brave Mercutio's dead:
  That gallant Spirit hath aspir'd the Clouds,
  Which too untimely here did scorn the Earth.   125
ROMEO   This Day's black Fate on moe Days doth
    depend:
  This but begins the Woe others must end.

Enter Tybalt.

BENVOLIO   Here comes the furious Tybalt back again.
ROMEO   Alive in Triumph, and Mercutio slain.
  Away to Heaven, respective Lenity,   130
  And fire-ey'd Fury be my Conduct now.
  — Now Tybalt, take the 'Villain' back again
  That late thou gavest me: for Mercutio's Soul
  Is but a little way above our Heads,
  Staying for thine to keep him Company.   135
  Either thou or I, or both, must go with him.
TYBALT   Thou wretched Boy that didst consort him
    here,
  Shalt with him hence.
ROMEO   This shall determine that.
                         They fight. Tybalt falls.
BENVOLIO   Romeo, away be gone:
  The Citizens are up, and Tybalt slain.   140
  Stand not amaz'd; the Prince will doom thee
    death
  If thou art taken. Hence be gone away.

143 **Fortune's Fool** victim of blind Fortune. At this moment Romeo
feels that he is at the mercy of forces beyond his control. In
Shakespeare's time, Fortune, Fate, and the Stars were all
referred to as ways of accounting for aspects of life that
seemed subject to something other than a person's free will.
There was a widespread conviction that what seemed like
chance frequently had a pattern. To understand those aspects
of 'Fortune' (chance) that seemed 'fated' (patterned), many
turned to astrology, a system that sought to discern how
various configurations of the stars and planets influenced
human life. Even orthodox Christians were generally inclined
to give astrology its due. But most thinkers of the period
assumed that, though 'the Stars' might affect the body and its
passions, they could not determine the fate of one whose
actions were governed by reason. To be a fool of Fortune,
then, was ultimately to be a victim of one's own failure to use
reason in such a way as to rise above the sway of the Stars.
Romeo's phrasing recalls the Nurse's words in II.iii.173–77. It
anticipates *King Lear*, IV.vi.189.

stay wait. Benvolio's line suggests that Romeo is to be played
here as a man momentarily rapt in reflection on the
consequences of what he has just done. Compare II.v.36.

147 **Up, Sir** This may be directed to Tybalt, with the arresting
Citizen watchman not yet realizing that he cannot obey. But it
seems more likely to be delivered to Benvolio, who may now
be kneeling over the fallen Tybalt.

148 **Fray** scene of civil disturbance. Compare I.i.119–20. Lines
148–52 recall I.i.107–18. *Vile* echoes II.ii.15–22.

149 **discover** disclose. Compare I.i.153, II.i.148.

150 **Manage** course, direction. As a term normally used to convey a
sense of order and control, *Manage* has ironic connotations
here, just as it does in I.i.70–71.

fatal both (a) death-dealing, and (b) ordained by Fate (see line
143).

161 **nice** petty, insignificant. Compare V.ii.18.

withal in addition. This word echoes line 81.

164 **take Truce with** achieve peace with.

unruly Spleen ungovernable wrath. The spleen was one of the
seats of the irascible passions.

ROMEO   O I am Fortune's Fool.
BENVOLIO   Why dost thou stay?
                                                    Exit Romeo.

                        Enter Citizens.

CITIZEN   Which way ran he that kill'd
    Mercutio?
Tybalt, that Murderer, which way ran he?   145
BENVOLIO   There lies that Tybalt.
CITIZEN   Up, Sir, go with me:
I charge thee in the Prince's Name obey.

        *Enter Prince, old Mountague, Capulet, their Wives,
                        and all.*

PRINCE   Where are the vile Beginners of this Fray?
BENVOLIO   O Noble Prince, I can discover all
    The unlucky Manage of this fatal Brawl: 150
    There lies the Man, slain by young Romeo,
    That slew thy Kinsman, brave Mercutio.
CAPULET'S WIFE   Tybalt, my Cousin, O my Brother's
    Child.
    – O Prince, O Cousin, Husband, O the Blood is spill'd
    Of my dear Kinsman. Prince, as thou art true,   155
    For Blood of ours shed Blood of Mountague.
    – O Cousin, Cousin.
PRINCE   Benvolio, who began this bloody Fray?
BENVOLIO   Tybalt, here slain, whom Romeo's Hand did
    slay:
    Romeo, that spoke him fair, bid him bethink   160
    How nice the Quarrel was, and urg'd withal
    Your high Displeasure. All this uttered
    With gentle Breath, calm Look, Knees humbly
        bow'd,
    Could not take Truce with the unruly Spleen

165 **tilts** points menacingly. We should notice that Benvolio's
account of the altercation differs in some ways from what a
theatre audience would have just seen.

167 **hot** infuriated, intemperate. Compare lines 1–4, 12, 53–56,
130–31.

168– **with one Hand . . . aside** Benvolio's imagery suggests that
69 Mercutio (and presumably Tybalt) had a smaller sword in his
other hand with which to fend off blows while he sought an
opening for his own thrusts.

168 **martial Scorn** Mars-like contempt.

169 **Cold** Benvolio's adjective echoes line 55.

171 **Retorts** returns, replies in kind.

173 **fatal** mortally wounding. This word echoes line 150. It also
recalls line 126 and line 5 of the Prologue.

175 **envious** driven by enmity, malicious. Compare II.i.46, 49.

178 **entertain'd** considered, welcomed.

179 **Lightning** This word recalls II.i.159–62.

180 **stout** strong and brave.

185 **Some twenty . . . Strife** Capulet's Wife's reaction to Benvolio's
account is so extreme in its partisanship as to make us
disregard any minor distortions in what Romeo's friend has
just said. Compare *Othello*, I.ii.60–99, and I.iii.47–218,
where the wronged Brabantio forfeits credibility and respect
by his intemperance and irrationality.
Strife Compare II.i.194.

190 **owe** both (a) owe, as a debt, and (b) own, as a penalty to be
repaid with more 'Blood'. Compare II.i.88. *Dear* recalls
II.v.29. Here *Who* refers to Romeo. Many editors depart from
the early texts and punctuate line 190 as a question.

192 **Fault** error, transgression. Compare II.iii.130. In the Second
Quarto and First Folio texts lines 191–93 are assigned to
Capulet. The Fourth Quarto corrects what seems an obvious
error and gives them to Mountague.

195 **an Interest** a personal reason to be concerned.

196 **my Blood** the blood of my own family.

Of Tybalt, deaf to Peace, but that he tilts   165
With piercing Steel at bold Mercutio's Breast,
Who, all as hot, turns deadly Point to Point,
And with a martial Scorn, with one Hand beats
Cold Death aside, and with the other sends
It back to Tybalt, whose Dexterity   170
Retorts it. Romeo he cries aloud
'Hold, Friends, Friends, part,' and swifter than
   his Tongue
His agile Arm beats down their fatal Points
And twixt them rushes, underneath whose Arm
An envious Thrust from Tybalt hit the Life   175
Of stout Mercutio, and then Tybalt fled,
But by and by comes back to Romeo,
Who had but newly entertain'd Revenge,
And to 't they go like Lightning, for ere I
Could draw to part them was stout Tybalt slain;   180
And as he fell did Romeo turn and fly.
This is the Truth, or let Benvolio die.

CAPULET'S WIFE   He is a Kinsman to the Mountague:
  Affection makes him False, he speaks not True.
  Some twenty of them fought in this black Strife,   185
  And all those twenty could but kill one Life.
  I beg for Justice, which thou, Prince, must give:
  Romeo slew Tybalt, Romeo must not live.

PRINCE   Romeo slew him, he slew Mercutio,
  Who now the Price of his dear Blood doth owe.   190

MOUNTAGUE   Not Romeo, Prince; he was Mercutio's
  Friend.
  His Fault concludes but what the Law should end,
  The life of Tybalt.

PRINCE   And for that Offence
  Immediately we do exile him hence.
  I have an Interest in your Hate's proceeding: 195
  My Blood for your rude Brawls doth lie
    a-bleeding.

197 **amerce** penalize; a contraction of 'at the mercy of'.

200 **purchase out** buy absolution for.

201 **hast** haste (here spelled, and perhaps pronounced, to rhyme with *last*).

202 **Hour** here pronounced as a two-syllable word.

203 **attend our Will** abide by my wishes. Compare I.i.102–5. Line 204 is paralleled in *Measure for Measure*, I.iv.19–31, II.i.1–4, II.ii.92–106.

III.ii The setting is Juliet's bedroom.

2 **Phoebus' Lodging** the home of the God of the Sun. Juliet is eager for the Sun to set so that she and Romeo can consummate their marriage.
Wagoner charioteer, driver.

3 **Phaeton** son of the Sun God, who tried to drive Phoebus' chariot too fast and would have set the world on fire had not Zeus shot him down with a thunderbolt. Like Icarus (see the note to I.iv.20), Phaeton was an emblem of the moral embodied in the Friar's sentence 'they stumble that run fast' (II.ii.94). Shakespeare has alluded to the Phaeton myth in II.i.232–33 and II.ii.3–4. For other treatments of the story see *The Two Gentlemen of Verona*, III.i.153–60, and *3 Henry VI*, I.iv.33–34, II.vi.11–13.

5–6 **Spread . . . wink** One way to interpret this line is to assume that the 'fiery-footed Steeds' of the Sun's chariot are the 'Runaways' whose eyes would 'wink' (be put to sleep or be blindfolded or 'hoodwink'd', as in I.iv.4). If so, the 'close Curtain' of Night is the 'hood' covering the Steeds' eyes and making it possible for the lovers to meet 'unseen' (line 7). Juliet is yet to learn that her Phaeton-like husband (see III.i.130–31) is now a runaway (see III.i.142–43, 181, 201–2).

8 **Rights** both (a) rights (by virtue of their matrimonial bond), and (b) rites, ceremonies. Compare II.i.188. Line 9 echoes II.i.33.

10 **civil Night** 'Love-performing Night' (line 5) is now invoked as an emblem of propriety and sobriety. *Civil* recalls line 4 of the Prologue, as well as I.i.23–25, 92.

But I'll amerce you with so strong a Fine
That you shall all repent the loss of Mine.
I will be deaf to Pleading and Excuses:
Nor Tears nor Prayers shall purchase out Abuses,   200
Therefore use none. Let Romeo hence in hast,
Else when he's found that Hour is his last.
Bear hence this Body, and attend our Will:
Mercy but murders, pardoning those that kill.

Exeunt.

Scene 2

Enter Juliet alone.

JULIET   Gallop apace, you fiery footed Steeds,
Towards Phoebus' Lodging. Such a Wagoner
As Phaeton would whip you to the West
And bring in cloudy Night immediately.
Spread thy close Curtain, Love-performing Night,   5
That Runaways' Eyes may wink, and Romeo
Leap to these Arms untalk'd of and unseen.
Lovers can see to do their amorous Rights,
And by their own Beauties; or, if Love be blind,
It best agrees with Night. Come, civil Night,   10
Thou sober-suited Matron all in black,

12   **learn** teach. See I.iv.93.

 loose a winning Match (a) unleash, set loose, start, and (b) lose
 a 'match' (here both a competitive game and a triumphant
 pairing) in such a way as to win in reality. Juliet is affirming
 her role as a 'Weaker Vessel' (see I.i.17–20, and the final
 sentence of the note to III.i.123). *Match* can also mean 'fit
 together', of course, and in that sense the word recalls
 I.iii.80–95. Compare I.iii.95–96, II.Chorus.4.

14   **Hood . . . bating** Juliet compares her wanton blood to an
 'impatient' (line 30) and unrestrained ('unmann'd') falcon
 whose wings would flutter ('bate') unless the bird's head were
 hooded. In this image the hood would be the 'black Mantle'
 (line 15) of matronly Night, who would turn 'True-love acted'
 (line 16, echoing II.i.146) from something unrestrained and
 socially unacceptable to something embodying 'simple
 Modesty'. Her imagery recalls II.i.200–209.

18   **Whiter . . . Back** This line recalls such previous passages as
 I.i.233–34; I.ii.89–90; I.iv.159–64; II.i.60–65, 68–74;
 II.iii.15–19, II.iv.73–75.

21   **die** Juliet may be referring to the erotic 'death' she welcomes
 (see the note to II.Chorus.2), but she may also be thinking of
 her own mortality. Many editors follow the Fourth Quarto in
 this line and print *he* rather than *I*.

23   **fine** refined, sparkling with tiny ('fine') spangles.

25   **garish Sun** By contrast with the beauty of the Night, the Sun
 will be able to offer only a crudely glaring ('garish') light.
 Lines 20–25 echo II.i.45–48, 57–64, 68–74.

26–28 **O I have bought . . . enjoy'd** Juliet's imagery derives from the
 world of real estate transactions, and it foreshadows Romeo's
 use of similar phrasing in III.iii.106–7. Romeo has used a
 comparable metaphor in I.iv.106–11.

35   **Ay, ay** Here the early texts print *I, I* (as the 'I' sound for
 affirmation was represented in Shakespeare's time). In the
 next line, however, the early texts print *Ay*, as here. See the
 note to I.i.5, and compare II.iii.224. In lines 45–50 this
 edition retains the *I* in the original texts. The wordplay on *I*,
 Ay, and *Eye* is one of the dominant motifs of this scene.
 Compare line 6, and see the note to III.i.11.

 Cords the rope ladder by which Romeo will climb into Juliet's
 window. See II.iii.195–99.

And learn me how to loose a winning Match
Play'd for a pair of stainless Maidenhoods.
Hood my unmann'd Blood, bating in my Cheeks,
With thy black Mantle till strange Love grow
    bold,   15
Think True-love acted simple Modesty.
Come Night, come Romeo, come thou Day in
    Night,
For thou wilt lie upon the Wings of Night
Whiter than new Snow upon a Raven's Back.
Come gentle Night, come loving, black-brow'd
    Night,   20
Give me my Romeo, and when I shall die,
Take him and cut him out in little Stars,
And he will make the Face of Heaven so fine
That all the World will be in love with Night
And pay no Worship to the garish Sun.   25
O I have bought the Mansion of a Love
But not possess'd it; and though I am sold,
Not yet enjoy'd. So tedious is this Day
As is the Night before some Festival
To an impatient Child that hath new Robes   30
And may not wear them.

Enter Nurse with Cords.

                    O here comes my Nurse,
And she brings News; and every Tongue that
    speaks
But Romeo's Name speaks heavenly Eloquence.
– Now, Nurse, what News? What hast thou there,
    the Cords
That Romeo bid thee fetch?
NURSE   Ay, ay, the Cords.   35
JULIET   Ay me, what News? Why dost thou wring thy
    Hands?

37   **weraday**   welladay, roughly equivalent to 'alas'.

40   **envious**   both (a) jealous, and (b) malicious. Compare III.i.175.

43   **Divel**   Devil. Shakespeare often uses the *Divel* spelling.

44   **dismal**   Here the context reinforces the original sense of this
       word; it derives from *dies mali*, Latin for 'evil days'. Compare
       IV.iii.135–40.

47   **Cockatrice**   a mythical serpent (often called a basilisk) with the
       power to kill a victim by darting one glance from its eyes.
       Death-darting Eye echoes III.i.20–23. It also recalls
       I.i.208–16; I.iii.96–99; I.iv.19–28, 253–55; II.ii.48–52;
       II.iii.15–19; II.v.6–7.

49   **Or those Eyes shot**   or those eyes darted. An eye hit by the
       'Death-darting Eye of Cocakatrice' (line 47) could be
       described as 'shot' or fatally wounded, as by a dart (arrow).
       The Nurse's following speech, emphasizing what she 'saw . . .
       with [her] Eyes' and punctuated by 'God save the Mark' (an
       expression to ward off evil when one has seen, heard, or
       spoken something of ill omen), reinforces this reading of
       Juliet's line.

54   **Corse**   corpse. The Second Quarto spelling, *coarse*, is apt here.

56   **gore**   The Nurse may mean 'congealed' or 'clotted'; but *gore*
       also means blood, and her adjective may simply be intended
       by the playwright as a redundancy.
       sounded   swounded; that is, swooned. No doubt the Nurse also
       'sounded' (cried out), as she does now.

57   **Bankrout**   bankrupt (with a pun on 'break').

59   **Earth**   (a) Juliet's body, then (b) the ground. Juliet's phrasing
       recalls I.ii.14–15, I.iv.162, II.i.2, II.ii.9, 17–18, III.i.124–25.

60   **press on heavy Bier**   share a burial plinth. Here *on* may mean
       one (that word was often spelled without an *e*), as the Fourth
       Quarto printers inferred. *Press* recalls I.i.190 and anticipates
       V.iii.217; *heavy* echoes II.iv.17.

67   **Trumpet**   Juliet refers to 'the last trump' (1 Corinthians 15:52)
       signalling the Day of Judgement ('the general Doom').

NURSE   A weraday, he's dead, he's dead, he's dead.
We are undone, Lady, we are undone.
Alack the Day, he's gone, he's kill'd, he's dead.
JULIET   Can Heaven be so envious?
NURSE   Romeo can,   40
Though Heaven cannot. O Romeo, Romeo:
Who ever would have thought it Romeo?
JULIET   What Divel art thou that dost torment me
    thus?
This Torture should be roar'd in dismal Hell.
Hath Romeo slain himself? Say thou but 'I',   45
And that bare Vowel 'I' shall poison more
Than the Death-darting Eye of Cockatrice!
I am not I if there be such an 'I'
Or those Eyes shot that makes thee answer 'I'.
If he be slain, say 'I', or if not, 'No':   50
Brief Sounds determine of my Weal or Woe.
NURSE   I saw the Wound, I saw it with mine Eyes,
God save the Mark, here on his manly Breast.
A piteous Corse, a bloody, piteous Corse:
Pale, pale as Ashes, all bedaub'd in Blood,   55
All in gore Blood, I sounded at the Sight.
JULIET   O break, my Heart: poor Bankrout, break at
    once.
To Prison, Eyes: ne'er look on Liberty.
Vile Earth, to Earth resign: end Motion here,
And thou and Romeo press on heavy Bier.   60
NURSE   O Tybalt, Tybalt, the best Friend I had,
O curteous Tybalt, honest Gentleman,
That ever I should live to see thee dead.
JULIET   What Storm is this that blows so contrary?
Is Romeo slaught'red, and is Tybalt dead?   65
My dearest Cousin and my dearer Lord!
Then dreadful Trumpet, sound the general Doom:
For who is living if these two are gone?
NURSE   Tybalt is gone and Romeo banished:

73　**O Serpent Heart . . . flow'ring Face**　The Serpent was a primal image of Satan, owing to the manner of the Devil's first appearance in the Garden of Eden in Genesis 3, and some representations of the temptation of Eve showed the Serpent as a snake with a flower-like countenance. The images that follow (lines 74–85) all derive from the belief that the Devil had the power to transform himself into 'an angel of light' (2 Corinthians 11:14). *Dove* recalls I.iv.163, II.i.10, and II.iv.7. *Raven* echoes line 19.

77　**Despised . . . Show!**　most despicable person in reality despite your divine appearance. Like Romeo in I.i.193–97, Juliet uses oxymorons to convey her sense that seeming opposites are no longer distinguishable (line 78). *Substance* recalls II.i.183.

81　**bower**　shelter with overhanging boughs.

82　**mortal**　human (as distinguished from immortals such as God and his angels). But Romeo will prove *mortal* sooner than Juliet can imagine. *Paradise* recalls II.iii.175.

83–84 **Was . . . bound?**　Juliet's question recalls her mother's description of Paris in I.iii.81–92; it also echoes I.iv.7, 225, II.i.198–99, and III.i.107–8. *Vile* recalls I.iv.111; II.ii.17–18; III.i.76, 148, and III.ii.59. *Bound* echoes I.iv.17–22 and II.i.175. For Juliet, the Romeo she thought a dove is really a vengeful preying raven; the Romeo she thought a lamb (see I.iii.3) is really a wolf in sheep's clothing (see Matthew 7:15).

87　**naught**　naughty, evil; literally, nothing, worthless; having undone themselves by proving their word of no value.
　　Dissemblers　deceivers. In this context the Nurse's phrasing proves literally apt: Romeo no longer has the semblance he once did.

88　**Aqua-vitae**　a kind of brandy, drunk in Shakespeare's time as a restorative.

91　**borne**　both (a) carried, and (b) born. *Shame* recalls I.iv.197.

94　**universal**　entire. Juliet echoes what the Nurse has said in I.iii.75–76 and in II.iii.213–15. *Chide* (scold) recalls the Friar's words in II.v.1–2.

98　**smooth**　rearrange, reorder. *Smooth* can also mean 'compliment' (see II.i.131) or 'flatter' (speak fair, as in III.i.160). *Name* is a jolting reminder of how much has happened since the Balcony Scene; see II.i.75–103.

Romeo that kill'd him, he is banished.   70
JULIET   O God, did Romeo's Hand shed Tybalt's Blood?
NURSE   It did, it did, alas the Day, it did.
JULIET   O Serpent Heart, hid with a flow'ring Face:
  Did ever Dragon keep so fair a Cave?
  Beautiful Tyrant, fiend Angelical.   75
  Dove-feather'd Raven, wolvish, ravening Lamb.
  Despised Substance of divinest Show!
  Just Opposite to what thou justly seem'st:
  A damned Saint, an honourable Villain.
  – O Nature, what hadst thou to do in Hell   80
  When thou didst bower the Spirit of a Fiend
  In mortal Paradise of such sweet Flesh?
  Was ever Book containing such vile Matter
  So fairly bound? O that Deceit should dwell
  In such a gorgeous Palace.
NURSE   There's no Trust,   85
  No Faith, no Honesty in Men: all perjur'd,
  All forsworn, all naught, all Dissemblers.
  Ah, where's my Man? Give me some Aqua-vitae:
  These Griefs, these Woes, these Sorrows make me
    old.
  Shame come to Romeo.
JULIET   Blister'd be thy Tongue   90
  For such a Wish. He was not borne to Shame.
  Upon his Brow Shame is asham'd to sit:
  For 'tis a Throne where Honour may be crown'd
  Sole Monarch of the universal Earth.
  O what a Beast was I to chide at him!   95
NURSE   Will you speak well of him that kill'd your
    Cousin?
JULIET   Shall I speak ill of him that is my
    Husband?
  – Ah poor my Lord, what Tongue shall smooth thy
    Name
  When I, thy three-hours' Wife, have mangled it?

102 **native Spring** natural (born) source.

103 **tributary** paying tribute, belonging to, with an analogy to tributary streams and rivers.

104 **mistaking** mis-taking, misunderstanding. In lines 103–4 Juliet means that the tears she thought she was shedding in sorrow ('Woe') turn out instead to be more appropriate to 'Joy' (since Romeo is still alive. Compare *Macbeth*, I.iv.33–35.

107 **Wherefore** for what reason, why.

109 **would forget it fain** would like to forget it. *Fain* recalls II.iv.16.

116 **sower** sour. But, as in II.iv.24, the Second Quarto spelling reminds us that 'Woe' is also a sower, and that 'This but begins the Woe others must end' (III.i.127). Compare II.ii.9–30. In line 117 *rank'd with* can mean 'overgrown with', 'rotted with', or 'corrupted and diseased with'. See *Hamlet*, I.ii.135–37; *2 Henry IV*, III.i.37–39, IV.i.59–66; and *Troilus and Cressida*, I.iii.315–19.

117 **needly will be** needs or wishes to be.
   rank'd with in the company of.

120 **modern** present, everyday; ordinary.

121 **rearward** bringing up the rear, coming last.

125 **Limit** The word recalls II.i.109. *Bound* echoes lines 83–84.

126 **sound** measure the depth of. Compare line 56 and I.i.153.

128 **Course** corse (corpse). Again, however, the Second Quarto spelling is suggestive (see the note to line 54). Tybalt's 'course' (his way of proceeding), particularly his disregard of his uncle's will (see I.iv.180–207), has scathed him (I.iv.199) and converted his 'Intrusion' as well as Romeo's to 'bitt'rest Gall' (I.iv.206–7).

But wherefore, Villain, didst thou kill my
   Cousin?   100
– That villain Cousin would have kill'd my
   Husband.
– Back, foolish Tears; back to your native
   Spring:
Your tributary Drops belong to Woe,
Which you, mistaking, offer up to Joy.
– My Husband lives that Tybalt would have slain,   105
And Tybalt's dead that would have slain my
   Husband:
All this is Comfort, wherefore weep I then?
Some Word there was, worser than Tybalt's Death,
That murd'red me. I would forget it fain,
But O it presses to my Memory   110
Like damned guilty Deeds to Sinners' Minds:
'Tybalt is dead, and Romeo banished.'
That 'Banished', that one word 'Banished',
Hath slain ten thousand Tybalts. Tybalt's Death
Was Woe enough if it had ended there;   115
Or if sower Woe delights in Fellowship,
And needly will be rank'd with other Griefs,
Why followed not, when she said 'Tybalt's dead',
'Thy Father' or 'thy Mother', nay, or both,
Which modern Lamentation might have mov'd,   120
But with a rearward following Tybalt's Death,
'Romeo is banished'. To speak that Word
Is Father, Mother, Tybalt, Romeo, Juliet,
All slain, all dead. Romeo is 'Banished':
There is no End, no Limit, Measure, Bound,   125
In that Word's Death, no Words can that Woe
   sound.
– Where is my Father and my Mother, Nurse?
NURSE   Weeping and wailing over Tybalt's Course.
   Will you go to them? I will bring you thither.
JULIET   Wash they his Wounds with Tears? Mine shall
   be spent,   130

132   **beguil'd** deceived, cheated.

135   **Widowed** here pronounced with three syllables, to rhyme with 'to my Bed'. *Highway* recalls II.iii.198–99 and II.iv.9–10.

137   **Maidenhead** virginity. Juliet's phrasing recalls line 13 and I.i.23–34, I.iii.2–3, and anticipates III.v.141, IV.iii.122–26, and V.iii.101–5.

138   **Hie** hasten. Like *Highway* (line 134), this word echoes II.iv.69–79.

139   **wot** know.

III.iii   The setting is the cell of Friar Lawrence. Although the opening stage direction calls for the Friar and Romeo both to enter, the dialogue makes it clear that the audience hears, and probably sees, the Friar first.

2   **enamour'd of thy Parts** in love with you. *Parts* (physical and spiritual attributes) anticipates III.v.183. Lines 2–3 echo III.ii.136–37.

4   **Doom** judgement, sentence. So also in lines 8–9.

5   **craves . . . hand** wishes to be introduced to me.

6   **familiar** here pronounced as a four-syllable word.

7   **sowre** either (a) sour (compare III.ii.116) or (b) sore (compare I.iv.19 and *Macbeth*, II.ii.55).

9   **Doomsday** the Last Judgement.

When theirs are dry, for Romeo's Banishment.
Take up those Cords. – Poor Ropes, you are
  beguil'd,
Both you and I, for Romeo is exil'd:
He made you for a Highway to my Bed,
But I, a Maid, die Maiden Widowed.   135
Cords, Cords. – Come, Nurse, I'll to my Wedding
  Bed,
And Death, not Romeo, take my Maidenhead.
NURSE   Hie to your Chamber, I'll find Romeo
To comfort you: I wot well where he is.
Hark ye, your Romeo will be here at Night.   140
I'll to him: he is hid at Lawrence' Cell.
JULIET   O find him, give this Ring to my true
  Knight,
And bid him come, to take his last Farewell.

Exeunt.

Scene 3

Enter Friar and Romeo.

FRIAR   Romeo, come forth, come forth, thou fearful
  Man:
Affliction is enamour'd of thy Parts,
And thou art wedded to Calamity.
ROMEO   Father, what News? What is the Prince's
  Doom?
What Sorrow craves acquaintance at my hand   5
That I yet know not?
FRIAR   Too familiar
Is my dear Son with such sowre Company!
I bring thee Tidings of the Prince's Doom.
ROMEO   What less than Doomsday is the Prince's
  Doom?

16   **patient**   accepting of your lot, trusting in Providence to bestow grace on you. The Friar's attempts at consolation parallel what John of Gaunt tells his son Henry Bullingbrook in *Richard II*, I.iii.274–75.

17   **without Verona Walls**   outside Verona's walls. Compare lines 17–20 with *The Two Gentlemen of Verona*, II.i.170–87, where Valentine laments his banishment.

21   **misterm'd**   misnamed.

22   **Golden Axe**   an apt euphemism, as if a victim of execution would feel better knowing that his head will be going first class when it falls.

24   **rude**   ignorant, unsophisticated. Compare I.iv.166.

25   **Fault**   misdeed, crime. Compare III.i.192.

26   **rush'd aside**   a reference to the fact that the law was not only brushed aside but done so hastily. *Part* (here meaning 'side') echoes line 2.

33   **Validity**   legitimacy, fidelity to their natural state. The creatures enumerated in lines 30–31 recall those in III.i.106–7.

39   **Sin**   sinful. Romeo's phrasing recalls his initial encounter with Juliet; see I.iv.208–25. *Vestal* (line 38) recalls II.i.50, and *Modesty* echoes III.ii.16.

41   **fly**   flee. Romeo puns on *flies*. See the note to III.ii.5–6, and compare Romeo's language in II.i.108–10.

FRIAR   A gentler Judgement vanish'd from
    his Lips: 10
Not Body's Death, but Body's Banishment.
ROMEO   Ha, Banishment? Be merciful: say 'Death'.
For Exile hath more Terror in his Look,
Much more than Death. Do not say 'Banishment'.
FRIAR   Hence from Verona art thou banished: 15
Be patient, for the World is broad and wide.
ROMEO   There is no World without Verona Walls
But Purgatory, Torture, Hell it self:
Hence 'Banished' is banish'd from the World,
And World's Exile is Death. Then 'Banished'   20
Is Death misterm'd: calling Death 'Banished',
Thou cut'st my Head off with a Golden Axe
And smilest upon the Stroke that murders me.
FRIAR   O deadly Sin, O rude
    Unthankfulness.
Thy Fault our Law calls Death, but the kind Prince,   25
Taking thy part, hath rush'd aside the Law
And turn'd that black word 'Death' to Banishment.
This is dear Mercy, and thou seest it not.
ROMEO   'Tis Torture and not Mercy. Heav'n is here
Where Juliet lives; and every Cat and Dog   30
And little Mouse, every unworthy thing,
Live here in Heaven and may look on her,
But Romeo may not. More Validity,
More honourable State, more Courtship lives
In carrion Flies than Romeo: they may seize   35
On the white Wonder of dear Juliet's Hand
And steal immortal Blessing from her Lips,
Who even in pure and vestal Modesty
Still blush, as thinking their own Kisses Sin.
But Romeo may not, he is Banished.   40
Flies may do this, but I from this must fly:
They are Freemen, but I am Banished.
And say'st thou yet that Exile is not Death?

45   **mean**   base, lowly.

49   **ghostly**   holy, spiritual (as in II.i.234, II.ii.45, and II.v.21).

51   **mangle**   Romeo's verb echoes what Juliet has said about him in the preceding scene (III.ii.98–99).

52   **fond**   foolish. Compare II.i.140.

55–56 **Adversity's sweet Milk, Philosophy . . . banished**   The Friar's remarks would have reminded Elizabethans of Bothius's classic *Consolation of Philosophy*, a work written while the author was in prison awaiting execution in the year 524. Boethius had been translated into English by the Queen herself, and his work was a standard treatment of how 'right reason' could rise above the worst that fickle Fortune could do to a person. According to Lady Philosophy, who visits Boethius in his adversity, a man should view suffering as a blessing: a reminder of how fleeting all temporal happiness can be, and God's way of telling him to turn his thoughts to eternity in Heaven, beyond the ups and downs of life on Earth. Compare Duke Senior's observation that 'Sweet are the Users of Adversity' in *As You Like It*, II.i.12. And for another allusion to Boethian philosophy, see *King Lear*, IV.i.18–21.

59   **Displant**   transplant, relocate.

61   **Ears**   The Friar is probably alluding to Matthew 11:15 ('He that hath ears to hear, let him hear'), a passage that underlies much of the action of *Henry IV*, Parts 1 and 2. *Eyes* evokes all the wordplay of the previous scene. It also recalls II.ii.67–68.

63   **dispute**   reason. Philosophical arguments were often referred to as disputations, and it is characteristic of the Friar to insist on fitting Romeo's emotional problems into the abstract categories of scholastic philosophy. Romeo, on the other hand, is so preoccupied with what he feels that he is unwilling to consider the possibility that there might be some value in attempting to think objectively about his situation.

67   **Doting**   loving obsessively. Here as in II.ii.82, the word refers to an affection that is not subject to the dictates of rationality. Compare *A Midsummer Night's Dream*, I.i.105–9, II.i.170–72, III.ii.1–3.

Hadst thou no Poison mix'd, no sharp ground
   Knife,
No sudden means of Death, though ne'er so mean,   45
But 'Banished' to kill me? 'Banished'?
O Friar, the Damned use that Word in Hell:
Howling attends it. How hast thou the Heart,
Being a Divine, a ghostly Confessor,
A Sin-absolver, and my Friend profess'd,   50
To mangle me with that word 'Banished'?
FRIAR   Thou fond, mad Man, hear me a little speak.
ROMEO   O thou wilt speak again of Banishment.
FRIAR   I'll give thee Armour to keep off that Word:
Adversity's sweet Milk, Philosophy,   55
To comfort thee though thou art banished.
ROMEO   Yet 'Banished'? Hang up Philosophy:
Unless Philosophy can make a Juliet,
Displant a Town, reverse a Prince's Doom,
It helps not, it prevails not. Talk no more.   60
FRIAR   O then I see that Mad Men have no Ears.
ROMEO   How should they when that Wise Men have no
   Eyes.
FRIAR   Let me dispute with thee of thy Estate.
ROMEO   Thou canst not speak of that thou dost not
   feel.
Wert thou as young as I, Juliet thy Love,   65
An Hour but married, Tybalt murdered,
Doting like me, and like me banished,
Then mightest thou speak, then mightest thou
   tear thy Hair
And fall upon the Ground as I do now,

70 **Taking the ... Grave** As Romeo prostrates himself on the floor of Friar Lawrence's cell, he suggests that he is determining the length of the grave he will need. Whether he is 'taking the Measure' of the grave in another sense (getting the better of it) is another question. *Measure* recalls I.i.129, I.iv.9–10, 165; II.v.24; and III.ii.125. Here it provides a vivid reminder that Romeo lacks measure (moderation, balance, control) in the Aristotelian sense that relates virtue to the avoidance of extremes (vices). See the note to line 14 of the Chorus to Act II. Also see the notes to II.i.95, 109, 156; II.ii.15–30, 94; II.iii.98–100, 198; II.iv.69; II.v.33; III.i.55, 130–31; III.ii.3, 5–6.

72 **Groans** this word recalls I.i.203–4, II.Chorus.1–4, II.ii.74, II.iii.95, and II.v.33.

73 **enfold me** hide me away. Romeo's imagery echoes I.i.134–56, II.i.94–95, 116–17.

76 **By and by** right away. Compare II.i.193.

77 **Simpleness** folly, simplemindedness. Compare III.i.33–36.

79 **Errant** the Nurse's pronunciation of *errand*, probably intended by the playwright as a comic malapropism, here one that sharpens our awareness that errant behaviour by the Nurse and the Friar has contributed to what has suddenly transformed itself from a comic to a tragic situation.

84 **Case** condition. But the Nurse's phrasing unintentionally suggests another meaning of *Case* as well (see the note to II.iii.51), an implication reinforced by the command to 'Stand up' in line 88 and the reference to 'so deep an O' in line 90. See the note to I.iv.96 for a pertinent sense of the 'Nothing' O represents arithmetically. *Case* derives from the same Latin root (*causa*) as *cause*, so the Nurse's phrasing also relates to the lovers' cause (both 'situation' and 'mission'); compare II.iii.26–28.

88 **and** if. *Stand up* recalls such previous passages as I.i.9–34, I.iii.36, II.i.23–29, 213–16, II.ii.93, and II.iii.155–69.

90 **an O** The Nurse refers to the despairing cry of Romeo in his misery. But the shape of the letter O was itself suggestive of a hole or pit such as the depression into which Romeo has fallen. See the note to II.iii.98–100.

Taking the Measure of an unmade Grave.   70
                          [*A Knock at the Door.*]
FRIAR   Arise, one knocks. Good Romeo, hide thy self.
ROMEO   Not I, unless the breath of Heartsick Groans,
  Mist-like, enfold me from the search of Eyes.
                                          They knock.

FRIAR   Hark, how they knock! – Who's
    there? – Romeo, arise:
  Thou wilt be taken. – Stay awhile. – Stand up,   75
                                          Still knock.
  Run to my Study. – By and by. – God's will,
  What Simpleness is this? – I come, I come.
                                          Knock.
  Who knocks so hard? Whence come you? What's
    your will?
NURSE   [*Within*] Let me come in, and you shall
    know my Errant:
  I come from Lady Juliet.
FRIAR   Welcome then.   80

                    Enter Nurse.

NURSE   O holy Friar, O tell me, holy Friar,
  Where's my Lady' Lord? Where's Romeo?
FRIAR   There on the Ground, with his own Tears made
    drunk.
NURSE   O he is even in my Mistress' Case,
  Just in her Case. O woeful Sympathy,   85
  Piteous Predicament. Even so lies she,
  Blubb'ring and weeping, weeping and blubb'ring.
  – Stand up, stand up. Stand and you be a Man,
  For Juliet's sake, for her sake, rise and stand:
  Why should you fall into so deep an O?   90
ROMEO   Nurse.
NURSE   Ah Sir, ah Sir, Death's the end of all.
ROMEO   Spakest thou of Juliet? How is it with her?

97   **conceal'd**   Both the metre and the parallelism with and play on
        cancell'd dictate a stress on the first syllable.

102   **deadly Level**   dead aim, shot at point blank range. Compare the
        'Shot' imagery in III.ii.45–50.

105–6 **In what vile part . . . lodge?**   This speech echoes in an
        excruciatingly ironic way Juliet's meditation on Romeo's
        name in II.i.75–103. Compare III.ii.98–99.
        sack   loot, pillage. Lines 105–7 echo III.iii.1–2, 26–28. Romeo
        would 'prick Love for pricking' (I.iv.28); compare what he
        essays to do here with what Juliet threatens in IV.i.50–67 and
        does in V.iii.172.

107   **Hold thy desperate Hand**   In the First Quarto, a stage direction
        indicates that after Romeo 'offers to stab himself' the Nurse
        'snatches the dagger away'. But the dialogue suggests that it is
        the Friar who intervenes to stop him from self-slaughter.
        Form recalls II.i.130 and II.iii.37–39.

110   **unreasonable**   unreasoning. Because reason was considered to
        be a faculty unique to mankind, and more prominent in males
        than in 'Weaker Vessels' (see the note to III.i.122), the Friar
        compares Romeo's 'Fury' to that of a 'Beast'.

112   **ill-beseeming Beast**   The Friar says that Romeo's behaviour is
        so 'unseemly' that it would ill become even a beast. Compare
        I.i.96. Also compare *The Merchant of Venice*, I.ii.19.

114   **temper'd**   (a) composed, mixed, (b) treated for durability, and
        (c) controlled, moderated. Compare III.i.122.

117   **doing . . . Self**   a reminder that suicide was regarded as a mortal
        sin, resulting from despair and leading to damnation. See
        Hamlet, I.ii.129–32.

118   **rail'st thou on**   complain about.

120   **loose**   both (a) set loose, release, forgo, and (b) lose.

122   **Usurer**   one who hoards his bounty and lends only at interest.
        The Friar's moral derives from such texts as Matthew
        25:14–30. *Wit* recalls I.i.212, I.iii.42, I.iv.45–49, and II.iii.68,
        74–84.

Doth not she think me an old Murtherer
Now I have stain'd the Childhood of our Joy
With Blood removed but little from her own?   95
Where is she? And how doth she? And what says
My conceal'd Lady to our cancell'd Love?

NURSE   O she says nothing, Sir, but weeps and weeps,
And now falls on her Bed, and then starts up,
And Tybalt calls, and then on Romeo cries,   100
And then down falls again.

ROMEO   As if that Name,
Shot from the deadly Level of a Gun,
Did murther her as that Name's cursed Hand
Murder'd her Kinsman. O tell me, Friar, tell me,
In what vile part of this Anatomy   105
Doth my Name lodge? Tell me that I may sack
The hateful Mansion.   *He offers to stab himself.*

FRIAR   Hold thy desperate Hand.
Art thou a Man? Thy Form cries out thou art.
Thy Tears are Womanish; thy wild Acts
Denote the unreasonable Fury of a Beast.   110
Unseemly Woman in a seeming Man,
And ill-beseeming Beast in seeming both,
Thou hast amaz'd me. By my holy Order,
I thought thy Disposition better temper'd.
Hast thou slain Tybalt? Wilt thou slay thy Self?   115
And slay thy Lady that in thy Life lives
By doing damned Hate upon thy Self?
Why rail'st thou on thy Birth, the Heaven, and
    Earth,
Since Birth and Heaven and Earth all three do
    meet
In thee at once, which thou at once wouldst loose?   120
Fie, fie, thou sham'st thy Shape, thy Love, thy
    Wit,
Which like a Usurer abound'st in all,
And usest none in that true Use indeed

124 **bedeck** adorn.

125 **a Form of Wax** a lifeless figure, resembling a man only in appearance. In I.iii.76, the Nurse commended Paris to Juliet as a 'Man of Wax'. See the notes to I.iv.20 and III.ii.3, 5–6.

126 **Digressing** deviating.

128 **vow'd to cherish** The Friar alludes to the marriage vow Romeo has just taken.

129 **Wit** mind, reason (as in line 121). But the Friar's words can also apply to Romeo's genital wit (see I.iii.42), a sense reinforced by 'dismemb'red' in line 133.

130 **Conduct** guidance. The Friar's phrasing in lines 129–33 recalls such passages as III.i.130–31 ('Conduct') and II.v.9–11 ('Powder').

131 **Flask** container.

132 **Ignorance** both (a) lack of knowledge or skill (line 131), and (b) disregard of the conduct of reason and its counsels of prudence. For this second sense of *ignorance*, which derives from *ignore* and refers to wilful neglect, see *Hamlet*, III.i.148–49, *Troilus and Cressida*, II.iii.31–34, *King Lear*, IV.v.9–10, and *Othello*, III.iii.392–95.

140 **light** alight (but do so in a way that makes your burden lighter than before). Compare I.iv.11–24.

141 **Array** raiment, dress.

145 **decreed** planned, decided.

147 **look thou** see (be heedful) that you. *Stay* recalls line 75 and III.i.143.
Watch the volunteer citizens' guard. See I.i.75–77, III.i.144–47.

150 **blaze** proclaim. Compare *blazon*, II.v.26. The Friar's phrasing keeps us mindful of the degree to which he himself is playing with inflammatory ingredients (see lines 129–33) in his efforts to produce a happy consummation.

157 **apt** predisposed.

Which should bedeck thy Shape, thy Love, thy Wit.
Thy Noble Shape is but a Form of Wax   125
Digressing from the Valour of a Man;
Thy dear Love sworn but hollow Perjury,
Killing that Love which hast vow'd to
    cherish;
Thy Wit, that Ornament to Shape and Love,
Misshapen in the Conduct of them both,   130
Like Powder in a skill-less Soldier's Flask,
Is set afire by thine own Ignorance,
And thou dismemb'red with thine own Defence.
What, rouse thee, Man: thy Juliet is alive,
For whose dear sake thou wast but lately dead.   135
There art thou happy. Tybalt would kill thee,
But thou slew'st Tybalt. There art thou happy.
The Law that threat'ned Death becomes thy Friend
And turns it to Exile. There art thou happy.
A pack of Blessings light upon thy Back;   140
Happiness courts thee in her best Array;
But like a misbehav'd and sullen Wench,
Thou pouts upon thy Fortune and thy Love.
Take heed, take heed, for such die miserable.
Go get thee to thy Love as was decreed;   145
Ascend her Chamber, hence and comfort her.
But look thou stay not till the Watch be set,
For then thou canst not pass to Mantua,
Where thou shalt live till we can find a Time
To blaze your Marriage, reconcile your Friends,   150
Beg Pardon of the Prince, and call thee back
With twenty hundred thousand times more Joy
Than thou went'st forth in Lamentation.
– Go before, Nurse; commend me to thy Lady,
And bid her hasten all the House to Bed,   155
Which heavy Sorrow makes them apt unto.
Romeo is coming.
NURSE   O Lord, I could have stay'd here all the
    Night

159   **Learning**   both (a) literacy (as in I.ii.45), and (b) the wisdom
        that reading conveys. Compare Gremio's ejaculation about
        the wonders of learning in *The Taming of the Shrew*, I.ii.163.

161   **chide**   scold, probably meant playfully. Compare II.ii.85,
        II.v.1–2, and III.ii.95.

162   **Ring**   The Nurse hands Romeo the ring Juliet gave her in
        III.ii.142–43. *Chide* (line 161) is a reminder of Juliet's initial
        reaction to his deed in the previous scene (see III.ii.95).

163   **Hie**   hasten. Compare II.iv.69–79 and III.ii.138. The reference
        to how late it is recalls I.iv.105, 241, 254, and anticipates line
        171.

165   **your State**   your situation (literally, your standing). Like *stay*
        (see line 158) and *stand*, upon which the Friar plays in this
        line, *State* derives from the Latin word *stare* (see the note to
        II.i.216, and compare line 88). Compare the imagery in
        II.ii.93–94.

167   **disguise from hence**   leave here under the cover of a disguise.

168   **Man**   manservant (Balthasar). The Friar's phrasing recalls
        . Tybalt's remarks and Mercutio's rejoinder, in III.i.59–64.

170   **good Hap**   good happening, happy occurrence.

172   **Joy past Joy**   an earthly joy that surpasses the Joy (bliss) of
        Heaven. *Joy* recalls II.i.158–59, II.iii.198, II.v.3–5, 24–25,
        III.ii.103–4, and III.iii.93–95.

173   **brief**   briefly.

III.iv   The setting is a room in Capulet's house.

2   **move**   persuade. Compare I.i.6–14, 93; I.iii.97; I.iv.16,
        220–21; III.i.12–14; III.ii.120.

4   **borne**   both (a) carried in the womb, and (b) given birth. *Late*
        (line 5) echoes III.iii.163, 171, and anticipates line 34.

5   **she'll . . . to night**   This line echoes what the Friar has advised
        in III.iii.154–57. It thus reminds us why Juliet is secluded in
        her bedroom; it also shows that despite the promptings of
        'heavy Sorrow', the Capulets have not hastened 'all the House
        to bed'.

To hear good Counsel. O what Learning is.
– My Lord, I'll tell my Lady you will come.   160
ROMEO   Do so, and bid my Sweet prepare to chide.
                    Nurse offers to go and turns again.
NURSE   Here, Sir, a Ring she bid me give you, Sir.
  Hie you, make haste, for it grows very late.   *Exit.*
ROMEO   How well my Comfort is reviv'd by this.
FRIAR   Go hence, goodnight. And here
    stands all your State: 165
  Either be gone before the Watch be set
  Or by the break of Day disguise from hence.
  Sojourn in Mantua; I'll find out your Man,
  And he shall signify from Time to Time
  Every good Hap to you that chaunces here.   170
  Give me thy Hand. 'Tis late: farewell, goodnight.
ROMEO   But that a Joy calls out on me,
  It were a Grief so brief to part with thee.
  Farewell.   *Exeunt.*

Scene 4

Enter old Capulet, his Wife, and Paris.

CAPULET   Things have fall'n out, Sir, so unluckily
  That we have had no time to move our Daughter.
  Look you, she lov'd her kinsman Tybalt dearly,
  And so did I. Well, we were borne to die.
  'Tis very late: she'll not come down to night.   5
  I promise you, but for your Company,
  I would have been abed an Hour ago.

8   **Woe** grief. The pun on *Woo* in this line is a reminder that in this play wooing has become inseparable from woe. Compare *Love's Labour's Lost*, IV.iii.372, where *woo* is spelled *woe*. Here *Woe* recalls I.iv.21, II.ii.46, III.i.127, III.ii.51, 103, 115–16, 126, and anticipates IV.iii.135, V.iii.13, 214, 311.

9   **commend** give my respects. Paris' phrasing echoes the Friar's in the previous scene (III.iii.154).

11   **mewed up to** enclosed in (from falconry).
     Heaviness despondency, mourning. Juliet is bearing up under more 'Heaviness' than her father realizes (see I.iv.17–31, 92–96). Compare III.ii.60 and III.iii.156.

12   **Tender** offer. Compare I.iv.23–27. Here *desperate* means 'rash', 'hasty', or 'bold', and it relates to what Capulet regards as a nearly desperate (hopeless) state of melancholy in Juliet. Compare I.i.134–58.

14   **respects** ways. Compare II.ii.90, III.i.130–31.

17   **mark you me?** This and other gestures make it clear that Capulet treats his wife in much the same way that he manages his servants.

18   **soft** wait, hush for a moment; hold it.

19   **ha, ha** Capulet is probably saying *hmmm* here as he deliberates, but it is possible that he chuckles as he does so.

20   **A' Thursday** on Thursday.

24   **so late** so recently. Compare lines 5, 34.

25   **held him carelessly** had no feelings for him or for his loved ones. Capulet's phrasing reminds us that his daughter is not holding her new husband 'carelessly'. Compare III.v.23, 75–78.

28   **and . . . end** and no more; that will suffice. Capulet speaks more accurately than he recognizes.

32   **against** in preparation for.

34   **Afore me** a mild oath, comparable in force to 'indeed'; its literal meaning is 'I swear on my own self'. Compare 'Ay me' (I.i.164, II.i.67) and 'By my Head' (III.i.37).

35   **by and by** soon. Compare III.iii.76. Capulet's remarks imply that the hour nears either (a) midnight or (b) dawn. The conclusion of the next scene suggests that Capulet means dawn.

PARIS   These Times of Woe afford no Times to Woo:
   – Madam, goodnight; commend me to your
   Daughter.
LADY   I will, and know her Mind early to morrow;   10
   To night she's mewed up to her Heaviness.
          Paris offers to go, and Capulet calls him again.
CAPULET   Sir Paris, I will make a desperate Tender
   Of my Child's Love: I think she will be rul'd
   In all respects by me; nay more, I doubt it not.
   – Wife, go you to her ere you go to Bed;   15
   Acquaint her here of my Son Paris' Love,
   And bid her (mark you me?) on Wednesday next –
   – But soft, what Day is this?
PARIS   Monday, my Lord.
CAPULET   Monday, ha, ha. well, Wednesday is too
     soon;
   A' Thursday let it be. A' Thursday, tell her,   20
   She shall be married to this Noble Earl.
   – Will you be ready? Do you like this Haste?
   We'll keep no great ado, a Friend or two,
   For hark you, Tybalt being slain so late,
   It may be thought we held him carelessly,   25
   Being our Kinsman, if we revel much.
   Therefore we'll have some half a dozen Friends,
   And there an end. But what say you to Thursday?
PARIS   My Lord, I would that Thursday were to morrow.
CAPULET   Well, get you gone: a' Thursday be it then.   30
   – Go you to Juliet ere you go to Bed;
   Prepare her, Wife, against this Wedding Day.
   – Farewell, my Lord. – Light to my Chamber, ho.
   Afore me, it is so very late that we
   May call it early by and by. Goodnight.   *Exeunt.*   35

III.v   The setting is Juliet's bedroom, probably represented by a
window above the main stage.

7–8   **what envious Streaks . . . East**   It is typical of Romeo's tendency
to allegorize experience that he sees the streaks of pre-dawn
light on the clouds as 'envious' of the lovers' happiness.
Envious recalls II.i.46–51 and III.i.175. *East* recalls II.i.45,
and it thereby reminds us of Romeo's first view of Juliet's
window.

8   **severing Clouds**   The clouds Romeo sees are 'severing' in three
senses: they are (a) dispersing, separating from one another,
(b) separating night from day, and (c) most importantly,
separating Romeo from Juliet. *Clouds* recalls III.i.123–25.

9   **Night's Candles**   the stars and planets.
jocund Day   cheerful, jocular Day; here personified as standing
on tiptoe to peer in on the lovers and expose their secret.
Compare III.ii.1–7.

13   **Meteor**   possibly a reference to a meteor in the usual modern
sense (a 'shooting star'), but more likely an allusion to the
'will o' th' wisp', a luminous gas thought to be 'exhaled' or
drawn by the Sun from low-lying marshes. Meteors too were
thought to be combustible vapours. Romeo's phrasing recalls
the Icarus and Phaeton imagery from earlier in the play; see
the notes to III.ii.3, 5–6.

20   **pale Reflex of Cynthia's Brow**   dim light reflected from the face
of the Moon (here identified with Cynthia, the Goddess of the
Moon). *Notes* (line 21) recalls I.i.238–40. Romeo's
description of the Goddess of Chastity and her 'Brow' recalls
II.i.46–51.

22   **vaulty Heaven**   the overarching sky; specifically, the crystalline
spheres believed to enclose the Globe in concentric circles.

23   **care**   desire, concern. This word echoes III.iv.25. *Stay* recalls
line 16 and III.iii.147; see the note to II.i.216.

26   **Hie**   hasten (again reverberating with *high*, line 22). Compare
II.iv.69–79 and III.iii.163.

27   **Lark . . . out of Tune**   The Lark now sings out of tune because
his notes are a breach of the harmony the lovers have enjoyed
during the night. *Discords* recalls III.i.49–50; in the process it
reminds us of the fray that has now frayed the harmony the
lovers sought for themselves. For other references to music,
see I.iv.19–22, 141; II.i.202–8; II.iii.21–25, 32–33; II.iv.
22–24; II.v. 24–29; III.i. 47–51; III.ii.67; IV.iii.174,
182–231.

Scene 5

Enter Romeo and Juliet aloft.

JULIET   Wilt thou be gone? It is not yet near Day.
It was the Nightingale and not the Lark
That pierc'd the fearful Hollow of thine Ear:
Nightly she sings on yond Pomegranate Tree.
Believe me, Love, it was the Nightingale.   5
ROMEO   It was the Lark, the Herald of the Morn,
No Nightingale. Look, Love, what envious Streaks
Do lace the severing Clouds in yonder East.
Night Candles are burnt out, and jocund Day
Stands tiptoe on the misty Mountaintops.   10
I must be gone and live, or stay and die.
JULIET   Yond Light is not Daylight, I know it, I:
It is some Meteor that the Sun exhales
To be to thee this Night a Torch-bearer
And light thee on thy way to Mantua.   15
Therefore stay yet, thou needst not to be gone.
ROMEO   Let me be ta'en; let me be put to death;
I am content, so thou wilt have it so.
I'll say yon Grey is not the Morning's Eye;
'Tis but the pale Reflex of Cynthia's Brow.   20
Nor that is not the Lark whose Notes do beat
The vaulty Heaven so high above our Heads.
I have more care to stay than will to go:
— Come, Death, and welcome; Juliet wills it so.
— How is't, my Soul? Let's talk, it is not Day.   25
JULIET   It is, it is. Hie hence; be gone away.
It is the Lark that sings so out of Tune,

29   **Division**   a musical term referring to a melodic phrase, and
       sometimes to melody in general. Juliet puns on the more
       common sense of the word, alluded to in line 30. Compare
       lines 7–8.

31   **change**   exchange. Compare II.i.169, II.v.3–5.

33   **affray**   both (a) make afraid, frighten, and (b) separate with a
       disturbing din.

34   **Hunting thee**   pursuing you.
       Hunt's-up   a morning song to wake up huntsmen. Compare *A
       Midsummer Night's Dream*, IV.i.141, and *Titus Andronicus*,
       II.ii.1–6.

37   **Woes**   This word recalls III.iv.8 and anticipates line 52.

40   **wary**   Compare I.i.127, II.i.145.

44   **every Day in the Hour**   a hyperbolic variation on the phrase
       'every hour in the day', indicating how slowly time will pass
       for Juliet while she is severed from Romeo. Compare II.i.211.

46   **Count**   This word recalls I.iii.71 and II.v.32.

49   **omit**   neglect, fail to avail myself of.

55   **Me thinks . . . low**   The Second Quarto and the First Folio set
       off 'thou art so low' in parenthetical commas, as here.
       Modern editions normally place the initial comma before
       now. The First Quarto provides no commas.

56   **bottom of a Tomb**   The position of the lovers at this point
       mirrors that of the initial Balcony Scene (II.i), with Romeo
       below and Juliet above.

Straining harsh Discords and unpleasing Sharps.
Some say the Lark makes sweet Division;
This doth not so, for she divideth us.   30
Some say the Lark and loathed Toad change Eyes;
O now I would they had chang'd Voices too,
Since Arm from Arm that Voice doth us affray,
Hunting thee hence with Hunt's-up to the Day.
O now be gone: more light and light it grows.   35
ROMEO   More light and light; more dark and dark our
Woes.

Enter Nurse, hastily.

NURSE   Madam.
JULIET   Nurse.
NURSE   Your Lady Mother is coming to your Chamber;
The Day is broke; be wary, look about.   [*Exit.*]   40
JULIET   Then Window, let Day in and let Life out.
ROMEO   Farewell, farewell; one Kiss and I'll
descend.   *He goeth down.*
JULIET   Art thou gone so? Love, Lord, ay, Husband,
Friend,
I must hear from thee every Day in the Hour,
For in a Minute there are many Days.
O by this Count I shall be much in Years   45
Ere I again behold my Romeo.
ROMEO   Farewell;
I will omit no Opportunity
That may convey my Greetings, Love, to thee.   50
JULIET   O think'st thou we shall ever meet again?
ROMEO   I doubt it not, and all these Woes shall
serve
For sweet Discourses in our Times to come.
JULIET   O God, I have an ill-divining Soul:
Me thinks I see thee now, thou art so low,   55
As one dead in the bottom of a Tomb.

59   **Dry Sorrow drinks our Blood**   It was thought that the sighs of
love drew blood away from the heart, an idea also echoed in
A Midsummer Night's Dream, III.ii.97 ('Sighs of Love, that
costs the fresh Blood dear'). Here those sighs are attributed to
a thirsty figure of Sorrow personified. *Pale* (line 57) echoes
line 20 and recalls II.iv.17 and III.ii.55. It anticipates V.i.28
and V.iii.96, 146.

67   **so**   The word here carries the weight of an intensifier meaning
'extraordinarily'. Juliet's phrasing echoes III.iv.34–35. It
thereby reminds us again that the lovers have been upstairs
boldly consummating their marriage at the same time that
Juliet's parents have been arranging for their daughter's
wedding to Paris.

68   **unaccustom'd**   unusual, departing from the customary norm.
procures   draws. *Cause* recalls III.iii.84.

69   **how now**   how are you?

72   **And if**   even if.

74   **still**   always.
want of Wit   lack of judgement. Juliet's mother would be
shocked to learn that her daughter has not been suffering
from 'want of Wit' in the conjugal sense. Compare III.iii.129,
and see the notes to I.i.212 and I.iii.42. Lines 73–77 parallel
Hamlet, I.ii.68–106.

75   **feeling Loss**   deeply felt death (see the note to II.Chorus.2).
Juliet's phrasing can refer to the 'Loss' she and Romeo have
just experienced. See III.ii.8–13, where she asks 'civil Night'
to teach her how to lose 'a winning Match' for 'a pair of
stainless Maidenhoods'. And see *All's Well That Ends Well*,
III.ii.43–45, for a reference to the 'Loss of Men' that results in
'the Getting of Children'. Juliet uses *feeling* in the 'Sense'
defined in I.i.23–32, and it is clear that the 'Friend' she weeps
for has been extremely 'civil with' her. Her *double entendres*
are by no means limited to the kinds of 'feeling Loss' that
bring joy to the senses and emotions (see lines 51–65), but
they include them.

Either my Eyesight fails or thou look'st pale.
ROMEO   And trust me, Love, in my Eye so do you:
Dry Sorrow drinks our Blood, Adieu, adieu.   *Exit.*
JULIET   O Fortune, Fortune, all Men call thee
Fickle.   60
If thou art Fickle, what dost thou with him
That is renown'd for Faith? Be fickle, Fortune:
For then I hope that wilt not keep him long,
But send him back.
LADY   [*Within*] Ho, Daughter, are you up?   65
JULIET   Who is't that calls? It is my Lady Mother.
Is she not down so late or up so early?
What unaccustom'd Cause procures her hither?
                    She goeth down from the Window.

                    Enter Mother.

LADY   Why how now, Juliet?
JULIET   Madam, I am not well.
LADY   Evermore weeping for your Cousin's
Death?   70
What, wilt thou wash him from his Grave with
Tears?
And if thou couldst, thou couldst not make him
live.
Therefore have done: some Grief shews much of
Love,
But much of Grief shews still some want of Wit.
JULIET   Yet let me weep for such a feeling Loss.   75
LADY   So shall you feel the Loss, but not
the Friend
Which you weep for.
JULIET   Feeling so the Loss,
I cannot choose but ever weep the Friend.
LADY   Well, Girl, thou weep'st not so
much for his Death

82 **Villain ... asunder** This line, almost certainly to be spoken as an aside, is most likely to be intended as a statement that the concepts of 'Villain' and 'Romeo' are miles apart ('asunder'). *Villain* recalls III.i.64, 132.

83 **God pardon** This was a formulaic phrase usually uttered as a pious expression, with the speaker giving little or no thought to its content. Juliet probably speaks it in the conventional manner while meaning it sincerely.

87 **Would ... Death** Again, Juliet says one thing to please her mother, but privately means something quite different.

90 **Runagate** both (a) renegade (traitor), and (b) runaway (a person banished or fled). Compare III.ii.5–7.

91 **unaccustom'd Dram** a potion that will be both unexpected and unprecedented in its potency. *Unaccustom'd* echoes line 68.

95–98 **With Romeo ... temper it** Most modern editions change the period (full stop) to a dash in line 95, to yield a reading in which Juliet tells her mother she will never be satisfied till she sees 'Romeo – dead'. This edition retains the punctuation in the Second Quarto and First Folio texts, based on the interpretation that 'dead' is an adjective Juliet applies to her grieving heart. Juliet plays on a non-vengeful sense of *satisfied* (compare II.i.167–69), and she puns on *hold* when she says 'behold him'.

97 **Man** Here and in line 104, the word probably means 'servingman' (as in III.iii.168).

98 **temper** mix in further ingredients. While saying this to her mother, Juliet is thinking that she would in fact dilute the potion so that its sole effect would be to help Romeo sleep contentedly. Compare III.iii.114.

102 **wreak** both (a) avenge (the meaning Juliet's mother hears), and (b) bestow or spend upon (Juliet's private meaning), probably with an erotic sense in 'come to him' (line 101), a sense that also suggests itself in III.iii.157, 160, and gives an unintended, amusingly ironic implication to Capulet's observation a moment later that 'we were borne to die' (III.iv.4). See the note to II.Chorus.2.

104 **Means** recalls lines 13–14 of the Chorus to Act II.

108 **careful** care-full, loving. This word recalls III.iv.25–26 and III.v.23, and anticipates lines 178–80.

As that the Villain lives which slaughter'd him.   80
JULIET   What Villain, Madam?
LADY   That same villain Romeo.
JULIET   Villain and he be many Miles
    asunder.
God pardon, I do with all
    my Heart;
And yet no Man like he doth grieve my Heart.
LADY   That is because the Traitor
    Murderer lives.   85
JULIET   I Madam, from the reach of these my Hands;
    Would none but I might venge my Cousin's death.
LADY   We will have Vengeance for it, fear
    thou not.
Then weep no more; I'll send to one in Mantua
(Where that same banish'd Runagate doth live)   90
Shall give him such an unaccustom'd Dram
That he shall soon keep Tybalt company;
And then I hope thou wilt be satisfied.
JULIET   Indeed I never shall be satisfied
    With Romeo till I behold him. Dead   95
Is my poor Heart, so for a Kinsman vex'd:
Madam, if you could find out but a Man
To bear a Poison, I would temper it
That Romeo should upon receipt thereof
Soon sleep in quiet. O how my Heart abhors   100
To hear him nam'd and cannot come to him
To wreak the Love I bore my Cousin
Upon his Body that hath slaughter'd him.
MOTHER   Find thou the Means, and I'll find
    such a Man.
But now I'll tell thee joyful Tidings, Girl.   105
JULIET   And Joy comes well in such a needy Time.
    What are they, I beseech your Ladyship?
MOTHER   Well, well, thou hast a careful
    Father, Child,

109 **put . . . Heaviness**   Given the implication *Heaviness* acquired in
III.iv.11, this phrase carries the unintended meaning 'separate
thee from thy Romeo' (compare lines 29–30).

110 **sorted out**   picked out, fixed upon.

112 **in happy Time**   just in time. Compare I.ii.46.

116 **happily**   Here its metrical position calls for *happily* to be
pronounced as a two-syllable word, thereby merging it with
haply, a word whose ironic connotations (by chance, by
accident) are even more appropriate to the context.

119 **I wonder**   I am astonished.

127 **drizzle Dew**   It is not certain whether Capulet is thinking of
dew in the normal sense (in which case *drizzle* would mean
'shed') or of *drizzle* in the normal sense (in which case *dew*
refers to its residue of fine, spray-like drops). The contrast
with 'rains downright' (line 129) is clear in either case.

130 **Conduit**   probably a reference to an elaborately designed
fountain in which the water spouts from a carved human
form in the centre.

132 **counterfeits**   resembles. Compare II.iii.51.
Bark   barque, a small sailing vessel. Romeo will compare
himself to a bark in V.iii.118–20.

137 **overset**   Capulet means 'overwhelm' or 'capsize'; but *overset* is
an apt term for what Juliet's 'Tempest-tossed Body' has just
been subjected to.

One who, to put thee from thy Heaviness,
Hath sorted out a sudden Day of Joy,   110
That thou expects not, nor I look'd not for.
JULIET   Madam, in happy Time, what Day is that?
MOTHER   Marry, my Child, early next
     Thursday morn
The gallant, young, and Noble Gentleman,
The County Paris, at Saint Peter's Church,   115
Shall happily make thee there a joyful Bride.
JULIET   Now, by Saint Peter's Church and Peter too,
He shall not make me there a joyful Bride.
I wonder at this Haste, that I must wed
Ere he that should be Husband comes to woo.   120
I pray you tell my Lord and Father, Madam,
I will not marry yet; and when I do I swear
It shall be Romeo, whom you know I hate,
Rather than Paris. These are News indeed.
MOTHER   Here comes your Father; tell him so
     your self,   125
And see how he will take it at your hands.

Enter Capulet and Nurse.

CAPULET   When the Sun sets, the Earth doth drizzle
     Dew;
But for the Sunset of my Brother's Son,
It rains downright.
How now, a Conduit, Girl, what, still in Tears?   130
Evermore show'ring in one little Body?
Thou counterfeits a Bark, a Sea, a Wind:
For still thy Eyes, which I may call the Sea,
Do ebb and flow with Tears; the Bark thy Body is,
Sailing in this salt Flood; the Wind's thy Sighs,   135
Who, raging with thy Tears and they with them,
Without a sudden Calm will overset
Thy Tempest-tossed Body. — How now, Wife,

139   **Decree**   Capulet probably means 'decision', but 'decree' conveys the nature of the situation with absolute precision. Compare III.iii.145.

140   **will none**   will have none of it. Line 141 recalls III.ii.137.

142   **Soft, take me with you**   Slow down, let me be sure I follow you. *Soft* echoes III.iv.18.

144   **Is she not proud?**   Capulet means 'Is she not proud of the match we have arranged for her?'

146   **Bride**   bridegroom.

148   **what I hate**   The next line suggests that Juliet refers not to Paris but to the way her parents have arranged the marriage without consulting her or considering her wishes.

150   **Chopp'd Logic**   sophistic wordplay (logical only in appearance).

152   **Minion**   here, a spoiled favourite.

154   **fettle your fine Joints**   prepare your refined limbs. Capulet uses alliteration here (fettle, fine) to give his words maximum emphasis. In this context, *fettle* suggests *fetters* (shackles).
       'gainst   in anticipation of. Compare III.iv.32.

156   **Hurdle**   a wooden sled on which criminals were conveyed to execution, an image that will prove prophetically apt.

157   **green-sickness Carrion**   the corpse of a girl who died of 'green sickness', a form of anaemia. See II.i.46–51.

158   **Tallow Face**   Tallow, from which candles were made, was pale in colour; Capulet is referring to Juliet's bloodless complexion. But compare I.iii.76, III.iii.125.
       Fie . . . mad?   Though these words would apply more aptly to Capulet, they are probably addressed to Juliet. Only later (line 176) does Capulet's Wife offer a mild word of protest to her husband. Compare lines 125–26, 140–41.

165   **My Fingers itch**   Capulet means that he is having difficult resisting the urge to strike Juliet.

166   **onely**   only, playing on *one* in the next line. Compare the description of Juliet in I.ii.14–15.

Have you deliver'd to her our Decree?

LADY   I Sir, but she will none, she
    gives you thanks.   140
  I would the Fool were married to her Grave.

CAPULET   Soft, take me with you, take me with you,
    Wife:
  How will she none? Doth she not give us Thanks?
  Is she not Proud? Doth she not count her Blest,
  Unworthy as she is, that we have wrought   145
  So worthy a Gentleman to be her Bride?

JULIET   Not Proud you have, but Thankful, that you
    have:
  Proud can I never be of what I hate,
  But Thankful even for Hate that is meant Love.

CAPULET   How, how, how, how, chopp'd Logic, what
    is this?   150
  'Proud' and 'I thank you', and 'I thank you not',
  And yet 'not Proud', Mistress Minion, you?
  Thank me no Thankings, nor proud me no Prouds,
  But fettle your fine Joints 'gainst Thursday next
  To go with Paris to Saint Peter's Church,   155
  Or I will drag thee on a Hurdle thither.
  Out, you green-sickness Carrion! Out, you
    Baggage,
  You Tallow Face.

LADY   Fie, fie, what, are you mad?

JULIET   Good Father, I beseech you on my Knees,
  Hear me with patience but to speak a Word.   160

CAPULET   Hang thee, young Baggage, disobedient
    Wretch.
  I tell thee what: get thee to Church a' Thursday,
  Or never after look me in the Face.
  Speak not, reply not, do not answer me.
  My Fingers itch. – Wife, we scarce thought us
    blest   165
  That God had lent us but this onely Child;

169 **Hilding** base wretch.

170 **too blame** too blameworthy.
   rate berate.

172 **smatter** prattle.
   Gossips garrulous old ladies. The original meaning of this
   word was 'godparents' (baptismal sponsors), from 'God-sibs'
   (relatives by virtue of spiritual affinity). There is a hint of that
   sense in 'Gossip's Bowl' (line 175).

173 **Treason** insubordination.
   O God'i'god-den O God give you good evening! Here used as
   a mild oath. Compare I.ii.59, II.iii.116–18.

175 **Utter . . . Bowl** mumble your grave wisdom over a cup of hot
   punch with your fellow gossips. *Hot* (line 176) recalls
   III.i.167.

177 **God's Bread** an oath referring to the wafer representing the
   body of Christ in the Communion service.

178 **Tide** Capulet may mean the interval determined by the tides,
   but it is more likely that he is using the word generically to
   refer to any indefinite period or season of time. *Still* (line 179)
   means 'always'.

180 **match'd** This word echoes III.ii.8–13, and it thus conveys
   another reminder that Juliet has already been 'match'd'.

182 **Demesnes** land holdings, domains. Compare II.i.20.
   Liand This word, from the Second Quarto, may be a coinage
   to combine (a) lined (descended), (b) aligned (connected), (c)
   allied, and (d) landed (propertied). Compare I.iii.83. The
   word in the First Quarto is *traind* and in the First Folio *allied*.

183 **Parts** aspects, qualities. Compare III.iii.2. *Stuff'd* echoes
   I.iii.76. Compare *Much Ado About Nothing*, I.i.57–61,
   III.iv.65–66.

185 **puling** whimpering.

186 **Mammet** puppet doll. Capulet is accustomed to treating Juliet
   as a mammet, but not to having her respond to him like a real
   human being with a mind and will of her own.
   tender fragile, not yet mature. Compare I.iv.22–30, III.iv.12.

190 **Graze** Capulet's use of this verb has the effect of reducing
   Juliet to the status of a farm animal.

But now I see this one is one too much,
And that we have a Curse in having her:
Out on her, Hilding.
NURSE   God in Heaven bless her.
    You are to blame, my Lord, to rate her so.   170
CAPULET   And why, my Lady Wisdom? Hold your
    Tongue,
Good Prudence, smatter with your Gossips, go.
NURSE   I speak no Treason.
CAPULET   O God'i'god-den.
NURSE   May not one speak?
CAPULET   Peace, you mumbling Fool:
    Utter your Gravity o'er a Gossip's Bowl,   175
    For here we need it not.
WIFE   You are too hot.
CAPULET   God's Bread, it makes me mad.
    Day, Night; Hour, Tide, Time; Work, Play;
    Alone, in Company: still my Care hath been
    To have her match'd. And, having now provided   180
    A Gentleman of Noble Parentage,
    Of fair Demesnes, Youthful and Nobly Liand,
    Stuff'd, as they say, with Honourable Parts,
    Proportion'd as one's Thought would wish a Man,
    And then to have a wretched, puling Fool,   185
    A whining Mammet, in her Fortunes tender,
    To answer 'I'll not wed, I cannot love,
    I am too young, I pray you pardon me'.
    — But and you will not wed, I'll pardon you:
    Graze where you will, you shall not house with
        me.   190

191 **I do not use to jest** I am not in the habit of speaking in jest. *Jest*
recalls II.iii.68–84.

192 **Lay Hand on Heart, advise** Speak to your heart. *Advise* echoes
II.i.160.

195 **I'll ne'er acknowledge thee** Capulet is threatening to disclaim
any relationship to Juliet, to disinherit her.

197 **forsworn** proven a liar or oathbreaker. Compare I.i.226,
III.ii.87.

203 **dim Monument** dark tomb.

208– **How . . . Earth?** How can I pledge my 'Faith' (fidelity in
10 marriage) to another man while the husband I've already
vowed it to remains alive and my promise to be faithful to
him is recorded in the Heaven that holds my religious faith?
See the notes to I.i.124, II.iii.198, III.ii.3, 5–6.

211 **practise Stratagems** play tricks. Juliet's words reflect
astonishment at a reversal of fortune so arbitrary as to seem
like a malicious cosmic jest.

212 **soft** weak, fragile.

215 **and all the World to Nothing** The Nurse seems to be saying
that the odds ('all the World' as opposed to 'Nothing') are
overwhelmingly against Romeo's ever coming back to claim
Juliet as his wife. Another possible reading is that, for all
practical purposes, Romeo has ceased to exist, both in the
eyes of the world and (if she is pragmatic in her thinking) in
the eyes of Juliet. The second reading would call for a comma
after *Nothing*. Either interpretation is consistent with the
Nurse's point of view. See the notes to I.iv.96, III.iii.84.

216– **That . . . by Stealth** The Nurse is assuming that Juliet will take
17 the practical course and marry Paris. If so, she says, Romeo
will be unable to 'challenge' the marriage publicly, only
privately ('by Stealth') if at all. Having seen Juliet 'married
once' (I.iii.61), the Nurse has no qualms about advising the
young lady to marry again; compare I.ii.10–13. In
Shakespeare's principal source for the play, Arthur Brooke's
Tragical History of Romeus and Juliet (1562), the Nurse
advises Juliet to marry the County and enjoy the 'wanton
love' of Romeus as a 'paramour'.

Look to't, think on't; I do not use to jest.
Thursday is near. Lay Hand on Heart, advise:
And you be mine, I'll give you to my Friend;
And you be not, hang, beg, starve, die in the
   Streets,
For by my Soul, I'll ne'er acknowledge thee,   195
Nor what is mine shall never do thee good.
Trust to't, bethink you, I'll not be forsworn.

                                             Exit.

JULIET   Is there no Pity sitting in the Clouds
   That sees into the Bottom of my Grief?
   – O sweet my Mother, cast me not away.   200
   Delay this Marriage for a Month, a Week;
   Or if you do not, make the Bridal Bed
   In that dim Monument where Tybalt lies.
MOTHER   Talk not to me, for I'll not speak a
      Word.
   Do as thou wilt, for I have done with thee.   *Exit.*   205
JULIET   O God. – O Nurse, how shall this be
      prevented?
   My Husband is on Earth, my Faith in Heaven:
   How shall that Faith return again to Earth
   Unless that Husband send it me from Heaven
   By leaving Earth? Comfort me, counsel me.   210
   Alack, alack, that Heaven should practise
      Stratagems
   Upon so soft a Subject as my self.
   What say'st thou? Hast thou not a word of Joy?
   Some Comfort, Nurse.
NURSE   Faith, here it is: Romeo
   Is banished, and all the World to Nothing   215
   That he dares ne'er come back to challenge you,
   Or if he do, it needs must be by Stealth.

218   **Case**   matter, situation. *Case* recalls III.iii.84, and here its association with *stands* gives the Nurse's phrasing an unintentionally erotic suggestiveness.

221   **Dishclout**   dishcloth. Compare II.iii.212–15.

223   **Beshrow**   beshrew (line 229), curse. This spelling reflects the way the word was frequently pronounced, by analogy with *sew*, *shew*, and *Shrewsbury*. *Match* (line 224) echoes line 180.

229   **Amen**   Juliet probably speaks this under her breath, or at least in such a way that the Nurse fails to understand that Juliet is commending the Nurse's willingness to 'beshrow' both her heart and her soul if she is not speaking with sincerity.

230   **Well . . . much**   Juliet means this ironically, but she delivers it in such a way that the Nurse takes it at face value.

235   **Auncient . . . Fiend**   Juliet is applying these names to the Nurse, but implicit in her remarks is the idea that it is Satan ('the Fiend' and the original source of the Fall that led to damnation) who speaks through her with the advice to forswear her marriage vows. When Juliet dismisses the Nurse with the words 'Go, Counsellor' (line 239), she is echoing 'Get thee behind me, Satan' (Matthew 16:23).

240   **Twain**   two, divided.

241   **Remedy**   prescription for this new malady. The root meaning of *remedy* is 'to heal again', and Juliet's phrasing is another reminder both of the Friar's familiarity with herbal drugs and of the role he has played in creating a situation that requires remediation.

Then, since the Case so stands as now it doth,
I think it best you married with the County.
O he's a lovely Gentleman;   220
Romeo's a Dishclout to him. An Eagle, Madam,
Hath not so green, so quick, so fair an Eye
As Paris hath. Beshrow my very Heart,
I think you are happy in this second Match,
For it excels your first; or if it did not,   225
Your first is dead, or 'twere as good he were,
As living here and you no use of him.

JULIET   Speak'st thou this from thy Heart?
NURSE   And from my Soul,
Too, else beshrew them both.
JULIET   Amen.
NURSE   What?
JULIET   Well, thou hast comforted me marvellous much.   230
Go in and tell my Lady I am gone,
Having displeas'd my Father, to Lawrence' Cell,
To make Confession and to be absolv'd.
NURSE   Marry, I will, and this is wisely done.   *Exit.*
JULIET   Auncient Damnation: O most wicked Fiend,   235
Is it more Sin to wish me thus forsworn
Or to dispraise my Lord with that same Tongue
Which she hath prais'd him with above compare
So many thousand times? – Go, Counsellor:
Thou and my Bosom henceforth shall be Twain.   240
I'll to the Friar to know his Remedy;
If all else fail, my self have power to die.

                                              Exit.

IV.i   The setting is the cell of Friar Lawrence.

3   **And . . . Haste** and I am no impediment ('Stop', as in II.i.111) to retard his impetuosity. Although this line can be interpreted to mean that Paris is reluctant to interfere with Capulet's haste, the context suggests that what Paris is telling the Friar is that he is powerless or unwilling to do anything to cross his future father-in-law. True to the effeminacy implicit in his title (see the note to I.iii.71), the ineffectual County Paris presents himself here as one of the 'Weaker Vessels' (I.i.15–20) of the world. *Slow* recalls II.v.15; compare II.ii.94, II.iv.17. Compare lines 2–3 with V.iii.26–27.

5   **Uneven . . . Course** The Friar's image suggests (a) a rough, swirling current of water (one that can 'overset' small objects such as Paris or Juliet, III.v.134–38), or (b) an irregular terrain over which to make one's 'Course' or journey (compare III.ii.128). *Uneven* invites comparison with *A Midsummer Night's Dream*, III.ii.417, and *Richard II*, II.ii.119 and II.iii.4–5.

8   **Venus . . . House of Tears** Paris means that the Goddess of Love cannot be expected to be effectual in a household in the throes of mourning. His phrasing also carries an astrological play on words, based on the idea that the planet Venus does not have a beneficent influence ('smiles not') when she is in one of the 'houses' (zones) of the Zodiac associated with water (Aquarius or Pisces).

12   **stop** both (a) block off, and (b) halt. Compare II.i.111 (cited in the note to line 3 above), II.iii.101–4, V.iii.54. *Stop* can mean 'stuff up', and that sense recalls the phrasing in III.v.183.

13   **minded** attended. But *minded* can also refer to a person's 'mind' or will, as in line 4 (compare I.i.123, I.iv.106–7, III.iv.10), and it is now clear that neither Paris nor Juliet's parents, nor even her Nurse, will ever be privy to her mind again. See III.v.239–40.
   alone in solitude. Like *minded* this word refers to Juliet's tears rather than to Juliet herself.

14   **Society** association with other people.

15   **of** for. Line 16 is probably to be spoken as an aside.

17   **Happily met** This phrase recalls III.v.112, 116.

ACT IV

Scene 1

Enter Friar and County Paris.

FRIAR   On Thursday, Sir? The Time is very
   short.
PARIS   My Father Capulet will have it so,
   And I am nothing slow to slack his Haste.
FRIAR   You say you do not know the Lady's Mind?
   Uneven is the Course, I like it not.   5
PARIS   Immoderately she weeps for Tybalt's Death,
   And therefore have I little talk'd of Love:
   For Venus smiles not in a House of Tears.
   Now Sir, her Father counts it dangerous
   That she do give her Sorrow so much Sway,   10
   And in his Wisdom hastes our Marriage
   To stop the inundation of her Tears,
   Which, too much minded by her self alone,
   May be put from her by Society.
   Now do you know the Reason of this Haste.   15
FRIAR   I would I knew not why it should be slow'd.

Enter Juliet.

   Look, Sir, here comes the Lady toward my Cell.
PARIS   Happily met, my Lady and my Wife.
JULIET   That may be, Sir, when I may be a Wife.

20   **must be** Like Juliet's parents, Paris assumes that Juliet has nothing to say about the matter.

21   **certain Text** sure saying (because it is tautological, asserting that something is identical with itself). The Friar calls it a 'Text' because it is a frequently cited proverb.

27   **Price** value, worth.

29   **abus'd** misused (see II.ii.19–20). Paris echoes the Nurse's *use* in III.v.227. *Tears* recalls lines 8, 12, and anticipates lines 30, 32.

31   **Spight** spite; contemptuous mistreatment.

32   **Report** both (a) statement of fact and (b) retort (as in the 'report' of the cannons that win a 'Victory').

34   **to my Face** both (a) to my own face, and (b) openly (not behind my back).

35   **Thy Face is mine** Paris is attempting to be gracious, but he succeeds only in sounding tedious and overbearing.

37   **at Leisure** able to spare time for me.

39   **pensive** reflective, sad. This word echoes *depend* in III.i.126–27.

40   **entreat** request.

41   **shield** forbid, prevent.

45   **Care** (a) the point at which attention will help, and (b) cure (the word in the First Quarto). Compare Sonnet 147, line 9 ('Past Cure I am, now Reason is past Care'), *Love's Labour's Lost*, V.ii.28 ('past Care is still past Cure'), and *Richard II*, II.iii.170 ('Things past Redress are now with me past Care'). *Care* recalls III.v.108.

47   **strains** both (a) constrains or forces, and (b) taxes. Line 47 echoes II.ii.19–20, and suggests that the Friar's 'Wits' are once again 'stumbling on Abuse'.
      compass reach, scope. *Wits* recalls III.v.74.

48   **prorogue** defer, postpone. Compare II.i.119–20.

PARIS   That 'may be' must be, Love, on Thursday
  next.   20
JULIET   What must be shall be.
FRIAR   That's a certain Text.
PARIS   Come you to make Confession to this Father?
JULIET   To answer that I should confess to you.
PARIS   Do not deny to him that you love me.
JULIET   I will confess to you that I love him.   25
PARIS   So will ye, I am sure, that you love me.
JULIET   If I do so, it will be of more Price
  Being spoke behind your Back than to your Face.
PARIS   Poor Soul, thy Face is much abus'd with
  Tears.
JULIET   The Tears have got small Victory by that,   30
  For it was bad enough before their Spight.
PARIS   Thou wrong'st it more than Tears with that
  Report.
JULIET   That is no Slaunder, Sir, which is a Truth,
  And what I spake, I spake it to my Face.
PARIS   Thy Face is mine, and thou hast sland'red it.   35
JULIET   It may be so, for it is not mine own.
  – Are you at Leisure, holy Father, now,
  Or shall I come to you at evening Mass?
FRIAR   My Leisure serves me, pensive
  Daughter, now.
  – My Lord, we must entreat the Time alone.   40
PARIS   God shield I should disturb Devotion.
  – Juliet, on Thursday early will I rouse ye;
  Till then adieu, and keep this holy Kiss.   *Exit*.
JULIET   O shut the Door, and when thou hast done so,
  Come weep with me: past Hope, past Care, past
  Help.   45
FRIAR   O Juliet, I already know thy Grief:
  It strains me past the compass of my Wits.
  I hear thou must, and nothing may prorogue it,
  On Thursday next be married to this County.

53 **Resolution** resolve, intention. By saying 'call my Resolution wise', Juliet is asking the Friar to bestow his blessing on her determination to commit suicide. Compare *Hamlet*, III.i.80–85, and *Macbeth*, V.v.41–43.

54 **presently** immediately, at this present moment.

57 **Label to an other Deed** Juliet probably means this phrase in a legal sense. Picking up on 'seal'd' in the preceding line, she appears to be using 'Label' to refer to a strip of parchment, bearing the official seal, that was attached to a deed.

58 **treacherous Revolt** traitorous insubordination. To break her vow to Romeo would be to violate her sworn obedience to both her earthly lord and her Lord in Heaven.

61 **present Counsel** instant guidance.

63 **Umpeer** umpire, judge. *Extremes* (line 62) recalls line 14 of the Chorus to Act II. Compare I.iii.102–3, II.v.33, III.iii.70.

64 **Commission** authority vested in the Friar. But Juliet's word is also a reminder that the Friar is already 'long experienc'd' in 'Commission' (actions committed) with Romeo and Juliet.

65 **Issue** outcome; here, the conclusion of a legal proceeding. But *Issue* can also mean 'offspring'; compare II.ii.9–22. *Honour* recalls II.i.185–90.

69 **desperate** done only in extreme, apparently hopeless situations. *Desperate* is derived from *despair*, the absence of hope in theological terms, and that is probably why the Friar calls his remedy 'a kind of Hope'. Compare III.iv.12–13.

72 **stay** stop, slay (the word in the First Quarto). Compare II.ii.26, and see *A Midsummer Night's Dream*, II.i.190. *Stay* recalls III.v.23.

75 **cop'st** contends with, rivals. The Friar's meaning is that the shame Juliet seeks to escape is as terrible as death itself would be. Lines 77–78 invite comparison with Matthew 4:5–7.

79 **Thievish Ways** pathways where robbers lurk.

81 **Charnel-house** originally a tomb (with *charnel* derived from the Latin word for flesh), but by Shakespeare's time a building next to a graveyard for the housing of unearthed skulls and bones.

JULIET   Tell me not, Friar, that thou hearest of this   50
   Unless thou tell me how I may prevent it.
   If in thy Wisdom thou canst give no Help,
   Do thou but call my Resolution wise,
   And with this Knife I'll help it presently.
   God join'd my Heart and Romeo's, thou our Hands,   55
   And ere this Hand, by thee to Romeo seal'd,
   Shall be the Label to an other Deed,
   Or my true Heart with treacherous Revolt
   Turn to an other, this shall slay them both.
   Therefore, out of thy long experienc'd Time,   60
   Give me some present Counsel, or behold,
   'Twixt my Extremes and Me this bloody Knife
   Shall play the Umpeer, arbitrating that
   Which the Commission of thy Years and Art
   Could to no Issue of true Honour bring.   65
   Be not so long to speak: I long to die
   If what thou speak'st speak not of Remedy.
FRIAR   Hold, Daughter, I do spy a kind of Hope,
   Which craves as desperate an Execution
   As that is desperate which we would prevent.   70
   If, rather than to marry County Paris,
   Thou hast the strength of Will to stay thy self,
   Then it is likely thou wilt undertake
   A thing like Death to chide away this Shame,
   That cop'st with Death himself, to scape from
     it.   75
   And if thou dar'st, I'll give thee Remedy.
JULIET   O bid me leap, rather than marry Paris,
   From off the Battlements of any Tower,
   Or walk in Thievish Ways, or bid me lurk
   Where Serpents are; chain me with roaring Bears,   80
   Or hide me nightly in a Charnel-house,
   O'ercover'd quite with Dead-men's rattling Bones,

83 **reeky Shanks** foul-smelling limbs.
  chaples either (a) chapels' (see line 81) or (b) chapless, jaw-less.

88 **unstain'd** spotless, immaculate. Compare III.ii.12–13. Also see
  II.ii.75–76, III.i.118–20, III.iii.93–95, V.iii.142–43.

89 **consent** This word recalls II.ii.64.

91 **look** see.

93 **Vial** small bottle.

94 **distilling** trickling down and flowing through the body.
  Compare I.i.197.
  Liquor medicinal solution.

95 **presently** instantly.

96 **drowsy Humour** sleep-inducing fluid. *Cold* recalls III.i.169.

97 **native Progress** inborn, natural movement. Compare III.ii.102
  and *Hamlet* IV.vii.173–75.
  surcease suspend operation. Compare *Macbeth*, I.vii.2–7.

101 **Like . . . Life** Compare Sonnet 73, lines 5–8.

102 **supple Government** resiliency, flexibility. *Government* recalls
  I.iv.181–83. *Part* carries ominous echoes of II.ii.23–30.

103 **stark** barren of life.

104 **shrunk** shrunken. Compare *As You Like It*, II.vii.161. *Likeness*
  recalls II.i.8.

107 **Bridegroom** The Friar means Paris, of course, but lines 102–7
  will also be fulfilled in a perverse way by Juliet's real
  bridegroom. Compare V.i.17–19.

109 **Manner** custom. Line 111, which appears in the Second
  Quarto and in all the subsequent early texts, is omitted in
  most modern editions as a redundancy that should have been
  deleted by the original typesetters. Compare the textual
  problem in II.i.230–33 and II.ii.1–4.

114 **against thou shalt awake** in preparation for your waking.
  Compare the use of *against* in III.iv.32 and III.v.154. For a
  different sense of the word see II.iii.102–3, 158–60.

With reeky Shanks and yellow chaples Skulls;
Or bid me go into a new made Grave,
And hide me with a Dead-man in his Shroud   85
(Things that, to hear them told, have made me
    tremble),
And I will do it without Fear or Doubt,
To live an unstain'd Wife to my sweet Love.
FRIAR   Hold then, go home, be merry, give consent
To marry Paris. Wednesday is to morrow;   90
To morrow night look that thou lie alone
(Let not the Nurse lie with thee in thy Chamber).
Take thou this Vial, being then in Bed,
And this distilling Liquor drink thou off,
When presently through all thy Veins shall run   95
A cold and drowsy Humour: for no Pulse
Shall keep his native Progress, but surcease;
No Warmth, no Breath shall testify thou livest;
The Roses in thy Lips and Cheeks shall fade
To many Ashes, thy Eyes' Windows fall,   100
Like Death when he shuts up the Day of Life;
Each Part, depriv'd of supple Government,
Shall stiff and stark and cold appear like Death.
And in this borrowed Likeness of shrunk Death
Thou shalt continue two and forty Hours,   105
And then awake as from a pleasant Sleep.
Now when the Bridegroom in the Morning comes
To rouse thee from thy Bed, there art thou dead;
Then, as the Manner of our Country is,
In thy best Robes uncover'd on the Bier,   110
Be borne to Burial in thy Kindred's Grave;
Thou shalt be borne to that same auncient Vault
Where all the Kindred of the Capulets lie.
In the mean time, against thou shalt awake,

115   **our Drift**   our intentions, the direction of our plans. In a way that will prove tellingly ironic, *Drift* echoes II.ii.55–56.

117   **watch**   wait for vigilantly, stay awake for (compare IV.iii.66). *Watch* recalls III.iii.147, 166–67. It also reverberates with a number of New Testament admonitions, among them Mark 13:34–37, where Jesus says 'Watch ye therefore: for ye know not when the master of the house cometh'. Compare *Macbeth*, II.ii.67–68, and see 1 Thessalonians 5:1–10, Hebrew 13:17, 1 Peter 4:7, 1 Corinthians 16:13, 2 Timothy 4:5, and Revelation 16:15.

118   **inconstant Toy**   trifle or doubt that interferes with one's 'constancy' or resolve. Compare *A Midsummer Night's Dream*, V.i.3.

120   **womanish Fear**   The Friar's phrasing echoes III.iii.109–10. *Valour* recalls III.i.122.

121   **Abate**   diminish (literally, beat down). Compare III.ii.13.

123   **prosperous**   fortunate, full of success.

124   **Resolve**   echoes lines 53–54.

126   **afford**   carry forward.

IV.ii   The setting for this scene is a room in Capulet's house.

2   **cunning**   skilled (literally, knowing). Line 1 recalls I.ii.34–45.

6   **ill Cook**   here *ill* probably means both 'bad' and 'unwell'.

8   **lick his Fingers**   It was proverbial that one who would not lick his fingers had no faith in his own work. With a bad cook, it might mean that he lacked confidence in the ingredients. With an 'ill Cook' (line 6), it might also mean that he was unwilling to eat food his own hands had contaminated. Compare I.iv.115–20.

10   **unfurnish'd**   unprepared. Compare line 35.

12   **forsooth**   in truth.

Shall Romeo by my Letters know our Drift,   115
And hither shall he come, and he and I
Will watch thy Waking, and that very Night
Shall Romeo bear thee hence to Mantua.
And this shall free thee from this present Shame
If no inconstant Toy nor womanish Fear   120
Abate thy Valour in the acting it.
JULIET   Give me, give me, O tell me not of Fear.
FRIAR   Hold, get you gone, be strong and prosperous
In this Resolve. I'll send a Friar with Speed
To Mantua with my Letters to thy Lord.   125
JULIET   Love give me Strength, and Strength shall
    help afford.
Farewell, dear Father.   *Exeunt.*

Scene 2

Enter Father Capulet, Mother, Nurse, and Servingmen, two or
three.

CAPULET   So many Guests invite as here are writ.
                              [*Exit Servingman.*]
– Sirrah, go hire me twenty cunning Cooks.
SERVINGMAN   You shall have none ill, Sir: for I'll
try if they can lick their Fingers.
CAPULET   How canst thou try them so?   5
SERVINGMAN   Marry Sir, 'tis an ill Cook that cannot
lick his own Fingers; therefore he that cannot
lick his Fingers goes not with me.
CAPULET   Go, be gone.   *Exit Servingman.*
– We shall be much unfurnish'd for this Time.   10
– What, is my Daughter gone to Friar Lawrence?
NURSE   Ay forsooth.

14 **self-wield** both (a) self-wielded, self-made, and (b) self-willed.
The Folio prints *self-wild*, a reminder that an ungoverned will
was considered wild, as opposed to 'Civil' (see line 4 of the
Prologue, and compare I.i.92) or civilized.
Harlotry worthlessness, disobedience. Compare *Hilding*
(III.v.169) and *Minion* (III.v.152).

15 **merry** cheerful. Compare I.iii.40.

16 **gadding** going idly about, like an unmanageable jade.
Headstrong carries the same implication of unruliness as the
phrasing in line 14. Compare *The Taming of the Shrew*,
IV.i.209–10, V.ii.126–27; *The Comedy of Errors*, II.i.15; *2
Henry IV*, IV.iv.62–66; and *Measure for Measure*, I.iv.19–20.

18 **learnt me** both (a) learned, and (b) taught myself. Compare
III.ii.12–13.

19 **Behests** commands.
enjoin'd commanded (see IV.i.89–90). Juliet's verb is a
reminder that she has also been 'enjoin'd' to Romeo by 'holy
Lawrence'.

23–24 **Send for the County ... morning** Before Capulet addresses a
word to Juliet, he orders that Paris be notified of her change
of mind; he also moves up the wedding date by a day. His
actions keep us aware that in the world of Shakespeare's
Verona everyone tends to 'stand on sudden Hast' (II.ii.93).
The words *stand up* (line 28) echo III.iii.75, 88, 165. Juliet's
posture recalls III.i.160–65.

26 **becomed** becoming, seemly, maidenly. Juliet's phrase *bounds
of Modesty* (line 27) recalls II.i.175 and III.ii.15–16. It
anticipates line 32, where *bound to him* offers an ironic
reminder of how much Verona is both indebted and
connected to the 'holy Friar'.

33 **Closet** private chamber.

34 **sort** select.

CAPULET   Well, he may chance to do some good on
    her:
  A peevish, self-wield Harlotry it is.

                Enter Juliet.

NURSE   See where she comes from Shrift with merry
    Look.   15
CAPULET   How now, my Headstrong, where have you
    been gadding?
JULIET   Where I have learnt me to repent the Sin
  Of disobedient Opposition
  To you and your Behests, and am enjoin'd
  By holy Lawrence to fall prostrate here   20
  To beg your Pardon.   *She kneels down.*
                Pardon, I beseech you;
  Henceforward I am ever rul'd by you.
CAPULET   Send for the County: go tell him of this.
  I'll have this Knot knit up to morrow morning.
JULIET   I met the youthful Lord at Lawrence' Cell   25
  And gave him what becomed Love I might,
  Not stepping o'er the bounds of Modesty.
CAPULET   Why I am glad on't, this is well, stand
    up;
  This is as't should be. – Let me see the County:
  Ay marry, go, I say, and fetch him hither.   30
  Now, afore God, this reverend holy Friar,
  All our whole City is much bound to him.
JULIET   Nurse, will you go with me into my Closet
  To help me sort such needful Ornaments
  As you think fit to furnish me to morrow?   35
MOTHER   No, not till Thursday; there is
    Time enough.
CAPULET   Go, Nurse, go with her; we'll to Church
  to morrow.   *Exeunt Juliet and Nurse.*

38   **short in our Provision**   deficient in our preparations (compare line 10). Having been overruled by her husband a moment earlier, Capulet's Wife objects again. Significantly, however, her concerns centre on 'Provision' for the wedding guests rather than on preparing her daughter for an event to which Juliet herself seems all but incidental. In other words, like Juliet's other adult counsellors, her parents are – and have evidently long been – 'short in' their 'Provision' for her deepest needs. In this line *provision* would be pronounced as a full four-syllable word (pro-víz-ee-on).

39   **stir about**   make myself busy. *Stir* recalls I.i.9–11, 83; I.iv.112; and III.i.4.

40   **warrant**   assure. Compare II.iii.213, II.iv.44.

41   **deck up her**   Capulet emphasizes the word *her*, which is placed in a stressed position both syntactically and metrically. His point is that he, being the 'Huswife for this once' (line 43), will deck up the house while his wife helps the Nurse deck up Juliet.

42   **let me alone**   both (a) leave me to my own devices (don't worry about me), and (b) let me be by myself. Compare *Twelfth Night*, III.iv.105, 119–20.

45   **prepare up him**   Capulet stresses the word *him*, which parallels the emphasis in the similar phrasing of line 41.

46   **wondrous light**   wondrously cheerful.

47   **reclaim'd**   both (a) returned to the fold (compare Matthew 18:12–14), and (b) repaired, remedied (see III.v.241, IV.i.67, 76). Having been prepared to disclaim his daughter, Capulet is now rejoicing over her suitability for reclamation. What had seemed lost, he reflects, is now found. *Wayward* recalls *Headstrong* (line 16); it also echoes Capulet's imagery in III.v.188–96.

IV.iii   The setting now shifts to Juliet's private chamber.

3   **Orisons**   prayers.

5   **cross**   at cross purposes with Heaven's will. *State* recalls III.iii.165. *Sin* echoes I.iv.208–25 and III.v.236–39.

7   **cull'd**   picked out.

8   **behooveful**   appropriate, required for the occasion.
         State   both (a) social station, and (b) public ceremony.

MOTHER   We shall be short in our Provision:
   'Tis now near Night.
CAPULET   Tush, I will stir about,
   And all things shall be well, I warrant thee,
      Wife.   40
   Go thou to Juliet, help to deck up her.
   I'll not to Bed to night, let me alone:
   I'll play the Huswife for this once. – What ho!
   – They are all forth. Well, I will walk my self
   To County Paris, to prepare up him   45
   Against to morrow. My Heart is wondrous light,
   Since this same wayward Girl is so reclaim'd.

                                 Exeunt.

Scene 3

Enter Juliet and Nurse.

JULIET   Ay, those Attires are best. But gentle
   Nurse,
   I pray thee leave me to my self to night:
   For I have need of many Orisons
   To move the Heaven to smile upon my State,
   Which, well thou know'st, is cross and full of
      Sin.   5

Enter Mother.

MOTHER   What, are you busy, ho? Need you my
   help?
JULIET   No, Madam, we have cull'd such Necessaries
   As are behooveful for our State to morrow.

9   **alone** Juliet's phrasing echoes IV.ii.42. Once her mother and the Nurse leave, Juliet will find herself more truly alone than she has ever been: see line 19. *Alone* recalls I.iv.180; II.i.36; II.v.36–37; III.v.179–80; IV.i.13–14, 40, 91. It anticipates V.ii.23 and V.iii.10, 137, 254.

11   **full all** completely full.

15   **cold** chilling. Compare IV.i.96. *Faint* carries an ominous echo of III.i.112–13. It also recalls *A Midsummer Night's Dream*, I.i.73.
       thrills a wonderfully apt verb, combining a sense of intense apprehension with the sensation of shivering.

19   **dismal** This word recalls the 'dismal Hell' Juliet evoked in III.ii.44.

22   **Lie thou there** Juliet probably addresses the knife she has brandished in IV.i.

25   **Subtly** craftily, cunningly.
       minist'red administered, prescribed for me. Juliet's phrasing is a reminder of the Friar's ministerial profession.

28   **not** not be.

29   **still** always.
       tried proven to be. Line 29 recalls IV.ii.31–32 and anticipates V.iii.272.

32   **redeem** both (a) rescue, deliver, and (b) reclaim (see IV.ii.47, and compare III.v.214–17 and IV.i.107–8). Juliet's imagery echoes the theological vocabulary of I.iv.208–25 and II.i.92–93, 97–98, 154–57.

33   **stifled** suffocated.

36   **like** likely; also the meaning in line 45.

37   **Conceit** thought, concept.

So please you, let me now be left alone,
And let the Nurse this Night sit up with you: 10
For I am sure you have your Hands full all
In this so sudden Business.
MOTHER   Goodnight.
Get thee to Bed and rest, for thou hast need.
JULIET   Farewell.   *Exeunt [Mother and Nurse].*
                    God knows when we shall meet again.
I have a faint, cold Fear thrills through my
    Veins,   15
That almost freezes up the Heat of Life.
I'll call them back again to comfort me.
– Nurse. – What should she do here?
My dismal Scene I needs must act alone.
– Come, Vial.   20
– What if this Mixture do not work at all?
Shall I be married then to morrow morning?
No, no, this shall forbid it. – Lie thou there.
– What if it be a Poison which the Friar
Subtly hath minist'red to have me dead,   25
Lest in this Marriage he should be dishonour'd
Because he married me before to Romeo?
I fear it is, and yet me thinks it should not:
For he hath still been tried a Holy Man.
How if when I am laid into the Tomb,   30
I wake before the time that Romeo
Come to redeem me? There's a fearful Point.
Shall I not then be stifled in the Vault,
To whose foul Mouth no healthsome Air breathes
    in,
And there die strangled ere my Romeo comes?   35
Or if I live, is it not very like
The horrible Conceit of Death and Night,
Together with the Terror of the Place,
As in a Vault, an auncient Receptacle
Where for this many hundred Years the Bones   40

42   **green** newly placed. The word *green* suggests both the colour of rotting flesh and the colour of fresh shoots.

43   **fest'ring** decomposing. *Shroud* recalls IV.i.85.

44   **resort** come, spend time.

47   **Shrikes** shrieks. The original spelling preserves a more strident-sounding word than the one conveyed by modern spelling.

    Mandrakes' . . . Earth It was widely believed that the mandrake plant (the *mandragola* or *mandragora* mentioned in *Othello*, III.iii.320, and *Antony and Cleopatra*, I.v.2) shrieked when pulled from the earth, and there were some who thought that madness or death, or both, came to anyone who heard that shriek. It is fitting that Juliet should think about mandrakes at this moment, because it is likely that the sleeping potion she is about to drink was extracted from a type of mandrake plant. Compare the effect ascribed to the Cockatrice in III.ii.45–51.

49   **distraught** distracted, crazed (a stronger term in Shakespeare's time than in our own).

50   **Environed** surrounded. *Joints* (line 51) refers to bone joints. But in other contexts this word is a term for the male member. See *Love's Labour's Lost*, V.i.137–39. The word echoes III.v.154–56. *Mangled* (line 52) echoes III.ii.98–99.

53   **Rage** mad frenzy. Compare Prologue. 10, I.i.87, and III.i.66.

56   **spit** impale, run through.

57   **stay** both (a) stop, and (b) remain where you are. Juliet is succumbing to a hallucinatory 'Rage'. *Stay* recalls IV.i.72. As Juliet falls behind the 'Curtains' around her bed, the setting shifts to one of the larger rooms of the house, but with Juliet remaining at the back of the stage. Most editors begin a new scene (IV.iv) at what is here designated line 59. But it is important to note that the action continues uninterrupted. Compare I.iv and II.i in this edition.

60   **Pastry** the chamber where pastry was baked.

61   **second Cock** A sixteenth-century book on *Husbandry* notes that cocks crowed 'at midnight, at three, and an hour before day'. *Stir* (line 61) recalls IV.ii.39.

Of all my buried Auncestors are pack'd,
Where bloody Tybalt, yet but green in Earth,
Lies fest'ring in his Shroud, where, as they say,
At some Hours in the Night Spirits resort —
Alack, alack, is it not like that I,   45
So early waking (what with loathsome Smells,
And Shrikes like Mandrakes' torn out of the
     Earth,
That living Mortals, hearing them, run mad) —
O if I wake, shall I not be distraught,
Environed with all these hideous Fears,   50
And madly play with my Forefathers' Joints,
And pluck the mangled Tybalt from his Shroud,
And in this Rage, with some great Kinsman's Bone,
As with a Club, dash out my desp'rate Brains?
— O look! Me thinks I see my Cousin's Ghost   55
Seeking out Romeo, that did spit his Body
Upon a Rapier's Point. — Stay, Tybalt, stay!
— Romeo, Romeo, Romeo, here's Drink: I drink to thee.
             She falls upon her Bed within the Curtains.

             Enter Lady of the House and Nurse.

LADY   Hold take these Keys and fetch more
   Spices, Nurse.
NURSE   They call for Dates and Quinces in the Pastry.   60

             Enter old Capulet.

CAPULET   Come, stir, stir, stir: the second Cock hath
   crow'd,

62   **Curfew bell . . . o'clock** Just as a bell was rung in the evening to alert people that it was time to cover their fires (the original meaning of the word *curfew*) and retire, another bell was rung in the morning to signal that it was time to rise.

    roong rung.

63   **Bak'd-meats** meat pies.

    Angelica evidently the name of the Nurse.

64   **Cot-quean** a man who does household chores as if he were a wife.

66   **watching** staying up rather than going to bed. This word recalls IV.i.117.

69   **Mouse-hunt** one who hunts mice (specifically, a cat or a weasel); an allusion to Capulet's earlier days as a woman-chaser. Compare I.iv.137–40, 146–47; II.iii.74–108.

71   **Jealous Hood** a jealous person. Capulet's response is probably meant to be a good-humoured reply to his wife's teasing dig, and is no doubt spoken while she is still within earshot.

78   **Mass** by the Mass, a mild oath.

79   **Loggerhead** blockhead, stupid person. Whether the servant's comment about a 'Head . . . that will find out Logs' (line 18) is meant to suggest that he is calling himself a loggerhead (blockhead) is unclear. He may simply be saying that he knows how to find logs without Peter's help. Or he may be making another joke, perhaps one that has to do with a hangover. In any case, it is obvious that Capulet enjoys both the servant's comment and his own jest in reply to it. Compare the banter in I.iv.115–31, 142–45.

    Father an oath in the name of God the Father. Many editors follow the Fourth Quarto and emend to *faith*; compare I.iv.241.

    'tis Day When it suits his purpose, Shakespeare contrives to make time move very rapidly in his dramatic scenes.

The Curfew Bell hath roong, 'tis three a'clock:
Look to the Bak'd-meat, good Angelica;
Spare not for Cost.
NURSE   Go, you Cot-quean, go,
Get you to Bed: faith, you'll be sick to morrow   65
For this Night's watching.
CAPULET   No, not a whit. What, I have watch'd ere
   now
All Night for lesser cause, and ne'er been sick.
LADY   Ay, you have been a Mouse-hunt in
   your Time,
But I will watch you from such Watching now.   70
                              Exeunt Lady and Nurse.
CAPULET   A Jealous Hood, a Jealous Hood.

*Enter three or four Fellows with Spits and Logs and
                        Baskets.*

Now, Fellow, what is there?
FELLOW   Things for the Cook, Sir, but I know
   not what.
CAPULET   Make haste, make haste, Sirrah, fetch drier
   Logs.
Call Peter: he will shew thee where they are.   75
FELLOW   I have a Head, Sir, that will find
   out Logs,
And never trouble Peter for the matter.
CAPULET   Mass, and well said, a merry Whoreson, ha.
Thou shalt be Loggerhead.   *Exit* [*Servingman.*]
                        Good Father, 'tis Day;
The County will be here with Music straight,   80
For so he said he would.   *Play Music.*
                  I hear him near.
– Nurse! – Wife! – What, ho, what, Nurse, I say!

Enter Nurse.

84 **Hie** hasten. Compare III.v.26. The dialogue makes it clear that as Capulet exits the Nurse goes to the curtains that designate the entrance to Juliet's chamber and surround her bed. By doing so, the Nurse shifts the setting into Juliet's bedroom. Here again modern editions normally indicate a scene break, with IV.v commencing at what is line 87 in this text.

87 **Fast** fast asleep (literally, locked in slumber). *Warrant* recalls IV.ii.40. And lines 87–97 contain many echoes of I.iii.1–95.

88 **Sluggabed** a person who habitually oversleeps.

92 **set up his Rest** set his hopes, resolved to himself. The phrase has associations (a) from primero, a card game in which one who 'sets up his Rest' wagers all on one hand; (b) from military life, where one used a 'rest' to support the heavy barrel of a musket before firing; and (c) from tilting, where one held a lance aloft for the charge. And of course the Nurse engages in wedding-night wordplay when she puns on *set up* and *Rest* in line 93. *Rest* echoes line 13.

96 **take you** greet you. The Nurse jests on the copulative meaning of the phrase. Her words recall, and reinforce the erotic suggestiveness of, line 85 (see the note to III.v.102). They also echo III.v.108–16, IV.i.107–8, IV.ii.23–24, 44–47.

97 **fright you up** both (a) stir you to life when you see how 'up' he is, and (b) make you bear up his 'freight' (punning on a lower-class pronunciation of this word). Compare I.iv.17–31, 92–96; III.iv.11; III.v.109–10.

98 **down** back in bed. Evidently the Nurse has just drawn back the curtains to see Juliet for the first time.

101 **weraday** welladay. Compare III.ii.37.
borne both (a) borne (carried) and (b) born. The Nurse's call for Aqua-vitae (line 102) recalls III.ii.88.

105 **my onely Life** The disparity between what Juliet's mother says here and what we have seen in earlier scenes should not lead us to assume that her grief is necessarily to be regarded as insincere. It is more likely that Shakespeare is simply portraying the Capulets as parents who are unaware of what their past treatment of their daughter reveals about their values. As the scene progresses, however, it becomes clear that the family's lamentations are ludicrously excessive.

Go waken Juliet; go and trim her up.
I'll go and chat with Paris. Hie, make haste,
Make haste: the Bridegroom he is come already.   85
Make haste, I say.   *Exit.*
NURSE   Mistress. What, Mistress. Juliet. – Fast, I
    warrant her, she.
Why, Lamb. Why, Lady. Fie, you Sluggabed.
Why, Love, I say. Madam. Sweetheart. Why, Bride.
What, not a Word? You take your Pennyworth's now,   90
Sleep for a week; for the next Night, I warrant,
The County Paris hath set up his Rest
That you shall rest but little, God forgive me.
– Marry and amen: how sound is she asleep.
I needs must wake her. – Madam, Madam, Madam.   95
Ay, let the County take you in your Bed:
He'll fright you up, i'faith, will it not be?
What, dress'd and in your Clothes, and down
    again?
I must needs wake you. Lady, Lady, Lady.
– Alas, alas, help, help, my Lady's dead!   100
O weraday, that ever I was borne.
Some Aqua-vitae, ho. My Lord! My Lady!

Enter Mother.

MOTHER   What Noise is here?
NURSE   O lamentable Day!
MOTHER   What is the matter?
NURSE   Look, look! O heavy Day!
MOTHER   O me, O me, my Child, my onely
    Life.   105
Revive, look up, or I will die with thee.
Help, help! Call help.

Enter Father.

111   **Out**   here, roughly equivalent to O.

112   **settled**   congealed. This word echoes *set* in line 92. *Joints* recalls line 51.

114   **Frost**   This image recalls the 'cold Death' of III.i.169; compare line 15.

115   **Flower**   Capulet echoes such previous passages as I.iii.77–78, II.i.163–64, II.ii.5–30, II.iii.64–67, II.iv.43–45, and III.ii.73. His words also evoke memories of 'the lilies of the field' (Matthew 6:28). *Field* recalls III.i.61.

122   **Death . . . thy Wife**   Capulet's personification of Death as a grim bridegroom is in keeping with his basic tendency to abstract from experience only what relates to his own concerns. Its effect is to divert attention from Juliet and focus it on Paris, who has been denied a bride, and on Capulet himself, who has been denied an heir and an opportunity to advance socially by means of his alliance with a Count. Compare I.ii.6–15, III.v.138–46.

123   **deflow'red**   Capulet doesn't yet realize that the 'Death' who has taken his daughter's maidenhead is Romeo. See the note to III.v.75.

127   **thought long**   long anticipated. *Face* recalls IV.i.29–36. Compare I.ii.89–90; I.iii.41, 55, 81; I.iv.170–72; II.i.80–84, 127–29; II.iii.114–15; II.iv.24, 40; III.ii.23,73; III.v.163; V.iii.29, 74.

131   **In lasting Labour**   in the lengthy toil.

133   **solace**   take comfort, joy.

134   **catch'd**   snatched.

FATHER   For shame, bring Juliet forth: her Lord is
  come.
NURSE   She's dead, deceas'd; she's dead, alack the Day.
MOTHER   Alack the Day, she's dead, she's
  dead, she's dead.   110
FATHER   Ha, let me see her. Out, alas, she's cold.
  Her Blood is settled, and her Joints are stiff;
  Life and these Lips have long been separated.
  Death lies on her like an untimely Frost
  Upon the sweetest Flower of all the Field.   115
NURSE   O lamentable Day!
MOTHER   O woeful Time!
FATHER   Death, that hath ta'en her hence to make
  me wail,
  Ties up my Tongue and will not let me speak.

    Enter Friar and the County [with the Musicians].

FRIAR   Come, is the Bride ready to go to Church?
FATHER   Ready to go, but never to return.   120
  O Son, the Night before thy Wedding Day
  Hath Death lain with thy Wife. There she lies,
  Flower as she was, deflow'red by him.
  Death is my Son-in-Law, Death is my Heir:
  My Daughter he hath wedded. I will die   125
  And leave him all: Life, Living, all is Death's.
PARIS   Have I thought long to see this Morning's
  Face,
  And doth it give me such a Sight as this?
MOTHER   Accurs'd, unhappy, wretched,
  hateful Day!
  Most miserable Hour that e'er Time saw   130
  In lasting Labour of his Pilgrimage.
  But one, poor one, one poor and loving Child;
  But one thing to rejoice and solace in;
  And cruel Death hath catch'd it from my Sight.

141 **Beguil'd** cheated. Compare III.ii.132.

145 **martyr'd** Capulet is probably using the term in its broad sense, to refer to murder and mutilation. But the word would also have had its usual modern sense, derived from the Greek word for 'witness'. In that sense ('sacrificed') it foreshadows Capulet's concluding speech in the play (V.iii.305–6).

146 **Uncomfortable** bringing no comfort. By contrast in V.iii.150 Friar Lawrence is described as 'comfortable'.

151 **Confusion's Cure** The Latin root of the word *confusio* allows for meanings that range from a mild mix-up to total devastation. *Cure* recalls IV.i.45.

152 **Confusions** The Friar here refers to the chaotic medley of outcries.

153 **Had part** shared equally. Similarly, in line 155 *part* means 'half interest'.

156 **part** Here, while retaining the implications of its previous uses, the word shades into a different meaning, more or less equivalent to 'commitment'. The Friar is now presenting Heaven as Juliet's advocate, taking her part and keeping its part of the bargain in a way her earthly friends could not.

158 **advanc'd** The word here means both 'advantaged' (benefited) and 'elevated' in social rank. In the next line, the Friar plays on both meanings with his observation that Juliet, in death, has now been granted the ultimate 'Promotion' (line 157). Compare II.ii.5.

162 **well** It was customary to speak of the dead as 'well' (in a beatific afterlife). See V.i.14–19, and compare *Macbeth*, IV.iii.176–79.

168 **some Nature** The Friar seems to be referring to Nature primarily in the sense of 'human nature' (the feelings that are a part of being human), which is unable to see what Reason perceives – that life in the sublunary world is only a pilgrimage to eternal life 'above the Clouds' (line 160).

NURSE   O woe, O woeful, woeful, woeful Day,   135
   Most lamentable Day, most woeful Day
   That ever, ever I did yet behold.
   O Day, O Day, O Day, O hateful Day,
   Never was seen so black a Day as this.
   O woeful Day, O woeful Day.   140
PARIS   Beguil'd, divorced, wronged, spited, slain.
   Most detestable Death, by thee beguil'd,
   By cruel, cruel Thee quite overthrown.
   O Love, O Life; not Life, but Love in Death.
FATHER   Despis'd, distressed, hated, martyr'd,
    kill'd.   145
   – Uncomfortable Time, why cam'st thou now
   To murther, murther our Solemnity?
   – O Child, O Child, my Soul and not my Child,
   Dead art thou. – Alack, my Child is dead,
   And with my Child my Joys are buried.   150
FRIAR   Peace ho, for shame, Confusion's Cure lives not
   In these Confusions. Heaven and your self
   Had part in this fair Maid; now Heaven hath all,
   And all the better is it for the Maid.
   Your Part in her you could not keep from Death,   155
   But Heaven keeps his Part in eternal Life.
   The most you sought was her Promotion,
   For 'twas your Heaven she should be advanc'd;
   And weep ye now, seeing she is advanc'd
   Above the Clouds as high as Heaven it self?   160
   O in this Love you love your Child so ill
   That you run mad, seeing that she is well.
   She's not well married that lives married long,
   But she's best married that dies married young.
   Dry up your Tears, and stick your Rosemary   165
   On this fair Corse and, as the Custom is,
   In all her best Array, bear her to Church;
   For though some Nature bids us all lament,
   Yet Nature's Tears are Reason's Merriment.

170   **ordained** planned, ordered. Here pronounced as a
        three-syllable word.

171   **Office** intended or proper function.

172   **Instruments** the musical instruments represented in the consort
        of minstrels commissioned for the wedding celebration.

173   **Cheer** the food to be provided for the wedding guests. This
        word recalls II.ii.5–6, 23–26.

174   **Sullen Dirges** mournful funeral marches. *Flowers* echoes lines
        114–15, 122–23. *Corse* (line 175) recalls III.ii.128 and IV.i.5.
        Here, as in III.ii.54, it is spelled *Coarse* in the Second Quarto;
        so also in lines 166, 179.

180   **lowre** frown. Compare II.iv.5–6.
        Ill sin, failing.

184   **put up** put away your instruments (with *put up* echoing I.i.66
        and III.i.87 and anticipating lines 208–9). But as usual the
        Nurse's words can also carry a bawdy implication, here one
        that appears to suggest that the way a woman's 'Case may be
        amended' is for 'good Fellows' to 'put up' their 'Pipes' (lines
        182–86). Compare lines 92–97, and see the notes to II.iv.44;
        III.iii.84, 88; III.v.218.

186   **the Case may be amended** The Fiddler may be taking the
        Nurse's use of 'Case' in the preceding line (where it means
        'instance' or 'situation') and applying it to his instrument case,
        pretending that the Nurse is telling him it is 'pitiful' and in
        need of repair. (Compare *The Winter's Tale*, IV.iv.847–53.)
        The Fiddler's phrase alludes to a proverbial saying, 'the case is
        altered' (see *3 Henry VI*, IV.iii.31), another variation on 'all
        things change them to the contrary' (line 176). But the Fiddler
        may also be punning on the genital sense of 'Case' (see the
        note to II.iii.51). Here as elsewhere, *I* means 'Ay', but in this
        context there may be phallic letter-play on the upright posture
        of the Roman numeral for *I*. See the note to II.iii.72–73.

187   **'Heart's Ease'** like 'My Heart is Full' in line 106, a popular
        song.

192   **merry Dump** A 'dump' was a mournful or plaintive melody,
        written from the point of view of someone 'down in the
        dumps'. In effect, Peter is requesting the Musicians to play a
        merry sad song. Compare I.i.179–84, III.ii.73–85.

FATHER   All things that we ordained Festival   170
Turn from their Office to black Funeral:
Our Instruments to Melancholy Bells,
Our Wedding Cheer to a sad Burial Feast,
Our Solemn Hymns to sullen Dirges change,
Our Bridal Flowers serve for a Burial Corse,   175
And all things change them to the contrary.
FRIAR   Sir, go you in; and Madam, go with him;
And go, Sir Paris; every one prepare
To follow this fair Corse unto her Grave.
The Heavens do lowre upon you for some Ill;   180
Move them no more by crossing their high Will.

*They all but the Nurse go forth, casting Rosemary on her
and shutting the Curtains.*

MUSICIANS   Faith, we may put up our Pipes and
be gone.
NURSE   Honest good Fellows, ah, put up, put up;
For well you know this is a pitiful Case.   185
FIDDLER   I, by my troth, the Case may be amended.
                                           Exit Nurse.

Enter Peter.

PETER   Musicians, O Musicians: 'Heart's Ease',
'Heart's Ease'. O and you will have me live,
play 'Heart's Ease'.
FIDDLER   Why 'Heart's Ease'?   190
PETER   O Musicians, because my Heart it self plays
'My Heart is Full'. O play me some merry Dump to
comfort me.
MINSTRELS   Not a Dump we; 'tis no time to play now.
PETER   You will not then?   195
MINSTRELS   No.

197   **give it you soundly** Peter alludes to the practice of giving a tip to musicians in appreciation of their 'sounds'. But what he means is that he will 'let them have it', and resoundingly.

199   **the Gleek** here, an insulting gibe or jeer at the Minstrel's expense. Compare *A Midsummer Night's Dream*, III.i.147–48.

200   **the Minstrel** In all likelihood, Peter's insulting words are accompanied by a rude gesture (see I.i.43–54) to which the musician replies in kind with one to signify the 'Serving-creature' (line 116). Compare III.i.47–52.

205   **carry no Crotchets** A crotchet was, among other things, a quarter note in music. Here Peter is reducing the Minstrel to a crotchet, just as the Minstrel in the preceding line has reduced Peter from a servingman to a serving-creature. Peter is saying that he will bear or put up with no crotchety musicians, and he probably emphasizes his words with a gesture resembling the hook-like shape of a quarter note. The phrase 'carry no Crotchets' is here equivalent to 'not carry Coals' (I.i.1). Lines 204–5 recall II.iii.210–11.

205–6 *re* **you . . . note me** As Peter names the two notes, *re* and *fa*, he probably points his dagger at the two Minstrels.

210   **put out your Wit** The Second Minstrel is telling Peter to put away his dagger and display ('put out') his 'Wit' (common sense) instead. *Wit* plays on the sense that can be represented by 'Dagger'. See the notes to III.v.74 and I.i.6–36, and compare line 184 and IV.i.47. In lines 211–12 Peter is probably declining the Second Minstrel's challenge to a 'Wit' combat (compare *Much Ado About Nothing*, I.i.62–65) by resorting to his own 'iron Wit' (dagger). *Dry beat* echoes III.i.80–83.

214   **griping** clutching, distressing.

221   **Prates** [He] prattles, speaks idle nonsense.
       Hugh Rebick Peter is naming the Minstrels after their instruments. A *Catling* (line 218) was a lute string made of catgut; a *Rebick* or rebeck (line 221) was a three-stringed forerunner of the violin; and a *Soundpost* (line 224) was a peg under the bridge of a stringed instrument.

PETER I will then give it you soundly.

MINSTRELS What will you give us?

PETER No Money, on my faith, but the Gleek; I will
give you the Minstrel.   200

1 MINSTREL Then will I give you the
Serving-creature.

PETER Then will I lay the
Serving-creature's Dagger on your Pate. I will
carry no Crotchets; I'll *re* you, I'll *fa* you, do   205
you note me?

1 MINSTREL And you *re* us and *fa* us, you note
us.

2 MINSTREL Pray you put up your Dagger, and
put out your Wit. Then have at you with my Wit.   210

PETER I will
dry-beat you with an iron Wit, and put up my
iron Dagger. Answer me like Men:
    When griping Griefs the Hart doth wound
    And doleful Dumps the Mind oppress   215
    Then Music with her silver Sound –
Why 'silver Sound'? Why 'Music with her silver
Sound'? – What say you, Simon Catling?

1 MINSTREL Marry Sir, because Silver hath a
sweet Sound.   220

PETER Prates. – What say you, Hugh Rebick?

228– **no Gold for Sounding** Peter says that he will give the
29   Musicians no payment for playing ('Sounding'). The only
      'Redress' (line 231) or compensation they can expect, in other
      words, is the 'speedy Help' that Music's own 'silver Sound'
      provides. In other words, like Virtue, Music is its own reward.
      Silver Sound echoes II.i.207–8.

231   **Redress** (a) remedy (an echo of III.v.241, IV.i.67, 76), (b)
      comfort, solace (see lines 184–93), (c) retaliation (see lines
      197–213), and (d) compensation, payment (see lines 226–29).

234   **Jack** a coarse, unrefined fellow. Compare II.iii.158–60,
      III.i.12–14.

235   **stay** wait for. This word recalls line 58.
      Dinner It is now approaching noon.

2 MINSTREL   I say 'silver Sound' because
Musicians sound for Silver.
PETER   Prates too. – What say you, James Soundpost?
3 MINSTREL   Faith, I know not what to say.   225
PETER   O I cry you mercy, you are the Singer. I
will say for you: it is 'Music with her silver
Sound' because Musicians have no Gold for
Sounding.

   Then Music with her silver Sound   230
    With speedy Help doth lend Redress.   *Exit.*

1 MINSTREL   What a pestilent Knave is this
same!
2 MINSTREL   Hang him, Jack. Come, we'll in
here, tarry for the Mourners, and stay Dinner.   235

                         Exeunt.

V.i   The scene shifts to Mantua, where the banished Romeo awaits some word from Juliet.

1-2   **If I . . . hand**   Romeo is saying that dreams sometimes deceive us by making us think that things are better than they are in reality. Ironically, the dream he describes proves to be a 'flattering' version of the play's final scene. Compare I.iv.50–114 and especially II.i.181–83.

2   **presage**   foreshadow.

3   **Bosom's Lord**   heart. *Unaccustom'd* (line 4) evokes the word Juliet's mother has spoken in III.v.89–92.

5   **Lifts me above the Ground**   Romeo's phrasing echoes what he said in I.iv.19–22, just before he entered the Capulet party and met Juliet. It also recalls Capulet's words in IV.ii.46. And it provides yet another illustration of the aptness of Romeo's surname (see the notes to I.i.124; II.iii.198; III.ii.3, 5–6; III.v.208–10). *Ground* recalls III.iii.82–83.

10-11   **Ah me . . . Joy**   If 'Love's Shadows' (Love's dreams and imaginings) are so 'rich in joy', how much more sweetness does 'Love it self' possess? *Possess'd* echoes III.ii.26–28.

17   **she is well**   Balthasar's words echo the Friar's in IV.iii.151–69, and carry the implication that, being in Heaven, Juliet is in bliss. Lines 16–17 recall IV.ii.40. Here Balthasar's name is spelled *Balthazer*, perhaps to indicate an accent on the second syllable rather than on the first and third.

18   **Her Body sleeps**   What the audience knows is that these words are true literally rather than metaphorically. *Angels* (line 19) recalls II.i.68–74 and III.ii.75.

21   **presently**   instantly. *Post* refers to post-horses; see line 26.

ACT V

Scene 1

Enter Romeo.

ROMEO If I may trust the flattering Truth of Sleep,
My Dreams presage some joyful News at hand.
My Bosom's Lord sits lightly in his Throne,
And all this Day an unaccustom'd Spirit
Lifts me above the Ground with cheerful Thoughts.   5
I dreamt my Lady came and found me dead
(Strange Dream that gives a Dead-man leave to
   think)
And breath'd such Life with Kisses in my Lips
That I reviv'd and was an Emperor.
Ah me, how sweet is Love it self possess'd   10
When but Love's Shadows are so rich in Joy.

Enter Romeo's Man.

News from Verona. – How now, Balthazer?
Dost thou not bring me Letters from the Friar?
How doth my Lady? Is my Father well?
How doth my Lady Juliet? That I ask again,   15
For nothing can be ill if she be well.
MAN Then she is well and nothing can be ill:
Her Body sleeps in Capel's Monument,
And her Immortal Part with Angels lives.
I saw her laid low in her Kindred's Vault   20
And presently took post to tell it you.

23   **Office** responsibility. Compare IV.iii.171.

24   **deny you, Stars** This is the reading in both the Second Quarto and the First Folio. The First Quarto reads 'defy my Stars'. The two phrases mean much the same: Romeo is declaring himself a cosmic rebel, and he says that henceforth he will take his destiny into his own hands. See the note to III.i.143. *Lodging* (line 25) recalls III.ii.1–2, III.iii.105–6.

26   **Post-horses** horses kept at a post-house for hire by travellers in need of getting somewhere 'post-haste'.

28–29 **import / Some Misadventure** foretell (literally, 'carry in') some mishap. *Wild* recalls IV.ii.14.

29   **Tush** a mild expression of dismissal.

32   **No matter** never mind, it doesn't matter.

34   **Well Juliet** Romeo means 'Well, Juliet'; but the absence of a comma in the early printings allows the phrase to be coloured by the sense *Well* has been given in lines 11–15.

35   **Let's . . . Means** Let's ponder how to effect my resolve to deny the Stars and lie with Juliet 'in Capel's Monument'. *Means* recalls II.Chorus.11–14, II.iii.188–89, and III.v.104–5.
         Mischief wrongdoing, harm.

36   **desperate** despairing; hopeless and thus reckless. Compare IV.i.69, where the Friar connects this word with a less severe expedient. The Apothecary Romeo's desperation leads him to resembles the figure of Despair in Edmund Spenser's *Faerie Queene* (1590); see Book I, Canto IX, stanzas xxviii–liv.

38   **'a** he.

39   **Weeds** clothes.
         overwhelming overhanging, beetling.

40   **Culling of Simples** gathering medicinal herbs. *Culling* recalls IV.iii.7–8.

45   **beggarly account** wretched and meagre assortment. *Beggarly* echoes III.v.32–34.

47   **Packthread** twine for parcels.
         Cakes of Roses rose petals compressed and used for perfume. Compare I.i.197, IV.i.94.

48   **Shew** show; display of wares.

    O pardon me for bringing these Ill News
    Since you did leave it for my Office, Sir.
ROMEO   Is it e'en so? – Then I deny you, Stars.
    – Thou knowest my Lodging; get me Ink and Paper,   25
    And hire Post-horses: I will hence to night.
MAN   I do beseech you, Sir, have Patience:
    Your Looks are pale and wild, and do import
    Some Misadventure.
ROMEO   Tush, thou art deceiv'd.
    Leave me, and do the thing I bid thee do.   30
    Hast thou no Letters to me from the Friar?
MAN   No, my good Lord.
ROMEO   No matter; get thee gone,
    And hire those Horses. I'll be with thee
      straight.   *Exit* [*Man.*]
    – Well Juliet, I will lie with thee to night.
    – Let's see for Means. – O Mischief, thou art
      swift   35
    To enter in the Thoughts of desperate Men:
    I do remember an Apothecary,
    And here abouts 'a dwells, which late I noted
    In tatt'red Weeds, with overwhelming Brows,
    Culling of Simples. Meagre were his Looks;   40
    Sharp Misery had worn him to the Bones;
    And in his needy Shop a Tortoise hung,
    An Alligator stuff'd, and other Skins
    Of ill-shap'd Fishes; and about his Shelves
    A beggarly account of empty Boxes,   45
    Green earthen Pots, Bladders and musty Seeds,
    Remnants of Packthread, and old Cakes of Roses
    Were thinly scatter'd to make up a Shew.

49   **Penury** abject poverty.

51   **Whose . . . Mantua** for which the penalty for anyone selling it
      in Mantua is immediate execution.

52   **caitiff** literally, captive; trapped in misery.

56   **Holy Day** holiday (a Wednesday in the play's time scheme).
      Given Romeo's disposition, it is anything but a 'holy day' for
      him.

59   **forty Duckets** A ducat was a gold coin, and forty of them
      would have been enough for a very expensive ring or its
      equivalent. Compare *The Merchant of Venice*, I.iii.1.

60   **soon-speeding Gear** quick-working compound. *Dram* recalls
      what Juliet's mother has promised to do in III.v.88–100. It is
      as if the Apothecary in this scene were the 'Man' Capulet's
      Wife threatened to send to Mantua to be sure that Romeo
      'shall soon keep Tybalt company'. *Gear* echoes II.iii.109.

63   **Trunk** body.

64–65 **hasty Powder . . . Womb** This image recalls what the Friar said
      in II.v.9–11 and in III.iii.131–33, 150. *Womb* echoes
      II.ii.9–30. *Fatal* recalls III.i.150.

67   **any he** any one.
      utters gives out.

68–75 **Art thou . . . Will** By depicting the Apothecary's situation in
      abstract terms, Romeo endeavours to obtain the poison he
      needs without seeming to implicate the poor Apothecary in a
      crime for which either must feel responsible.

73   **affoords** affords, provides.

76   **pray** entreat, solicit.

Noting this Penury, to my self I said
'An' if a Man did need a Poison now,   50
Whose Sale is present Death in Mantua,
Here lives a caitiff Wretch would sell it him.'
O this same Thought did but forerun my Need,
And this same needy Man must sell it me.
As I remember, this should be the House.   55
Being Holy Day, the Beggar's Shop is shut.
– What ho, Apothecary.

APOTHECARY [*Within*] Who calls so loud?
ROMEO Come hither, Man.

Enter Apothecary.

                         I see that thou art Poor.
Hold, there is forty Duckets: let me have
A Dram of Poison, such soon-speeding Gear   60
As will disperse it self through all the Veins,
That the Life-weary Taker may fall dead,
And that the Trunk may be discharg'd of Breath
As violently as hasty Powder fir'd
Doth hurry from the fatal Cannon's Womb.   65
APOTHECARY Such mortal Drugs I have, but Mantua's
    Law
    Is Death to any he that utters them.
ROMEO Art thou so bare and full of Wretchedness
    And fear'st to die? Famine is in thy Cheeks,
    Need and Oppression starveth in thy Eyes,   70
    Contempt and Beggary hangs upon thy Back:
    The World is not thy Friend, nor the World's Law.
    The World affoords no Law to make thee Rich:
    Then be not Poor, but break it and take this.
APOTHECARY My Poverty, but not my Will, consents.   75
ROMEO I pray thy Poverty and not thy Will.
APOTHECARY Put this in any Liquid Thing you will
    And drink it off; and if you had the Strength

82   **Compounds**   mixed drugs, as opposed to single-ingredient 'Simples' (line 40). Lines 80–82 anticipate *Timon of Athens*, IV.iii.1–42, where the protagonist depicts gold as the root of all of mankind's afflictions (1 Timothy 6).

84   **get thy self in Flesh**   This phrase suggests that the Apothecary is so emaciated as to be almost naked of flesh. His cadaverous appearance is no doubt intended to remind the audience of traditional images of such allegorical types as Despair and Death, both of which are pertinent to Romeo's spiritual state at this point in the play. See the note to line 36.

85   **Cordial**   a health-giving liquid, a drink or medicine to stimulate the heart (*cor* in Latin). See lines 1–5, and compare *Cymbeline*, I.vi.65, IV.ii.326, V.v.245–48, and *The Winter's Tale*, I.ii.314–15.

V.ii   The setting for this scene is the cell of Friar Lawrence. The stage direction suggests that Friar John and Friar Lawrence enter from different doors. Possibly Friar John's voice is to be heard within (that is, from behind the door he enters) before he emerges into view of Friar Lawrence and the audience. Compare the opening of III.iii.

5   **barefoot Brother**   a reminder that Franciscan friars were to take vows of poverty and live simply.

6   **to associate me**   to accompany me, be my associate.

8   **Searchers of the Town**   volunteers whose duty was to search out possible carriers of the plague and quarantine them to avoid spread of the infection. The London theatres had been closed for much of 1592–94 because of the plague; the situation described here would therefore have been familiar to Shakespeare's original theatregoers.

12   **stay'd**   suspended, delayed. Compare IV.v.235. *Speed* can mean both (a) rate of progress, and (b) success. Both senses echo III.i.94–95, where Mercutio says 'A Plague a' both your Houses: I am sped'. Mercutio's curse has been fulfilled with sickening precision.

13   **bare**   bore, carried.

Of twenty Men, it would dispatch you straight.
ROMEO   There is thy Gold: worse Poison to Men's
    Souls,   80
Doing more Murther in this loathsome World,
Than these poor Compounds that thou mayest not
    sell.
I sell thee Poison; thou hast sold me none.
Farewell; buy Food and get thy self in Flesh.
– Come, Cordial and not Poison: go with me   85
To Juliet's Grave, for there must I use thee.

Exeunt.

Scene 2

Enter Friar John to Friar Lawrence.

JOHN   Holy Franciscan Friar, Brother, ho.

Enter Lawrence.

LAWRENCE   This same should be the Voice of
    Friar John.
Welcome from Mantua. What says Romeo?
Or if his Mind be writ, give me his Letter.
JOHN   Going to find a barefoot Brother out,   5
One of our Order to associate me
Here in this City visiting the Sick,
And finding him, the Searchers of the Town,
Suspecting that we both were in a House
Where the infectious Pestilence did reign,   10
Seal'd up the Doors and would not let us forth,
So that my speed to Mantua there was stay'd.
LAWRENCE   Who bare my Letter then to Romeo?
JOHN   I could not send it – here it is again –

18   **nice** small, inconsequential, innocent. Compare III.i.161.
      Charge weight, command, importance.

19   **dear Import** inestimable importance. *Dear* recalls such
      passages as I.iv.162, 233; II.i.87–89, 235; II.ii.57–58; II.v.29;
      III.i.189–90; III.iii.28, 127. Compare V.iii.32.

21   **Crow** crowbar, a tool for prying things open.
      straight directly, immediately.

23   **Monument** the Capulets' burial monument, mausoleum.

24   **hours** here pronounced as a two-syllable word.

25   **beshrew** blame, upbraid. Compare, III.v.223, 229.

26   **Accidents** occurrences (specifically, the circumstances
      surrounding Juliet's 'death'). Here, of course, they are
      accidents in the usual modern sense. *Corse* (line 29) recalls
      IV.iii.166, 175, 179. The phrase 'living Corse' is a reminder of
      V.i.18–19, and of the crucial fact that the Friar alone is aware
      that Juliet's 'Body sleeps' but is not yet a corpse.

V.iii. The setting for this final scene is the Churchyard, with the
      Capulets' monument represented in a prominent position on
      the stage. Here the opening stage direction incorporates
      details from both the First Quarto and the Second Quarto.

S.D. **Sweet-water** perfumed water.

1   **aloof** at a distance. Compare line 26.

3   **lay thee all along** lie at full length to the ground.

6   **loose, unfirm** These adjectives refer to the Churchyard, whose
      ground is 'unfirm' from gravedigging.

Nor get a Messenger to bring it thee,   15
So fearful were they of Infection.

LAWRENCE   Unhappy Fortune. By my
   Brotherhood,
The Letter was not nice but full of Charge,
Of dear Import, and the neglecting it
May do much Danger. Friar John, go hence,   20
Get me an Iron Crow, and bring it straight
Unto my Cell.

JOHN   Brother, I'll go and bring it thee.

Exit.

LAWRENCE   Now must I to the Monument
   alone.
Within three Hours will fair Juliet wake;
She will beshrew me much that Romeo   25
Hath had no Notice of these Accidents;
But I will write again to Mantua,
And keep her at my Cell till Romeo come.
Poor living Corse, clos'd in a Dead-man's Tomb.

Exit.

Scene 3

*Enter County Paris and his Page, with Flowers and
Sweet-water.*

PARIS   Give me thy Torch, Boy. Hence and stand
   aloof.
Yet put it out, for I would not be seen.
Under yond Yew Trees lay thee all along,
Holding thy Ear close to the hollow Ground,
So shall no Foot upon the Churchyard tread,   5
Being loose, unfirm with digging up of Graves,

11   **adventure** take my chances (compare II.i.124–26). Lines 10–11
      are probably to be spoken as an aside as the Page steps away
      to obey his master.

12   **Flower** Paris addresses Juliet. His imagery recalls
          IV.iii.114–15, 122–23, 175.

14   **dew** sprinkle. Compare II.ii.5–8.

15   **wanting** lacking.
      distill'd by either (a) discharged by, or (b) mixed with, diluted
      by. The *Sweet-water* of line 14 would have been perfumed by
      distillations from roses or other flowers. Compare I.i.197,
      IV.i.94, V.i.47. The word *Tears* distils the memory of Paris'
      exchange with Juliet in IV.i.29–36. Compare IV.vi.6–14.

16   **Obsequies** rites for the dead.

19   **cursed** Without realizing it, Paris speaks with uncanny
      accuracy. See the note to V.ii.12. *Wanders* is a reminder that
      this 'cursed Foot' has lost its way and is proceeding on
      misleading directions; compare *A Midsummer Night's
      Dream*, III.ii.417.

20   **cross** both (a) impede, and (b) cast an evil spell upon. Compare
      IV.iii.5. *Right* (a rite Paris regards as his right, his just due as
      Juliet's fiancé) recalls II.i.188 and III.ii.8. Line 20 will be
      echoed in line 27, where *interrupt* means 'cross' and recalls
      Paris' remarks to the Friar in IV.i.2–3. *Course* (line 27) echoes
      IV.i.5.

21   **Muffle** wrap or cloak. Paris' phrasing echoes II.i.94, 117, 127,
      and III.iii.166–67.

22   **Mattock** a type of pickaxe, designed both to dig and to cut.
      wrenching Iron crowbar, 'Crow of Iron'.

25   **charge** command. Compare lines 1–8.

30–31 **take thence . . . Ring** Since Romeo does not in fact take a ring
      from Juliet's finger, it seems most likely that this explanation
      is offered merely to keep Balthasar from interfering. Paris,
      who is presumably too far away to hear Romeo, has no way
      of knowing Romeo's true intent; nor, of course, is he aware of
      Romeo's relationship with Juliet. *Dear* (line 33) means
      'precious' or 'indispensable'; it recalls V.ii.19.

33   **jealous** suspicious. Compare IV.iii.71. *Pry* is an apt verb here;
      Romeo is about to pry open Juliet's tomb.

But thou shalt hear it. Whistle then to me
As Signal that thou hearest some thing approach.
Give me those Flowers. Do as I bid thee, go.

PAGE   I am almost afraid to stand alone   10
Here in the Churchyard, yet I will adventure.

                    Paris strews the Tomb with Flowers.

PARIS   Sweet Flower, with Flowers thy Bridal Bed I
    strew.
O Woe, thy Canopy is Dust and Stones,
Which with Sweet-water nightly I will dew,
Or, wanting that, with Tears distill'd by Moans.   15
The Obsequies that I for thee will keep
Nightly shall be to strew thy Grave and weep.

                                    Whistle Boy.

The Boy gives Warning: something doth approach.
What cursed Foot wanders this way to night
To cross my Obsequies and True-love's Right   20
What, with a Torch? – Muffle me, Night, a while.

Enter Romeo and [his Man] Balthasar, with a Torch, a
        Mattock, and a Crow of Iron.

ROMEO   Give me that Mattock and the wrenching Iron.
Hold, take this Letter: early in the Morning
See thou deliver it to my Lord and Father.
Give me the Light. Upon thy Life I charge thee,   25
What e'er thou hearest or seest, stand all aloof,
And do not interrupt me in my Course.
Why I descend into this Bed of Death
Is partly to behold my Lady's Face,
But chiefly to take thence from her dead Finger   30
A precious Ring, a Ring that I must use
In dear Employment. Therefore hence be gone.
But if thou jealous dost return to pry
In what I farther shall intend to do,
By Heaven I will tear thee Joint by Joint   35

36 **strew** scatter, cover. The echo of line 17 is an indication of the difference between Romeo's mood and Paris'. *Joint* (line 35) recalls IV.iii.51; *wild* echoes V.i.28–29.

38 **inexorable** unrelenting, implacable.

39 **empty** famished, ravenously hungry. Compare line 36.

42 **that** Romeo probably hands his pouch of money to his faithful servant. *Prosperous* recalls IV.i.123–24.

43 **For all this same** for all that he and I have said. Balthasar shows true loyalty to and concern for Romeo when he decides to stand watch despite Romeo's stern warnings. Compare lines 10–11.

45 **Maw** mouth and throat of a voracious animal. Compare lines 36–39.

47 **enforce** force.

48 **in despight** in defiance, spite. Compare I.i.80–81, I.iv.177–78, II.i.27, IV.i.31.

54 **unhallowed Toil** unholy labours. *Unhallowed* echoes *hollow* (line 4), and it reminds us that Romeo is preparing to enter a space of 'hollow Ground'.

60 **Fly** flee. This verb recalls III.i.181; in the process it reminds us of one of the reasons for Romeo's presence here now.
   these gone these who have died. Romeo warns Paris (who is evidently younger than he is) to weigh what has happened to the corpses here, and avoid the fate of another not-so-gentle 'Youth' who tempted the protagonist's 'fire-ey'd Fury' (III.i.131) and suffered the consequences. *Desp'rate* echoes V.i.36, and it keeps us aware that Romeo has come here to do 'damned Hate' upon himself; see III.iii.107–17, IV.i.69, and *Hamlet*, I.ii.129–32, III.i.53–85. The clause 'Think upon these gone' calls to mind a later 'Paris', the Gabriel of James Joyce's *The Dead*, who discovers that his wife Greta has long mourned a passionate, gentle 'Romeo' (Michael Furey), who sacrificed his life for love of her.

62 **Sin** Romeo probably means 'reason for damnation'. Compare IV.iii.1–5. *Fury* (compare 'Rage', IV.iii.53) recalls III.i.131.

And strew this hungry Churchyard with thy Limbs.
The Time and my Intents are savage wild,
More fierce and more inexorable far
Than empty Tigers or the roaring Sea.

BALTHASAR   I will be gone, Sir, and not trouble ye.   40

ROMEO   So shalt thou shew me Friendship. Take thou
    that:
Live and be prosperous, and farewell, good
    Fellow.

BALTHASAR   For all this same, I'll hide me
    here about:
His Looks I fear, and his Intents I doubt.

ROMEO   Thou detestable Maw, thou Womb of Death,   45
Gorg'd with the dearest Morsel of the Earth,
                        Romeo opens the Tomb.
Thus I enforce thy rotten Jaws to open
And in despight I'll cram thee with more Food.

PARIS   This is that banish'd, haughty
    Mountague
That murd'red my Love's Cousin, with which Grief   50
It is supposed the Fair Creature died,
And here is come to do some villainous Shame
To the dead Bodies. I will apprehend him.
— Stop thy unhallowed Toil, vile Mountague.
Can Vengeance be pursued further than Death?   55
Condemned Villain, I do apprehend thee:
Obey and go with me, for thou must die.

ROMEO   I must indeed, and therefore came I hither.
Good, gentle Youth, tempt not a desp'rate Man;
Fly hence and leave me. Think upon these gone: 60
Let them affright thee. I beseech thee, Youth,
Put not an other Sin upon my Head
By urging me to Fury. O be gone.
By Heav'n I love thee better than my self,
For I come hither arm'd against my self.   65

68   **Conjurations**   entreaties. Paris may also be thinking of the
       'unhallowd' nature of Romeo's mission, in which case he is
       probably assuming that anyone who seeks to pursue
       vengeance 'further than death' is in league with evil spirits.
       This reading derives from the First Quarto; the Second
       Quarto reads *commiration*; later Quartos and the First Folio
       read *commiseration*.

70   **Boy**   Romeo's insult recalls Tybalt's in III.i.69.

76   **betossed**   unsettled, tormented. In line 77 *attend* means 'pay full
       attention'.

78   **should have**   was to have.

82   **sowre**   both (a) sour, and (b) sore. Compare III.iii.7, and see the
       note to II.iv.24.

84   **Lanthorn**   lantern. The old spelling is retained here partly as a
       guide to pronunciation, and partly as a reminder that
       windows (whether in lanterns or in buildings) were made of
       thin sheets of horn in Shakespeare's time. Here the word
       probably refers to the lantern dome designed to admit
       sunlight to a church or cathedral. Romeo's lantern image
       provides yet another link between this play and the 'Pyramus
       and Thisby' playlet in *A Midsummer Night's Dream*; see
       V.i.242–64 of that comedy.

86   **Feasting Presence**   probably a reference to the celebration of
       Holy Communion, a feast in which the Divine presence is
       made manifest.

89   **Keepers**   prison guards. *Merry* recalls IV.ii.15.

90   **Lightning**   The 'lightening' Romeo refers to is a sense of
       exhilaration similar to the state he described in V.i.1–5.
       Compare II.i.159–62, where Juliet portrays *Lightning* in a
       way that is ominously pertinent to Romeo's present condition.

94   **Ensign**   standard-bearer, officer who carried the royal insignia,
       here a 'pale Flag'. *Advanced* recalls IV.iii.158.

95   **crimson**   Romeo assumes that the hue in Juliet's features is still
       lingering despite her death. He has no way of knowing that
       the crimson is only now returning to her lips and cheeks as
       the effect of the Friar's potion wears off. Compare
       IV.i.99–108.

Stay not: begone, live, and hereafter say
A Madman's Mercy bid thee run away.
PARIS   I do defy thy Conjurations
And apprehend thee for a Felon here.
ROMEO   Wilt thou provoke me? Then have at thee,
Boy.   *They fight.*   70
PAGE   O Lord, they fight: I will go call the
Watch.   [*Exit.*]
PARIS   O I am slain. If thou be merciful,
Open the Tomb, lay me with Juliet.
ROMEO   In faith I will.
                            — Let me peruse this Face.
Mercutio's Kinsman, noble County Paris.   75
What said my Man when my betossed Soul
Did not attend him as we rode? I think
He told me Paris should have married Juliet.
Said he not so? Or did I dream it so?
Or am I mad, hearing him talk of Juliet,   80
To think it was so? — O give me thy Hand:
One writ with me in sowre Misfortune's Book.
I'll bury thee in a triumphant Grave.
A Grave? O no, a Lanthorn, slaught'red Youth:
For here lies Juliet, and her Beauty makes   85
This vault a Feasting Presence full of Light.
Death, lie thou there by a Dead-man interr'd.
— How oft when Men are at the point of Death
Have they been Merry? Which their Keepers call
A Lightning before Death. O how may I   90
Call this a Lightning? — O my Love, my Wife:
Death, that hath suck'd the Honey of thy Breath,
Hath had no power yet upon thy Beauty.
Thou art not conquer'd: Beauty's Ensign yet
Is crimson in thy Lips and in thy Cheeks,   95
And Death's pale Flag is not advanced there.
— Tybalt, liest thou there in thy bloody Sheet?
O what more Favour can I do to thee

103   **unsubstantial**   without substance or body. Compare
        II.i.181–83.

105   **Paramour**   royal mistress.

112   **set up . . . Rest**   establish my eternal resting place. This phrase
        echoes the Nurse's words about Paris (IV.iii.92–93). *Worms*
        (line 111) recalls III.i.113–14.

113   **shake the Yoke**   throw off the halter. Romeo's image suggests
        that he thinks of himself as an ox or other beast of burden. By
        taking his own life, he hopes to rid his 'Flesh' (line 112) of all
        the cares the World and the Stars have placed on his back.
        Compare *Hamlet*, III.i.64.
        inauspicious Stars   unlucky conjunction of the planets. An
        Elizabethan familiar with astrology would have observed that
        suicide normally indicated, not liberation from, but
        enslavement to and defeat by 'the Stars'. See the note to
        III.i.143.

116–   **seal . . . Death**   Romeo's imagery derives from the realm of
17   legal contracts. He is, in effect, completing a purchase and
        thus closing a deal (as one who is in a 'righteous' or legally
        entitled position to 'seal' a 'Bargain'). Death is 'engrossing'
        both in its role as purchaser (buying a 'gross' or large quantity
        of goods) and in its role as the one who writes ('engrosses')
        the contract. The bargain is 'dateless' because it will be for
        eternity. *Dateless* recalls I.iv.105–11. *Righteous* echoes *Right*
        (line 20); it thus reminds us that Romeo's kiss is also, for him,
        a ritual observance, a final consummation of the marriage rite.

118–   **Conduct . . . Pilot**   Romeo addresses the poison. *Conduct* (both
19   'guide' and 'means of conveyance') recalls III.i.131 and
        III.iii.130. It is 'bitter' both because it tastes like 'Gall' (see
        Tybalt's prophecy in I.iv.206–7) and because it brings
        Romeo's sweet dreams to an 'unsavoury' end, one that is as
        unhealthy and sinister as it is displeasing to the palate.

120   **Bark**   Romeo's body. Compare Capulet's use of the term in
        III.v.134–35.

122   **quick**   rapid. Ironically, *quick* also means 'alive', 'living'.
        Compare V.i.85.

S.D.   **Crow**   crowbar. See the note to line 22.

Than with that Hand that cut thy Youth in twain
To sunder his that was thine Enemy?   100
Forgive me, Cousin. – Ah dear Juliet,
Why art thou yet so Fair? I will believe, shall I believe,
That unsubstantial Death is amorous,
And that the lean, abhorred Monster keeps
Thee here in dark to be his Paramour?   105
For fear of that I still will stay with thee,
And never from this Pallet of dim Night
Depart again. Come lie thou in my arm:
Here's to thy Health, where e'er thou tumblest in.
Here, here will I remain,   110
With Worms that are thy Chambermaids; O here
Will I set up my everlasting Rest
And shake the Yoke of inauspicous Stars
From this World-wearied Flesh. – Eyes, look your
    last;
Arms, take your last Embrace; and Lips, O you   115
The Doors of Breath, seal with a righteous Kiss
A dateless Bargain to engrossing Death.
– Come, bitter Conduct; come unsavoury Guide.
Thou desperate Pilot, now at once run on
The dashing Rocks thy seasick, weary Bark.   120
Here's to my Love. O true Apothecary:
Thy Drugs are quick. Thus with a Kiss I die.

                                                    Falls.

Enter Friar with Lanthorn, Crow, and Spade.

123 **speed** As in V.ii.12, this word refers both to (a) a means of
prospering, and (b) a means of making rapid progress.
Compare lines 114–22 to what was almost certain meant to
be viewed as a burlesque of this scene, *A Midsummer Night's
Dream*, V.i.274–351.

124 **stumbled** The Friar's use of this verb is an ironic echo of his
earlier counsel to Romeo: 'Wisely and slow: they stumble that
run fast' (II.ii.94). See the notes to II.i.95, IV.i.47, 64, 115. As
the Friar lumbers in, he encounter's Romeo's man Balthasar.

128 **Grubs** either (a) the round wormlike larvae of beetles and
other insects, or (b) earthworms. As a verb, *grub* means 'dig',
and the Friar may also be thinking of the grub-like drudges
who labour in graveyards. Compare lines 110–11.

135 **fearfully** threateningly. *Intents* (line 136) recalls line 37.

137– **Fear . . . thing** The Friar probably speaks these lines to himself
38 as he rushes towards the tomb.

138 **unthrifty** unfortunate (literally, unthriving).

144 **Maister-less** separated from their masters or owners. Compare
I.i.68–71, III.i.149–50. *Gory* (blood-clotted) recalls III.ii.56.

FRIAR Saint Francis be my speed: how oft to night
  Have my old Feet stumbled at Graves? Who's there?
MAN Here's one a Friend, and one that knows
    you well.   125
FRIAR Bliss be upon you. Tell me, good my Friend,
  What Torch is yond that vainly lends his Light
  To Grubs and eyeless Skulls? As I discern,
  It burneth in the Capels' Monument.
MAN It doth so, Holy Sir, and there's my
    Maister,   130
  One that you love.
FRIAR   Who is it?
MAN   Romeo.
FRIAR How long hath he been there?
MAN   Full half an Hour.
FRIAR Go with me to the Vault.
MAN   I dare not, Sir:
  My Master knows not but I am gone hence,
  And fearfully did menace me with Death   135
  If I did stay to look on his Intents.
FRIAR Stay then, I'll go alone. Fear comes
    upon me;
  O much I fear some ill, unthrifty thing.
MAN As I did sleep under this Yew Tree here,
  I dreamt my Maister and another fought,   140
  And that my Maister slew him.
FRIAR   Romeo.
    Friar stoops and looks on the Blood and Weapons.
  – Alack, alack, what Blood is this which stains
  The stony Entrance of this Sepulchre?
  What mean these Maister-less and gory Swords
  To lie discolour'd by this place of Peace?   145
  Romeo, O pale! Who else? What, Paris too?
  And steep'd in Blood? Ah what an unkind Hour
  Is guilty of this lamentable Chance?
  The Lady stirs.   *Juliet rises.*

150 **comfortable** comforting, bearing comfort. This word echoes IV.iii.146–47. It also recalls I.ii.26–30; III.ii.107, 138–39; III.iii.55–56, 146, 164; III.v.210, 214; and IV.iii.17,192–93. *Stirs* (line 149) recalls IV.ii.39.

153 **Nest** The Friar's image recalls the Nurse's description (II.iv.75) of the setting for Romeo's 'Joy' (II.iii.198).

157 **Bosom** lap. Compare V.i.1–5. *Intents* (line 156) echoes line 136.

158– **Come . . . Nuns** The Friar's solution to Juliet's bereavement
59 parallels one of the options offered to Hermia in *A Midsummer Night's Dream*, I.i.62–78, 85–90, 117–21. Like Hermia, Juliet will prove unwilling to 'fit' her 'Fancies' to her 'Father's Will' (compare *Romeo and Juliet*, III.v.154–56), whether that 'Father is Capulet or her 'holy Father' (IV.i.37). *Stay* (lines 160–61) echoes lines 66, 136.

165 **Churl** lowborn servant. Normally a term of contempt, *churl* is here used scoldingly but with the deepest love. Compare III.iii.161, where Romeo tells Juliet's Nurse to 'bid my Sweet prepare to chide'.

167 **Haply** perhaps; but 'happily' may be implied as well.

168 **die with a Restorative** A restorative was a cordial or medicine to stimulate the heart. Juliet's words echo Romeo's description of the poison as 'Cordial and not Poison' in V.i.85. Compare lines 121–22.

169 **warm** another exquisitely painful reminder of how crucial a role timing plays in the tragic outcome of this action.

172 **Sheath** Juliet refers to her breast, where she plunges the dagger. In a play in which there have been so many references to knives and sheathes (both literal and metaphorical), this final gesture is surely intended by the playwright as a way of linking the imagery of copulation and violence – the two manifestations of 'hot blood' at the core of the tragedy. See the notes to II.Chorus.2, III.ii.21, and III.v.74, 75, 102. And compare the comic variations on the orgasmic sense of *die* in *A Midsummer Night's Dream*, V.i.309–50.

175 **attach** detain, arrest.

JULIET   O comfortable Friar, where is my Lord?   150
   I do remember well where I should be,
   And there I am. Where is my Romeo?
FRIAR   I hear some Noise, Lady: come from that Nest
   Of Death, Contagion, and unnatural Sleep.
   A greater Power than we can contradict   155
   Hath thwarted our Intents. Come, come away.
   Thy Husband in thy Bosom there lies dead,
   And Paris too. Come, I'll dispose of thee
   Among a Sisterhood of holy Nuns.
   Stay not to question, for the Watch is coming.   160
   Come, go, good Juliet, I dare no longer stay.
JULIET   Go get thee hence, for I will not away.

                        Exit [*Friar Lawrence*].

   – What's here? A Cup clos'd in my True-love's
     Hand?
   Poison I see hath been his timeless End.
   – O Churl, drink all, and left no friendly Drop   165
   To help me after. I will kiss thy Lips:
   Haply some Poison yet doth hang on them
   To make me die with a Restorative.
   Thy Lips are warm.

            Enter Boy and Watch.

WATCH   Lead, Boy: which way?   170
JULIET   Yea, Noise? Then I'll be brief. O happy
    Dagger,
   This is thy Sheath; there rust and let me die.

                 She stabs herself and falls.

BOY   This is the Place: where the Torch doth
   burn.
WATCH   The Ground is bloody; search
   about the Churchyard.
   Go, some of you: who e'er you find, attach.   175

           [*Exeunt some Watchmen.*]

180   **Raise up** arouse from sleep. Given the play's emphasis on the elevation of the younger Mountague (see II.i.29, where Mercutio says 'I conjure onely but to raise up him'), this order is grimly ironic. It once again calls attention to the appropriateness of Romeo's surname; see the notes to I.i.124; II.iii.198; III.ii.3, 5–6; III.v.208–10; V.i.5.

181–   **Ground . . . Ground** both (a) the earth of the Churchyard, and
82   (b) the basis or reason for what has happened.

183   **Circumstance** evidence, detail, information. This word recalls II.iv.36.
      descry perceive.

190   **Misadventure** terrible occurrence.

191   **our Person** The Prince employs a royal *we*. In the Renaissance a ruler was assumed to gather into his own person all his subjects (a tradition whose echoes still reverberate in the phrase 'the body politic'). *Rest* echoes line 112.

192   **shrike** shrieked. Compare IV.iii.47.

Pitiful Sight. Here lies the County slain,
And Juliet bleeding, warm, and newly dead,
Who here hath lain this two Days buried.
Go tell the Prince; run to the Capulets;
Raise up the Mountagues. Some others search: 180

                                [*Exeunt others.*]
We see the Ground whereon these Woes do lie,
But the true Ground of all these piteous Woes
We cannot without Circumstance descry.

Enter [one with] Romeo's Man.

WATCHMAN   Here's Romeo's Man; we found
  him in the Churchyard.
CHIEF WATCH   Hold him safety till the Prince
  come hither.   185

Enter Friar, and another Watchman.

3 WATCHMAN   Here is a Friar, that trembles, sighs, and
  weeps.
We took this Mattock and this Spade from him
As he was coming from this Churchyard's side.
CHIEF WATCH   A great Suspicion: stay the Friar too.

Enter the Prince with Others.

PRINCE   What Misadventure is so early up   190
  That calls our Person from our morning Rest?

Enter Capels.

CAPULET   What should it be that is so shrike abroad?
WIFE   O the People in the Street cry
    'Romeo',
  Some 'Juliet', and some 'Paris', and all run

226

205 **House** sheath, scabbard. But Capulet's phrasing is a reminder
that both his House and Mountague's are now 'empty' of
heirs.

208–9 **O . . . Sepulchre** The words of Capulet's Wife recall what Juliet
has said to the Nurse in III.ii.45–49.

211 **early down** fallen from the tree before he'd had time to ripen.
Compare the imagery of II.i.163–64 and I.iv.14–24; also see
I.iii.14–15. The Prince's words show that Romeo's initial
'Humour' was indeed 'portendous'; Mountague's son has
proven too 'heavy' to remain a 'light' fruit on the tree, and
'good Counsel' has removed the 'Cause' only too well
(I.i.140–45).

213 **stopp'd** halted. Mountague's verb recalls II.i.108–11 and
IV.i.3, 11–12.

216 **Untaught** Mountague's phrase alludes both to Romeo's youth
and to the lack of experience and wisdom his act exemplifies.
His point is that Romeo is guilty of a breach of 'Manners' to
rush ahead of his father in the queue to the 'Grave'. Compare
the emphasis on civility in Prologue. 4 and in I.i.92–98.

217 **press** shove ahead.

218 **Seal up the Mouth of Outrage** The Prince fears yet another
outbreak of feuding (see III.i.90), and he therefore wants to
close up the bloody 'Maw' before it can devour any more of
Verona's citizens. Compare the imagery in lines 36–39,
45–48, 117.

With open Outcry toward our Monument.   195
PRINCE   What Fear is this which startles in your
   Ears?
CHIEF WATCH   Sovereign, here lies the County
   Paris slain,
And Romeo dead, and Juliet, dead before,
Warm and new-kill'd.
PRINCE   Search, seek, and know how this foul Murder
   comes.   200
CHIEF WATCH   Here is a Friar, and slaughter'd
   Romeo's Man,
With Instruments upon them fit to open
These Dead-men's Tombs.

Enter Capulet and his Wife.

CAPULET   O Heavens! O Wife, look how our Daughter
   bleeds!
This Dagger hath mista'en, for lo his House   205
Is empty on the Back of Mountague
And it mis-sheathed in my Daughter's Bosom.
WIFE   O me, this sight of Death is as a
   Bell
That warns my Old Age to a Sepulchre.

Enter Mountague.

PRINCE   Come, Mountague, for thou art early up,   210
   To see thy Son and Heir, now early down.
MOUNTAGUE   Alas, my Liege, my Wife is dead to night;
   Grief of my Son's Exile hath stopp'd her Breath.
   What further Woe conspires against mine Age?
PRINCE   Look and thou shalt see.   215
MOUNTAGUE   O thou Untaught, what Manners is in this,
   To press before thy Father to a Grave?
PRINCE   Seal up the Mouth of Outrage for a while,

220 **Spring** source.

221 **General** commanding officer, chief mourner.

223 **Patience** forbearance, restraint (as in III.i.90), with no further rounds of retaliatory bloodshed. *Patience* recalls I.iv.204–5, III.v.159–60, and V.i.27.

224 **foorth** forth.

225 **greatest** both (a) highest ranking, and (b) 'most suspected' (line 226).

227 **make against me** testify against me, make me look suspect.

228 **impeach and purge** accuse and exonerate. *Stand* recalls line 1 (see the note to line 66).

230 **Date of Breath** remaining lifetime. *Date* echoes lines 116–17.

239 **Siege** seizure.

240 **perforce** by force.

242 **Wild** desperate, suicidal; unruly in her frenzy. Compare line 37.
   Mean means. Compare V.i.35.

247 **intended** The Friar's verb echoes lines 37, 156.

249 **as this dire Night** as he did on this terrible night.

Till we can clear these Ambiguities
And know their Spring, their Head, their true
   Descent;   220
And then will I be General of your Woes
And lead you even to Death. Mean time forbear,
And let Mischance be slave to Patience.
Bring foorth the Parties of Suspicion.

FRIAR   I am the greatest, able to do least,   225
   Yet most suspected, as the Time and Place
   Doth make against me, of this direful Murther:
   And here I stand, both to impeach and purge
   My self condemned and my self excus'd.

PRINCE   Then say at once what thou dost know in
   this.   230

FRIAR   I will be brief, for my short Date of Breath
   Is not so long as is a tedious Tale.
   Romeo there dead was Husband to that Juliet,
   And she there dead, that's Romeo's faithful Wife:
   I married them, and their stol'n Marriage Day   235
   Was Tybalt's Doomsday, whose untimely Death
   Banish'd the new-made Bridegroom from this City,
   For whom, and not for Tybalt, Juliet pin'd.
   You, to remove that Siege of Grief from her,
   Betroth'd and would have married her perforce   240
   To County Paris. Then comes she to me,
   And with Wild Looks bid me devise some Mean
   To rid her from this second Marriage,
   Or in my Cell there would she kill her self.
   Then gave I her (so tutor'd by my Art)   245
   A Sleeping Potion, which so took effect
   As I intended, for it wrought on her
   The Form of Death. Mean time I writ to Romeo
   That he should hither come, as this dire Night,
   To help to take her from her borrowed Grave,   250
   Being the Time the Potion's Force should cease.
   But he which bore my Letter, Friar John,

253 **stay'd**   prevented from proceeding. Compare lines 66, 136, 160–64.

255 **Hower**   hour (here disyllabic, as the Second Quarto spelling indicates).

257 **closely**   in hiding.

263 **bear . . . Patience**   accept Heaven's will without rebellion. Compare Romeo's resolve to 'deny' the 'Stars' (V.i.24) and 'shake' their 'yoke' (V.iii.113). *Desperate* (line 265, echoing line 59 and recalling V.i.36) makes it clear that the Friar believes that by 'doing damned Hate' upon himself Romeo has unwittingly induced his 'Lady' to do the same to herself (III.iii.115–17).

266 **Violence**   here pronounced glidingly so as to constitute two syllables metrically.

268 **ought**   anything.

270 **his**   its. Before *its* came into general use, the neuter possessive was normally represented by either *his* or *it*.

272 **still**   both (a) always, and (b) even yet. This line echoes IV.iii.29.

275 **in post**   in haste, riding post-horses. See V.i.21, 26.

278 **going**   here treated as a single syllable metrically.

282 **what made . . . place?**   What made your Master come to this place?

285 **Anon**   shortly.

Was stay'd by Accident, and yesternight
Return'd my Letter back. Then all alone
At the pre-fixed Hower of her Waking   255
Came I to take her from her Kindred's Vault,
Meaning to keep her closely at my Cell
Till I conveniently could send to Romeo.
But when I came, some Minute ere the Time
Of her Awakening, here untimely lay   260
The Noble Paris and true Romeo dead.
She wakes, and I entreated her come forth
And bear this Work of Heaven with Patience;
But then a Noise did scare me from the Tomb,
And she, too desperate, would not go with me,   265
But, as it seems, did Violence on her Self.
All this I know, and to the Marriage
Her Nurse is privy. And if ought in this
Miscarried by my Fault, let my old Life
Be sacrific'd some Hour before his Time   270
Unto the rigour of severest Law.
PRINCE   We still have known thee for a Holy Man.
  Where's Romeo's Man? What can he say to this?
BALTHASAR   I brought my Maister News of Juliet's
  Death,
And then in post he came from Mantua   275
To this same Place, to this same Monument.
This Letter he early bid me give his Father,
And threat'ned me with Death, going in the Vault,
If I departed not and left him there.
PRINCE   Give me the Letter; I will look on it.   280
  Where is the County's Page that rais'd the
  Watch?
  — Sirrah, what made your Maister in this Place?
PAGE   He came with Flowers to strew his Lady's
  Grave,
And bid me stand aloof, and so I did.
Anon comes one with Light to ope the Tomb,   285

288 **make good**   verify, corroborate.

291 **Pothecary**   an aphetic form of *apothecary*.

292 **die and lie**   These verbs echo what Romeo has said in V.i.34.
They also remind us yet again that under normal
circumstances a husband would 'lie and die' with his wife. See
the note to line 172, and compare lines 216–17.

294 **Scourge**   punishment; literally, a whip.

296 **Winking at**   closing my eyes to, failing to attend to. *Winking*
recalls III.ii.5–7. *Discords* echoes III.i.48–50, and III.v.27–28.

297 **brace**   pair (Mercutio and Paris).

299 **Jointure**   the sum reserved for the wife in the event that her
husband should die first and leave her widowed. By *This*
Capulet means Mountague's hand. Significantly their hands
are joined as Capulet speaks.

301 **raise her Statue**   erect a statue in her image. In a way
unintended by the Friar, these statues will 'blaze' the
'Marriage' of Romeo and Juliet and 'reconcile' their 'Friends'
(III.iii.150). *Raise* echoes line 180. In the process it reminds us
that the lovers have sought to raise themselves above the trials
and torments of this sublunary world by shaking off its 'Yoke'
(line 13) and aspiring to a 'timeless End' (line 164, echoing
line 11 of the Prologue) in a realm that transcends the 'Stony
Limits' (II.i.109) of the prison Verona has proven to be for
them.

303 **rate**   price, estimate.

306 **Poor**   Capulet means 'pitiable', but his adjective also plays on
rich in the previous line to continue the financial metaphor
introduced in line 303. Compare the insincere,
self-deprecatory use of *poor* in I.ii.24, where it means
'inadequate' or 'modest'. *Sacrifices* echoes line 270; it also
recalls the sacramental imagery the lovers have employed; see
the note to IV.iii.32.

S.D. **Exeunt omnes**   The stage direction probably indicates a
processional exit for everyone (omnes) remaining on stage.

And by and by my Maister drew on him,
And then I ran away to call the Watch.
PRINCE   This Letter doth make good the Friar's
    Words:
  Their Course of Love, the Tidings of her Death;
  And here he writes that he did buy a Poison   290
  Of a poor Pothecary and therewithal
  Came to this Vault to die and lie with Juliet.
  Where be these Enemies? – Capulet, Mountague,
  See what a Scourge is laid upon your Hate?
  That Heaven finds means to kill your Joys with
    Love.   295
  And I for Winking at your Discords too
  Have lost a brace of Kinsmen: all are punish'd.
CAPULET   O brother Mountague, give me thy Hand.
  This is my Daughter's Jointure, for no more
  Can I demaund.
MOUNTAGUE   But I can give thee more: 300
  For I will raise her Statue in pure Gold,
  That whiles Verona by that Name is known
  There shall no Figure at such rate be set
  As that of True and Faithful Juliet.
CAPULET   As rich shall Romeo's by his Lady's lie,   305
  Poor Sacrifices of our Enmity.
PRINCE   A glooming Peace this Morning with it
    brings;
  The Sun for Sorrow will not shew his Head.
  Go hence to have more Talk of these Sad Things.
  Some shall be pardon'd and some punished: 310
  For never was a Story of more Woe
  Than this of Juliet and her Romeo.   *Exeunt omnes.*

FINIS

PERSPECTIVES ON
Romeo and Juliet

In his 1765 edition of Shakespeare's works Samuel Johnson described *Romeo and Juliet* as 'one of the most pleasing of our Author's performances'. According to Dr Johnson,

> The scenes were busy and various, the incidents numerous and important, the catastrophe irresistibly affecting, and the process of the action carried on with such probability, at least with such congruity to popular opinions, as tragedy requires.
>
> Here is one of the few attempts of Shakespeare to exhibit the conversation of gentlemen, to represent the airy sprightliness of juvenile elegance. Mr Dryden mentions a tradition, which might easily reach his time, of a declaration made by Shakespeare, that he was obliged to kill Mercutio in the third act, lest he would have been killed by him. . . . Mercutio's wit, gaiety and courage, will always procure him friends that wish him a longer life; but his death is not precipitated, he has lived out the time allotted him in the construction of the play; nor do I doubt the ability of Shakespeare to have continued his existence. . . .
>
> The Nurse is one of the characters in which the Author delighted: he has, with great subtilty of distinction, drawn her at once loquacious and secret, obsequious and insolent, trusty and dishonest.
>
> His comic scenes are happily wrought, but his pathetic strains are always polluted with some unexpected depravations. His persons, however distressed, have a conceit left them in their wisery, a miserable conceit.

Three decades later, Walter Whiter was inclined to admire the 'conceit' (punning and other forms of licence in the use of figurative language) that Johnson found objectionable. In *A Specimen of a Commentary on Shakespeare* (London, 1794), Whiter observed that 'There is scarcely a play of our Author, where we do not find some favourite vein of metaphor or allusion by which it is distinguished.' By way of illustration Whiter compared Romeo's speech in I.iv.106–13 with his final words in V.iii.111–21.

> The curious reader will not fail to observe that the ideas drawn from the *Stars*, the *Law*, and the *Sea*, succeed each other in the same order, though with a different application, in both speeches. We may add likewise, that the bitter *cause* of Romeo's death is to be found in the [earlier] speech, though I am well aware that the word *bitterly* was suggested to the Poet by the impression on his mind of the peculiar species of death, which he had himself destined for the character; and that it was not intentionally selected for the purpose of attributing to Romeo a presentiment of the *mode*, by which the *date* of his existence was to *expire*. – This singular coincidence in the accumulation of images apparently so remote cannot surely be considered as the effect of chance, or as the product of imitation.

Samuel Taylor Coleridge was similarly impressed with the poetic complexity of *Romeo and Juliet*. In the lectures he delivered in London in 1811–12 Coleridge said that in this early tragedy 'were to be found' all of Shakespeare's 'excellencies such as they afterwards appeared in his more perfect drama, but differing from them in being less happily combined. All the parts were present,' Coleridge said, 'but they were not united with the same harmony.'

According to notes taken by John Payne Collier, who attended these lectures, Coleridge saw in Mercutio

> a man possessing all the elements of a Poet: high fancy, rapid thoughts. The whole world was, as it were, subject to his law of association. Whenever he wished to impress anything, all things became his servants; all things told the same tale and sound, as it were, in unison. This was combined with a perfect gentleman, himself unconscious of his powers. It was by his death contrived to bring

about the whole catastrophe of the play. It endears him to Romeo, and gives to Mercutio's death an importance which it otherwise could not have acquired.

Coleridge took issue with Dryden's comment 'that Shakespeare had carried on the character of Mercutio as far as he could, till his genius was exhausted, and then killed him to get him out of the way'.

> In truth, on the death of Mercutio the catastrophe depended, and it was produced by it; it served to shew how indifference and aversion to activity in Romeo may be overcome, and roused, by any deep feeling that is called forth to the most determined actions. Had not Mercutio been made so amiable and so interesting an object to every reader, we could not have felt so strongly as we do the necessity of Romeo's interference or connected it so passionately with the future fortunes of the lover and his mistress.

Commenting on the relationship between Romeo and Juliet, Coleridge noted that Shakespeare began with

> its first elements: that sense of imperfection, that yearning to combine itself with something lovely. Romeo became enamoured of the ideal he formed in his own mind, and then, as it were, christened the first real being as that which he desired. He appeared to be in love with Rosaline, but in truth he was in love only with his own idea. He felt the necessity of being beloved, which no noble mind can be without: Shakespeare then introduced Romeo to Juliet, and made it not only a violent but a permanent love at first sight, which had been so often ridiculed in Shakespeare.

A few years after Coleridge's lectures, the sixth President of the United States, John Quincy Adams, wrote a letter to the actor James Henry Hackett (published in Hackett's *Notes, Criticisms and Correspondence upon Shakespeare's Plays and Actors*, 1863) in which he observed that

> The age of Juliet seems to be the key to her character throughout the play, an essential ingredient in the intense sympathy which she inspires; and Shakespeare has marked it, not only in her discourse, but even in her name, the diminutive of tender affections applied only in childhood. If Shakespeare had exhibited upon the stage a woman of

nineteen, he would have dismissed her nurse and called her Julia. She might still have been a very interesting character, but the whole color and complexion of the play must have been changed. An intelligent, virtuous woman, in love with a youth of assorted age and congenial character, is always a person of deep interest in drama. But that interest is heightened and redoubled when, to the sympathy with the lover, you add all the kind affections with which you share in the joys and sorrows of the child. There is childishness in the discourse of Juliet, and the poet has shown us why; because she had scarcely ceased to be a child.

At about the same time that President Adams was reflecting on Juliet in Washington, an eminent German writer was considering her from the perspective of literary Romanticism. Notwithstanding our attachment to the heroine, Johann Ludwig Tieck concluded (in *Dramaturgische Blätter*, 1826), we should acknowledge that

> Shakespeare was eminently right in not closing the tragedy with [her] death. . . . Not only do the affecting reconciliation of the two old foes and the vindication of Friar Lawrence make the continuation necessary, but so it must be chiefly in order that, after misfortune has done its worst, the true idea of the tragedy, its glorified essence, may rise before our souls that up to this point have been too sorely tried and too violently affected to perceive the inmost meaning of the poem, or to take a painful yet clear survey of it.

A century later, one of the most gifted of all Shakespearean directors, Harley Granville-Barker, distilled his vast theatrical experience into an illustrious series of *Prefaces to Shakespeare*. In his remarks on *Romeo and Juliet* (Vol. 2, Princeton, 1947), Granville-Barker spoke eloquently about the lovers' initial meeting.

> It is hard to see what better first encounter could have been devised. To have lit mutual passion in them at once would have been common-place; the cheapest of love tragedies might begin like that. But there is something sacramental in this ceremony, something shy and grave and sweet; it is a marriage made already. And she is such a child; touched to earnestness by his trembling earnestness, but breaking into

fun at last (her defence when the granted kiss lights passion in him) as the last quatrain's meter breaks for its ending into 'You kiss by the book.' The tragedy to come will be deepened when we remember the innocence of its beginning. The encounter's ending has significance too. They are not left to live in a fool's paradise for long. Romeo hears who she is and faces his fate. An hour ago he was affecting melancholy while Mercutio and his fellows laugh round him. Then, as the guests and Maskers depart and the laughter dies, Juliet grows fearful. She hears her fate and must face it too. . . . The child is no more a child.

Granville-Barker stressed the 'vivid contrast between scene and scene', and the technique involved in having the scenes 'swiftly succeeding each other'. He also emphasized the importance of long, varied sequences such as the one (IV.iii) that begins with Juliet taking the medicine Friar Lawrence has given her.

The curtains of the inner stage are drawn back to show us Juliet's bed. Her nurse and her mother leave her; she drinks the potion, and . . . *She falls upon the bed within the curtains*. There has been argument upon argument whether this means the curtains of the bed or of the inner stage – which would then close on her. The difference in dramatic effect will be of degree and not kind. What Shakespeare aims at in the episodes that follow is to keep us conscious of the bed and its burden; while in front of it, Capulet and the servants, Lady Capulet and the Nurse pass hither and thither, laughing and joking over the preparation for the wedding, till the bridal music is playing, till, to the very sound of this, the Nurse bustles up to draw back the curtains and disclose the girl there stark and still.

This is one of the chief dramatic effects of the play; and it can only be gained by preserving the continuity of the action, with its agonies and absurdities cheek by jowl, with that bridal music sharpening the irony at the last. It is a comprehensive effect, extending from the drinking of the potion to the Nurse's parrot scream when she finds Juliet still and cold; and even beyond, to the coming of the bridegroom and his train, through the long-spoken threnody, to the farce of the ending – which helps to remind us that, after all, Juliet is not dead. It is one scene, one integral stretch of action; and its common mutilation by *Scene iv. Hall in Capulet's house . . . Scene v. Juliet's chaber. Enter Nurse . . .*, with the consequences involved, is sheer editorial murder.

Most of the play's commentators in the twentieth century have remarked upon the urgency with which things happen in *Romeo and Juliet*. After a discussion of the 'premonitions' and 'foreshadowings' that mark the early scenes, H. B. Charlton (*Shakespearian Tragedy*, Cambridge, 1948) notes that

> Shakespeare not only hangs omens thickly round his play. He gives to the action itself a quality apt to conjure the sense of relentless doom. It springs mainly from his compression of the time over which the story stretches. In all earlier versions there is a much longer lapse. Romeo's wooing is prolonged over weeks before the secret wedding; then, after the wedding, there is an interval of three or four months before the slaying of Tybalt; and Romeo's exile lasts from Easter until a short time before mid-September when the marriage with Paris was at first planned to take place. But in Shakespeare all this is pressed into three or four days. The world seems for a moment to be caught up in the fierce play of furies revelling in some mad supernatural game. . . . This earth, it would seem, has no place for passion like Romeo's and Juliet's. And so, stirred to sympathy by Shakespeare's poetic power, we tolerate, perhaps even approve, their death.

Caroline F. E. Spurgeon (*Shakespeare's Imagery and What It Tells Us*, Cambridge, 1935) speaks similarly.

> In *Romeo and Juliet* the beauty and ardour of young love are seen by Shakespeare as the irradiating glory of sunlight and starlight in a dark world. The dominating image is *light*, every form and manifestation of it: the sun, moon, stars, fire, lightning, the flash of gunpowder, and the reflected light of beauty and of love; while by contrast we have night, darkness, clouds, rain, mist, and smoke. . . . There can be no question, I think, that Shakespeare saw the story in its swift and tragic beauty, as an almost blinding flash of light, suddenly ignited, and as swiftly quenched. . . . The sensation of swiftness and brilliance, accompanied by danger and destruction, is accentuated again and again. . . .

Mark Van Doren (*Shakespeare*, New York, 1939) says that the relationship between Romeo and Juliet derives its luminosity

> from the contrast we are made to feel between their notion of day and night and the normal thought about such things. Normality is their foe, as it is at last their nemesis; the artificial night of Juliet's feigned

death becomes the long night of common death in which no private planets shine. The word normality carries here no moral meaning. It has to do merely with notions about love and life; the lovers' notion being pathetically distinguished from those of other persons who are not in love and so consider themselves realistic or practical. One of the reasons for the fame of *Romeo and Juliet* is that it has so completely and clearly isolated the experience of romantic love. It has let such love speak for itself; and not alone in the celebrated wooing scenes, where the hero and heroine express themselves with a piercing directness, but indirectly also, and possibly with still greater power, in the whole play in so far as the whole play is built to be their foil. Their deep interest for us lies in their being alone in a world which does not understand them. . . .

Wolfgang Clemen (*The Development of Shakespeare's Imagery*, London, 1951) brings similar perceptions to the poetic drama of the Balcony Scene.

Romeo stands below in the dark garden, above which slow-sailing clouds move in a star-strewn sky (all this is conjured up by his words!); Juliet appears above at the window. Romeo lifts his eyes, just as one must glance upward in order to perceive the heavenly bodies (the white-upturned eyes are his own eyes). When, in the first lines, the eyes of the beloved appear to Romeo as 'two of the fairest stars in all the heaven,' then, this is no conventional phrase but is based on the reality of the moment, on the fact that he has raised his eyes to heaven and to Juliet at the same time. And when Juliet now appears to him – in the image quoted – as 'winged messenger of heaven,' this, too, results from the metaphorical character of the situation itself. So everything in this image has a double function: the clouds and the heavenly *messengers* may be reality, and at the same time they are symbols. The deeply organic nature of this image is to be seen also in the fact that it coincides as a poetic enhancing element with Romeo's ecstatically uplifted mind. . . . In this image three functions merge, which we usually meet separately: it is the enhanced expression of Romeo's own nature, it characterizes Juliet (light, the most important symbol for her, occurs here), and it fills the night with clouds and stars, thus creating atmosphere.

Meanwhile (in 'Shakespeare's Tragedies', an essay in

Shakespeare's World, ed. James Sutherland and Joel Hurstfield, London, 1964) Winifred Nowottny notes that there is

> very good reason why Romeo the lover, and Juliet, too, should talk like a sonneteer. The play was written in the heyday of the sonnet, and the language of the sonnet was the language of love. The kind of love Petrarch had celebrated was often regarded as an experience which lifted a man above himself, as an exaltation of the spirit so spectacular that only religious experience could compete with it for intensity. It would hardly have been possible for Shakespeare, writing about idealistic passion at a time when the sonnet vogue was at its height, to ignore the sonneteers' language for it.

Within the context of the play, however, to be in Romeo and Juliet's

> state of mind is to be in a world of one's own. Their world, to Mercutio, is absurd; it is a closed world to the Nurse; it is a world Capulet has no time for, and one of whose wilfulness the Friar disapproves. This contrast between the world of lovers and the world of other people is itself a universal feature of the experience of being in love, and the plot of the play gives a dramatic heightening to this universal fact by placing this love in the midst of a feud between the lovers' families, so that it is the development of the feud, not the characters of the lovers, which destroys them.

In *The Living World of Shakespeare* (New York, 1964), John Wain offers the provocative suggestion that

> the psychological premises of *Romeo and Juliet* are those of the early comedies. Characteristically, those comedies concern themselves with the inborn, unargued stupidity of older people and the life-affirming gaiety and resourcefulness of young ones. The lovers thread their way through obstacles set up by middle-aged vanity and impercipience. Parents are stupid and do not know what is best for their children or themselves. . . . *Romeo and Juliet* is in essence a comedy that turns out tragically. . . .
>
> To put it another way, the form of *Romeo and Juliet* is that of a shattered minuet. The two lovers first come together in a dance. . . , and it is noteworthy that the first words they address to each other are in the form of a sonnet. A dance; a sonnet; these are symbols of a

formal, constrained wholeness. This wholeness is already threatened. Tybalt has recognized Romeo; and though his demand for instant combat has been restrained by his host (a rare case of the older generation's being wiser than the younger), he is glowering and planning revenge. The worm is already in the fruit.

Susan Snyder develops this notion further. In 'Romeo and Juliet: Comedy into Tragedy' (Essays in Criticism, 1970), she says that

> Romeo and Juliet is different from Shakespeare's other tragedies in that it becomes, rather than is, tragic. Other tragedies have reversals, but in Romeo and Juliet the reversal is so radical as to constitute a change of genre: the action and the characters begin in familiar comic patterns, and are then transformed – or discarded to compose the pattern of tragedy.
>
> Comedy and tragedy, being opposed ways of apprehending the real world, project their own opposing worlds. The tragic world is governed by inevitability, and its highest value is personal integrity. In the comic world 'evitability' is assumed; instead of heroic or obstinate adherence to a single course, comedy endorses opportunistic shifts and realistic accommodations as means to an end of new social health. The differing laws of comedy and tragedy point to opposed concepts of law itself. Law in the comic world is extrinsic, imposed on society *en masse*. Its source there is usually human, so that law may either be stretched ingeniously to suit the characters' ends, or flouted, or even annulled by benevolent rulers. . . . Even deep-rooted social laws, like the obedience owed to parents by their children, are constantly overturned. But in the tragic world law is inherent: imposed by the individual's own nature, it may direct him to a conflict with the larger patterns of law inherent in his universe. Tragic law cannot be altered. . . .

Snyder goes on to argue, however, that

> It is not only the shift from comedy to tragedy that sets Romeo and Juliet apart from the other Shakespeare tragedies. Critics have often noted, sometimes disapprovingly, that external fate rather than character is the principal determiner of the tragic outcome. For Shakespeare, tragedy is usually a matter of both character and circumstance, a fatal interaction of man and moment. But in this play,

although the central characters had their weaknesses, their destruction does not really stem from those weaknesses. One may agree with Friar Laurence that Romeo is rash, but it is not his rashness that propels him into the tragic chain of events but an opposite quality. In the crucial duel between Mercutio and Tybalt, Romeo tries to make peace. Ironically, this very intervention contributes to Mercutio's death. . . . If Shakespeare wanted to implicate Romeo's rashness in his fate, this scene is handled with unbelievable ineptness. Judging from the resultant effect, what he wanted to convey was an ironic dissociation between character and the direction of events. . . . For this once in Shakespearean tragedy, it is not what you are that counts, but the world you live in.

In *The Shakespearean Metaphor* (London, 1978) Ralph Berry takes a cue from Winifred Nowottny and ponders 'The Sonnet-world of Verona'.

The sonnet is the channel through which the play flows. Acts I and II are preceded by a choric sonnet; Romeo and Juliet at their first encounter compose a sonnet, charmingly, together. Several quatrains and sestets are scattered throughout the play, which closes with the Prince's sestet. . . . The sonnet material helps to establish Verona as a country of the mind, a locale whose inhabitants place themselves through their mode of discourse. In the Veronese language, the most obvious adjunct to the sonnet is the rhymed couplet. It is an easier mode than the cross-rhymes of the sonnet, and the Veronese fall into it naturally. . . . Rhyme is the shared possession of this society. . . . But rhyme is psychologically more interesting than it looks. I discern two main varieties of the mode. With the elders, the heavy, jogging rhymes have the effect of a self-fulfilling prophecy. *Night* must follow *light* with the same inevitability that it does the day. The rhymes figure a closed system. The younger people, apt to confuse facility with penetration, seize on the other aspect of rhyme – that it can pick up the loose ends of a companion's speech. Thus, to the stimulus of Benvolio's 'I rather weep . . . At thy good heart's oppression', Romeo instantly reacts 'Why such is love's transgression'. . . . It is a kind of game. . . .

One of the most distinctive features of *Romeo and Juliet* is its almost journalistic flair in identifying the literary movement of the 1590s and the ways in which people modelled themselves upon that movement. Shakespeare's conception, then, synthesises the physical world of Renaissance Italy, the most famous literary expression of that world, and the Elizabethan reception to the expression.

But is it healthy to inhabit the kind of milieu that Mark Van Doren describes as 'furiously literary'? Berry's answer is no, because

> Verona is a wrong-choice society. It is a community fascinated with names, forms, rituals. Its citizens are passionate, impulsive, intolerant, impulsive. It lacks a capacity for appraising its own values. Its Prince does not tell the community that the Montague–Capulet feud is an absurdity, he merely forbids brawling in the streets. The fatal chance of the thrust under Romeo's arm is bad luck: true. But someone would get killed in a duel, sometime; it was inevitable. Fate, then, is diffused back into the entire society. . . . What we have in *Romeo and Juliet* is a complete social context for an action, a society that is unable to cope with consequences of its own deficiencies.

In her essay on 'Patterns and Paradigms' in the tragedy (in *The Shakespeare Plays: A Study Guide*, 1979) Marjorie Garber observes that

> From the first, the audience is made aware that there is something seriously wrong in the play's world. The Chorus delivers a Prologue in the form of a sonnet, a fourteen-line poem usually devoted in Shakespeare's time to a private declaration of love. But here we have a sonnet gone public, and a sonnet that speaks not of love but of civil war: 'Where civil blood makes civil hands unclean'. Moreover, the Prologue is followed by the appearance of two servants of the house of Capulet who seem to have no object in life except to quarrel with their rivals, the servants of Montague. Lewdly jesting about the heads of maids and their maidenheads, the two servants continue the confusion between love and war, sexuality and violence, which was first suggested by the sonnet. Their squabble inevitably expands to envelop their masters, as Old Capulet, still wearing his nightgown, rushes into the street calling for his sword. There could be no more visible sign of the disorder endemic in Verona than the fact that servants draw masters into battle rather than the other way around.

In such an environment, Garber asserts, it is to be expected that the lovers can

find reality and comfort only in darkness. All of the play's intimate scenes take place at night: the Capulet ball, the orchard or 'balcony' scene, the night of marital consummation in Juliet's chamber, and the final night in the graveyard. Daylight brings public brawls, murderous duels, and the unwelcome threat of a bigamous marriage with Paris. Yet such is the tenuousness of their situation that light is continually breaking in on the lovers – either by the coming of day, or by the images in which they speak of one another.

Garber points out that 'Silver is mentioned three times in the play', and that it is consistently associated with things that are pleasant. 'By contrast', she says, 'the play's references to gold are frequently negative and debasing, connected with things that appear to be of questionable value.'

Having experienced – and remembered – all of this, what is the audience to make of the plan for atonement put forward by Old Capulet and Old Montague at the end of the play? Montague will 'raise [Juliet's] statue in pure gold'. . . . Capulet, competitive to the last, will do the same for Romeo. But are the gold statues an adequate and appropriate memorial – or have those persons left on stage missed the point of the tragic happenings in Verona? Guided by the clues the playwright has given us, we may be justified in thinking that Shakespeare has provided us with an opportunity to be wiser than that other audience of these events, the surviving characters on the stage, and to realize that his play, rather than the golden statues, is the fit monument by which Romeo and Juliet will be remembered, and their tragedy understood.

In her article on 'Coming of Age in Verona' (*Modern Language Studies*, 8), Coppelia Kahn notes that the play's action develops in a setting that

is distinctly patriarchal as well as domestic. Much of it takes place within the Capulet household, and Capulet's role as *paterfamilias* is apparent from the first scene, in which his servants behave as members of his extended family. That household is a charming place: protected and spacious, plentiful with servants, food, light, and heat, bustling with festivity, intimate and informal even on great occasions, with a cosy familiarity between master and servant. In nice contrast to it stands the play's other dominant milieu, the streets of Verona. It is there that those fighting the feud are defined as men, in contrast to those who would rather love than fight, who in terms of the feud are less than men. Gregory and Sampson ape the machismo of their masters, seeking insults on the slightest pretext so that they may prove their valor. . . . As male servants their position resembles that of the sons bound by their honor to fight for their families' names. More important, their obvious phallic competitiveness in being quick to anger at an insult to their status or manhood, and quick to draw their swords and fight, shades into competitiveness in sex as well. . . . (In the opening scene) the many puns on 'stand' as standing one's ground in fighting and as erection attest that fighting in the feud demonstrates virility as well as valor. Sampson and Gregory also imply that they consider it their prerogative as men to take women by force as a way of demonstrating their superiority to the Montagues. . . .

It is against this background, Kahn says, that we must appraise what Romeo does at the turning-point of the action.

In that moment, caught between his radically new identity as Juliet's husband, which has made him responsible (he thinks) for his friend's death, and his previous traditional identity as the scion of the house of Montague, he resumes the latter and murders Tybalt. . . . As much as we want the love of Romeo and Juliet to prosper, we also want the volatile enmity of Tybalt punished and the death of Mercutio, that spirit of vital gaiety, revenged, even at the cost of continuing the feud. Romeo's hard choice is also ours. Though the play is constantly critical of the feud as the medium through which criteria of patriarchally oriented masculinity are voiced, it is just as constantly sensitive to the association of those criteria with more humane principles of loyalty to family and friends, courage, and personal dignity. . . . In patriarchal Verona, men bear names and stand to fight for them; women, 'the weaker vessels,' bear children and 'fall backward' to conceive them, as the Nurse's husband once told the young Juliet.

Marianne Novy builds upon Kahn's observations in *Love's Argument: Gender Relations in Shakespeare* (Chapel Hill, NC, 1984).

Why do Romeo and Juliet keep their love secret not only from their parents but also from their peers? ... It is in part because of the difference between their experience of love and Verona's distortion of it. ... Yet this secrecy is avoidance of a problem that they cannot ultimately escape. When Romeo tries to act according to his secret love of Juliet instead of according to the feud, Tybalt and Mercutio insist on fighting. And when Romeo's intervention – to stop the fight – results in Mercutio's death, it is clear that Verona's definition of masculinity by violence is partly Romeo's definition as well. ...

Just before their crucial fight, Tybalt and Mercutio, speaking of Romeo, quibble on the point that 'man,' a word so important as an ideal, has from the opening scene the less honorific meaning of 'manservant.' ... This pun is an analogue of the irony that it is precisely in his 'manly' vengeance for Mercutio's death that Romeo most decisively loses control of his own fate and becomes, as he says, 'fortune's fool'. ... In a sense, as Mercutio's elaboration of his pun suggests without his awareness, a commitment to proving manhood by violence makes one easily manipulated by whoever offers a challenge. ... In the larger sense, the code of violence that promises to make Romeo a man actually makes him its man – its pawn.

In an essay about 'Language and Sexual Difference in *Romeo and Juliet*' (in *Shakespeare's Rough Magic*, ed. Peter Erickson and Coppelia Kahn, Newark, Del., 1985), Edward Snow observes 'an opposition' between the ways in which Romeo and Juliet experience and express love. Snow argues that

The imaginative universe generated by Romeo's desire is dominated by eyesight, and remains subject to greater rational control than Juliet's. His metaphors assemble reality 'out there,' and provide access to it through perspectives that tend to make him an onlooker rather than a participant. There is a kind of metonymic fascination in his language with parts and extremities, especially when viewed from a distance, against a backdrop that heightens the sensation of outline and boundary. Juliet 'hangs upon the cheek of night / As a rich jewel in an Ethiop's ear'. ... Contact with Juliet tends to be a matter of reaching out, and gently touching, while the idea of union with her generates imagery of parts securely fitted to each other rather than wholes merging and boundaries dissolving. ... His imagination fixes objects in stable Euclidian space, and keeps them separate and distinct, even while entertaining fantasies of metamorphosis. . . .

Juliet, however, is the locus of affirmative energies that can't be contained within a tragic frame of reference. Her imaginative universe, in contrast to Romeo's, is generated by all the senses, and by a unity of feeling that is more than just the sum of their parts. Her desire generates images of whole, embodied selves, and extravagant gestures of giving and taking: 'Romeo, doff thy name, / And for thy name, which is no part of thee, / Take all myself.'. . . Juliet's sensations tend in general to be more 'piercing' and ontologically dangerous than Romeo's. . . . Even vision is for her an armed faculty that penetrates the field of perception instead of gazing into it from a wistful distance: 'But no more deep will I endart mine eye / Than your consent gives strength to make it fly.'. . . Even when Juliet's language seems to place her in the same imaginative world with Romeo, there is often a contrast between the tendency of his metaphors to keep love distant and remote, and hers to bring it up close, and make it possible. . . .

The impression, then, is of two distinct modes of desire – one reaching out, the other unfolding – exquisitely fitted to each other, but rarely meeting in the same phenomenological universe. . . . Always, it seems, there is a lack in Romeo that corresponds to an overflowing in Juliet.

But if there is a difference between the way Romeo and Juliet think and speak, there is even more difference between their discourse and that of the other characters. In an essay on 'How the Characters Talk' (in the *Shakespeare's World* anthology cited earlier), James Sutherland contrasts the 'bawdy jokes' and bad puns of Sampson and Gregory with the 'grandiloquence' of the Prince's pronouncements in the opening scene. Sutherland goes on to discuss the 'excess and hyperbole' that punctuates the 'mocking' discourse of 'the libertine gallant' Mercutio. He analyses the 'fussy and bustling' conversation of Old Capulet. But the character who interests him most is the Nurse. Commenting on her long discourse in Act I, scene iii, he says:

> She has the animal vitality of healthy old age: once she is off on a reminiscence she is as irrepressible as the Wife of Bath, and has the same hearty vulgarity and confident femininity. Her lack of education is seen in the way that she joins her narrative together with a series of

'Ands' and 'Buts' and 'Fors,' the 'Buts' and 'Fors' being usually no more than simple connectives, and not really adversative or causal. She is endlessly repetitive, sometimes consciously so. . . , more often unconsciously. . . . She has the uneducated speaker's constant striving for emphasis, obtained characteristically by means of oaths ('marry,' 'by the rood'), by her wager, . . . and by frequent exclamations. . . . She keeps interrupting herself, breaking off as some irrelevant idea enters her head. . . . Her whole speech, of course, is one vast irrelevance: the sole point at issue is the question, How old is Juliet?

Stanley Wells has also written on the 'The Uses of Inconsequentiality' in Shakespeare's portrayal of the Nurse (in *Shakespeare's Styles*, ed. Philip Edwards et al., Cambridge, 1980). As Wells notes, speaking of the same discourse in I.iii:

Part of the comedy of the Nurse's utterance lies in the fact that what she interrupts has in itself no logical sequence. The information that she has to convey in her main speech is entirely contained in its second line:

Come Lammas Eve at night shall she be fourteen.

This fact might well be pointed by stage business, Lady Capulet endeavouring to resume the conversation after this statement. But the Nurse's well of recollection has been tapped, and the flow cannot be quenched. . . .

The very fact that Susan's relationship with the Nurse is not explicitly stated is itself an aspect of Shakespeare's dramatic style here. It tells us obliquely of the Nurse's intimacy with the family in which she lives, an intimacy which the performers can use by suggesting a sympathetic, if bored, acceptance that once the Nurse has embarked on this tack, she must be indulged. And it engages the audience by requiring them to make the inference. The death of an infant has an inevitable poignancy, and one which must link the Nurse to the Capulets since Juliet has thriven on the milk which should have reared Susan.

. . . The Nurse's ramblings do indeed give us a sense of the past; and they do so in a particularly poignant context. The stage situation shows us a girl poised on the brink of womanhood. We have not met her before, and one function of the Nurse's speech is to engage our sympathetic interest in the play's heroine. As the Nurse talks, her memories not only throw our minds back to the infancy of this girl, they also recall a prediction made at that time of how Juliet would react when she had 'more wit' and came 'to age'. The child who is talked about as an innocent infant is now before us, the subject of marriage plans. . . . The temporary complexities of the situation are subtle and ironical.

How does the Nurse's role look from the inside? In *Players of Shakespeare* (ed. Philip Brockbrank, Cambridge, 1985), Brenda Bruce, who played the part in a Royal Shakespeare Company production in 1980, says:

Nurse is no country bumpkin. She holds a very important position with an important family in Verona. She is the Italian equivalent of a bright Cockney with all the same energetic vulgarity and warmth, and the only interest in her life is Juliet and Juliet's happiness. A fairly simple premise. However the complications within the part are tremendous. . . . In almost every scene she reports happenings to the other characters, most often repeating what has already been seen by the audience. She nudges Juliet sexually as Mercutio nudges Romeo in the same manner. . . .

Nurse's bawdiness is part of her character. She cannot resist sexual innuendo. It is a running joke; often after a bawdy remark she says 'May God forgive me.'. . .

Morally, how does Nurse stand? Does one protect, in fact encourage one's child to harbour, a convicted murderer? The answer must be yes, if, like Nurse, one believes that happiness with one's chosen man, however fleeting, is the very essence of life. There have been murderers and deserters since the beginning of history who have gained respite because of the loyalty of their women. . . .

But what about the Nurse's counsel to her charge once Juliet is told that she must marry Paris?

Nurse is incapable of sending Juliet out into the world; Juliet's parents are moreover full of grudge against the Montagues, a 'continuing rage'. Nurse has only one answer and it is immoral and against the law. It is damnation in the eyes of the church, but better than starving on the streets. Her solution is *bigamy*. . . . Anything is better than family rejection, starvation. . . . Parental control and approval and marriage were the only possibilities for a woman. Independence for the Juliets of that time was out of the question.

At the end of Act IV

Nurse comes to awaken Juliet. All fears allayed, a conscience stifled; teasing, bawdy Nurse once again. Juliet is dead. Here Shakespeare abandons Nurse. She joins in a formal lament and disappears from the story. In V.iii, the Friar confesses his part in the tragedy and says, 'and to the marriage / Her nurse is privy'. Nurse is not in the scene to put *her* case. Why? Might it be that she is the epitome of the woman who lives on the fringe of other people's lives, helping to shape their destiny, but no more than that?

FURTHER READING

Many of the works quoted in the preceding survey (or excerpts from those works) can be found in modern collections of criticism. Of particular interest are two anthologies:

Andrews, John F. (ed.), *'Romeo and Juliet': Critical Essays*, New York and London: Garland Publishing, 1993 (25 articles, including the ones quoted above by Ralph Berry, Brenda Bruce, Marjorie Garber, Coppelia Kahn, Marianne Novy, Edward Snow, Susan Snyder, Mark Van Doren, and Stanley Wells).

Cole, Douglas (ed.), *Twentieth Century Interpretations of 'Romeo and Juliet'*, Englewood Cliffs, NJ: Prentice-Hall, 1970 (15 articles, including the ones quoted above by H. B. Charlton, Wolfgang Clemen, Harley Granville-Barker, Winifred Nowottny, Caroline F. E. Spurgeon, James Sutherland, and John Wain).

Other studies of Shakespeare that include discussions of *Romeo and Juliet*:

Battenhouse, Roy, *Shakespearean Tragedy: Its Art and Its Christian Premises*, Bloomington: Indiana University Press, 1969.

Brooke, Nicholas, *Shakespeare's Early Tragedies*, London: Methuen, 1968.

Calderwood, James L., *Shakespearean Metadrama*, Minneapolis: University of Minnesota Press, 1971.

Coghill, Nevill, *Shakespeare's Professional Skills*, Cambridge: Cambridge University Press, 1964.

Dickey, Franklin M., *Not Wisely But Too Well: Shakespeare's Love Tragedies*, San Marino, Cal.: Huntington Library, 1957.

Goddard, Harold C., *The Meaning of Shakespeare*, Chicago: University of Chicago Press, 1951.

Jorgens, Jack, *Shakespeare on Film*, Bloomington: Indiana University Press, 1977 (includes a fine chapter on Franco Zeffirelli's film).

Lawlor, John, *'Romeo and Juliet'*, in *Early Shakespeare*, Stratford-upon-Avon Studies 3, ed. John Russell Brown and Bernard Harris, London: Edward Arnold, 1961.

Mahood, M. M., *Shakespeare's Wordplay*, London: Methuen, 1957.

Rabkin, Norman, *Shakespeare and the Common Understanding*, New York: Free Press, 1967.

Ribner, Irving, *Patterns in Shakespearean Tragedy*, London: Methuen, 1960.

Stauffer, Donald A., *Shakespeare's World of Images*, New York: Norton, 1949.

Stirling, Brents, *Unity in Shakespearean Tragedy*, New York: Columbia University Press, 1956.

Traversi, D. A., *An Approach to Shakespeare*, 2nd edn, New York: Doubleday, 1956.

Background studies and useful reference works:

Abbott, E. A., *A Shakespearian Grammar*, New York: Haskell House, 1972 (information on how Shakespeare's grammar differs from ours).

Allen, Michael J. B., and Kenneth Muir (eds), *Shakespeare's Plays in Quarto: A Facsimile Edition*, Berkeley: University of California Press, 1981.

Andrews, John F. (ed.), *William Shakespeare: His World, His Work, His Influence*, 3 vols, New York: Scribners, 1985 (articles on 60 topics).

Bentley, G. E., *The Profession of Player in Shakespeare's Time, 1590–1642*, Princeton: Princeton University Press, 1984.

Brown, John Russell, *Shakespeare's Plays in Performance*, London: Edward Arnold, 1966.

Bullough, Geoffrey (ed.), *Narrative and Dramatic Sources of Shakespeare*, 8 vols, New York: Columbia University Press, 1957–75 (printed sources, with helpful summaries and comments by the editor).

Campbell, O. J., and Edward G. Quinn (eds), *The Reader's Encyclopedia of Shakespeare*, New York: Crowall, 1966.

Cook, Ann Jennalie, *The Privileged Playgoers of Shakespeare's London*: Princeton: Princeton University Press, 1981 (argues that theatre audiences at the Globe and other public playhouses were relatively well-to-do).

De Grazia, Margreta, *Shakespeare Verbatim: The Reproduction of Authenticity and the Apparatus of 1790*, Oxford: Clarendon Press, 1991 (interesting material on eighteenth-century editorial practices).

Fastman, Arthur M., *A Short History of Shakespearean Criticism*, New York: Random House, 1968.

Gurr, Andrew, *Playgoing in Shakespeare's London*, Cambridge: Cambridge University Press, 1987 (argument for changing tastes, and for a more diverse group of audiences than Cook suggests).

—— *The Shakespearean Stage, 1574–1642*, 2nd edn, Cambridge: Cambridge University Press, 1981 (theatres, companies, audiences, and repertories).

Hinman, Charlton (ed.), *The Norton Facsimile: The First Folio of Shakespeare's Plays*, New York: Norton, 1968.

Muir, Kenneth, *The Sources of Shakespeare's Plays*, New Haven: Yale

254

University Press, 1978 (a concise account of how Shakespeare used his sources).

Onions, C. T., *A Shakespeare Glossary*, 2nd edn, London: Oxford University Press, 1953.

Partridge, Eric, *Shakespeare's Bawdy*, London: Routledge & Kegan Paul, 1955 (indispensable guide to Shakespeare's direct and indirect ways of referring to 'indecent' subjects).

Schoenbaum, S., *Shakespeare's Lives*, 2nd edn, Oxford: Oxford University Press, 1992 (readable, informative survey of the many biographers of Shakespeare, including those believing that someone else wrote the works).

—— *William Shakespeare: A Compact Documentary Life*, New York: Oxford University Press, 1977 (presentation of all the biographical documents, with assessments of what they tell us about the playwright).

Speaight, Robert, *Shakespeare on the Stage: An Illustrated History of Shakespearian Performance*, London: Collins, 1973.

Spevack, Marvin, *The Harvard Concordance to Shakespeare*, Cambridge, Mass.: Harvard University Press, 1973.

Wright, George T., *Shakespeare's Metrical Art*, Berkeley: University of California Press, 1988.

PLOT SUMMARY

Prologue   The Chorus sets the scene. A bitter feud has existed for many years between two families who live in Verona. The play deals with the bloody conclusion of this enmity; two lovers, one from each family, take their own lives.

1.1   In a street in Verona, a sword-fight develops between servingmen of the Capulet and Mountague households. Benvolio, a nephew to Mountague, tries to end it. But Tybalt, a nephew to Capulet's wife, attacks Benvolio, thinking Benvolio is fighting the Capulets' servingmen. The city Watch enter and attack both parties.

Old Capulet arrives with his wife, followed shortly by old Mountague and his wife. Both men offer to fight each other. Finally Escalus, Prince of Verona, arrives and stops the brawl. He declares that if Verona's peace is disrupted again by the Mountagues' and the Capulets' feud, then the heads of those households will be executed.

Everyone else having left, Benvolio tells old Mountague how the affray began. Mountague's wife inquires after her son's, Romeo's, whereabouts, and Benvolio tells her that he saw Romeo before dawn in a sycamore grove outside the city. Mountague notes that such behaviour is habitual; he wishes that he knew the cause of his son's unhappiness. Benvolio offers to try to discover it.

As Romeo enters, his parents depart. Romeo tells Benvolio that he loves a woman who does not love him. Benvolio urges Romeo to forget her, but Romeo declares that he cannot.

1.2   Outside his house, old Capulet talks to Paris, a young Count, and kinsman to Prince Escalus. Paris wishes to marry Capulet's daughter. As his daughter is not yet fourteen, Capulet will not insist that she marry. But if she wishes to marry Paris, he will happily consent. Capulet invites Paris to a feast he is giving that night. Handing his servingman a list of those to be invited, Capulet leaves with Paris.

      Romeo and Benvolio enter, and the servingman, as he cannot read, asks Romeo what names are on the list. Romeo reads them out, and the servingman tells him what the invitations are to. Benvolio points out that Rosaline, Romeo's beloved, will be at the feast. Benvolio suggests that they go, so that he can show Romeo that there are more beautiful women than Rosaline. Romeo agrees.

1.3   Within Capulet's house and just before the feast, Capulet's wife tells her daughter, Juliet, that Paris wishes to marry her. Juliet's Nurse adds her own comments. Juliet says that she will try to love Paris.

1.4   Outside the Capulet house, Romeo, Benvolio and Mercutio, a kinsman of Prince Escalus and friend of Romeo, are preparing to put on their masks and enter. Mercutio insists that they should all dance when they get inside. Romeo gives his reasons why he does not want to; but he enters with the rest.

      Inside, Romeo falls in love with one of the women he sees dancing. Tybalt, overhearing him trying to find out who she is, recognizes him and sends for a sword. However, old Capulet insists that Tybalt do nothing.

      Romeo declares his love to the woman, who is then called away by the Nurse. The Nurse tells Romeo that the woman is Juliet. He leaves with Benvolio and Mercutio.

      Juliet has also fallen in love; she finds out from her Nurse that the man was Romeo.

2 Prologue   The Chorus notes that although Romeo and Juliet both love each other, their love is beset with difficulties because of the feud between their families.

2.1   Romeo eludes his friends by hiding within the Capulets' orchard. Juliet comes to her window, and he overhears her speaking to herself of her love for him. He tells her that he loves her. Juliet arranges to send a messenger to Romeo the next day, so that he can let her know if he will marry her. She is called away by her Nurse.

2.2   Romeo visits Friar Lawrence, finding him outside his cell. The Friar agrees to marry the pair, as he hopes the marriage will end their families' feud.

2.3   In a street at midday, Romeo meets Benvolio and Mercutio, who have been wondering where he went after the feast. Shortly afterwards, the Nurse comes in and asks to speak to Romeo alone. Mercutio and Benvolio leave.

     Romeo tells the Nurse to ask Juliet to come to Friar Lawrence's cell that afternoon. There they will be married. He also asks the Nurse to wait behind the abbey wall, where his man, within the hour, will bring her a rope-ladder.

2.4   In the Capulets' orchard, the Nurse gives Juliet Romeo's message. Juliet leaves for the Friar's cell, and the Nurse goes to fetch the rope-ladder.

2.5   In Friar Lawrence's cell, the Friar and Romeo are waiting. When Juliet arrives, they go offstage to be married.

3.1   In a street, Mercutio, Benvolio and their men meet Tybalt, Petruchio and others. Romeo arrives and declines Tybalt's challenge to a fight. Mercutio accepts, and he and Tybalt fight. As Romeo tries to stop them fighting, Tybalt fatally wounds Mercutio and then leaves. When he returns, Romeo kills him, and then himself flies.

     First the citizens, and then the Prince, the Mountagues, the Capulets and others arrive. Benvolio gives his account of events. The Prince banishes Romeo.

3.2   In her bedroom, Juliet waits impatiently for the night. Her Nurse arrives with the rope-ladder and the news that Romeo has killed Tybalt and been banished. Juliet is upset. The Nurse goes to fetch Romeo.

3.3   In his cell, the Friar tells Romeo of his sentence and tries to comfort him. The Nurse enters with news of Juliet. The Friar advises Romeo to visit Juliet and then to leave for Mantua. While Romeo is in Mantua, the Friar will keep him informed about what is happening in Verona and will try to secure his recall. The Nurse returns to Juliet with the message that Romeo will soon arrive.

3.4　Within Capulets' house, old Capulet tells Paris that he may marry Juliet on Thursday and tells his wife to inform Juliet.

3.5　As dawn breaks on Tuesday, Romeo leaves Juliet's bedroom. Her mother comes to tell her that she will be marrying Paris on Thursday. Juliet protests. When her father arrives, he threatens to throw her out of his house if she refuses. After her parents have left, the Nurse advises Juliet to marry Paris. Juliet leaves to go to confession at Friar Lawrence's cell.

4.1　When Juliet arrives, Paris is making arrangements with the Friar to marry her. Paris leaves to allow her to confess. Friar Lawrence gives Juliet a liquor to drink on Wednesday night which will make her appear to have died. This effect lasts for forty-two hours. In this time she will be placed in the Capulets' tomb. Meanwhile, the Friar will have recalled Romeo to Verona, so that when Juliet awakes Romeo can take her back with him to Mantua.

4.2　Having gone home, Juliet announces to her parents and Nurse that she is happy to marry Paris. Her father decides that she shall marry on the next morning, a day earlier than planned.

4.3　In her bedroom, Juliet dismisses her Nurse and her mother. Then she drinks the liquor.
　　The next morning all are busy with preparations. The Nurse discovers that Juliet is 'dead'. While the family laments, the Friar offers comfort and sets the preparations for the funeral in motion. The Nurse dismisses the musicians, whom Peter, a servant, refuses to pay.

5.1　In a street in Mantua, Romeo hears of Juliet's death from Balthasar, his servant. Having sent Balthasar for horses by which to travel to Verona, he buys poison from an impoverished apothecary.

5.2　In his cell, Friar Lawrence learns from Friar John that Romeo has not received his message that Juliet is not truly dead. He sends Friar John for a crow bar, and sets off himself for the Capulets' tomb, where Juliet has been interred.

5.3　In the churchyard, Paris is placing flowers on Juliet's tomb.

Warned by his page that someone is coming, he hides. Romeo enters and dismisses Balthasar, who decides to remain in the churchyard. Then Romeo opens the tomb. Recognizing Romeo, Paris attacks him and is killed. Romeo lays Paris beside Juliet, as he had requested, and, after kissing Juliet, drinks poison and dies.

The Friar enters the tomb as Juliet awakes. She refuses to leave Romeo, and the Friar departs, fearing the arrival of the watch. When they arrive, Juliet stabs herself and dies.

The watch discover the dead and then search the churchyard, where they find Balthasar and the Friar. The Prince arrives, followed by the old Capulet and his wife, and finally old Mountague. Mountague's wife, made unhappy by Romeo's banishment, has died earlier that night.

The Friar, Balthasar and Paris's Page in turn recount what they know of events. A letter Romeo had written to his father explains what they cannot know. Capulet and Mountague give up their feud and agree to raise statues to commemorate their children's love for one another. The Prince dismisses everyone.

ACKNOWLEDGEMENTS

Acknowledgements are due to the copyright holders of the extracts reprinted in the Perspectives on *Romeo and Juliet* section of this edition.

DRAMA
IN EVERYMAN

A SELECTION

Everyman and Medieval Miracle Plays

EDITED BY A. C. CAWLEY
A selection of the most popular medieval plays **£3.99**

Complete Plays and Poems

CHRISTOPHER MARLOWE
The complete works of this fascinating Elizabethan in one volume **£5.99**

Complete Poems and Plays

ROCHESTER
The most sexually explicit – and strikingly modern – writing of the seventeenth century **£5.99**

Restoration Plays

Five comedies and two tragedies representing the best of the Restoration stage **£7.99**

Female Playwrights of the Restoration: Five Comedies

Rediscovered literary treasures in a unique selection **£5.99**

Poems and Plays

OLIVER GOLDSMITH
The most complete edition of Goldsmith available **£4.99**

Plays, Poems and Prose

J. M. SYNGE
The most complete edition of Synge available **£6.99**

Plays, Prose Writings and Poems

OSCAR WILDE
The full force of Wilde's wit in one volume **£4.99**

A Doll's House/The Lady from the Sea/The Wild Duck

HENRIK IBSEN
A popular selection of Ibsen's major plays **£3.99**

£2.99

£2.99

£2.99

AVAILABILITY

All books are available from your local bookshop or direct from
Littlehampton Book Services Cash Sales, 14 Eldon Way, LinesideEstate, Littlehampton, West Sussex BN17 7HE. PRICES ARE SUBJECT TO CHANGE.

To order any of the books, please enclose a cheque (in £ sterling) made payable to Littlehampton Book Services, or phone your order through with credit card details (Access, Visa or Mastercard) on 0903 721596 (24 hour answering service) stating card number and expiry date. Please add £1.25 for package and postage to the total value of your order.

POETRY
IN EVERYMAN

A SELECTION

Silver Poets of the Sixteenth Century

EDITED BY
DOUGLAS BROOKS-DAVIES
A new edition of this famous
Everyman collection **£6.99**

Complete Poems

JOHN DONNE
The father of metaphysical verse in
this highly-acclaimed edition **£4.99**

Complete English Poems, Of Education, Areopagitica

JOHN MILTON
An excellent introduction to
Milton's poetry and prose **£6.99**

Selected Poems

JOHN DRYDEN
A poet's portrait of Restoration
England **£4.99**

Selected Poems

PERCY BYSSHE SHELLEY
'The essential Shelley' in one
volume **£3.50**

Women Romantic Poets 1780-1830: An Anthology

Hidden talent from the Romantic era,
rediscovered for the first time **£5.99**

Poems in Scots and English

ROBERT BURNS
The best of Scotland's greatest lyric
poet **£4.99**

Selected Poems

D. H. LAWRENCE
A newly-edited selection spanning
the whole of Lawrence's literary
career **£4.99**

The Poems

W. B. YEATS
Ireland's greatest lyric poet
surveyed in this ground-breaking
edition **£6.50**

£5.99

£4.99

£3.50

AVAILABILITY

All books are available from your local bookshop or direct from
**Littlehampton Book Services Cash Sales, 14 Eldon Way, LinesideEstate,
Littlehampton, West Sussex BN17 7HE.** PRICES ARE SUBJECT TO CHANGE.

To order any of the books, please enclose a cheque (in £ sterling) made payable to
Littlehampton Book Services, or phone your order through with credit card details (Access,
Visa or Mastercard) on 0903 721596 (24 hour answering service) stating card number and
expiry date. Please add £1.25 for package and postage to the total value of your order.

PHILOSOPHY AND RELIGIOUS WRITING IN EVERYMAN

A SELECTION

An Essay Concerning Human Understanding

JOHN LOCKE
A central work in the development of modern philosophy **£4.99**

Philosophical Writings

GOTTFRIED WILHELM LEIBNIZ
The only paperback edition available **£3.99**

Critique of Pure Reason

IMMANUEL KANT
The capacity of the human intellect examined **£6.99**

A Discourse on Method, Meditations, and Principles

RENE DESCARTES
Takes the theory of mind over matter into a new dimension **£4.99**

Philosophical Works including the Works on Vision

GEORGE BERKELEY
An eloquent defence of the power of the spirit in the physical world **£4.99**

The Social Contract and Discourses

JEAN-JAQUES ROUSSEAU
Rousseau's most influential works in one volume **£3.99**

Utilitarianism/OnLiberty/ Considerations on Representative Government

J. S. MILL
Three radical works which transformed political science **£4.99**

Utopia

THOMAS MORE
A critique of contemporary ills allied with a visionary ideal for society **£2.99**

Ethics

SPINOZA
Spinoza's famous discourse on the power of understanding **£4.99**

The Buddha's Philosophy of Man

Ten dialogues representing the cornerstone of early Buddhist thought **£4.99**

Hindu Scriptures

The most important ancient Hindu writings in one volume **£6.99**

Apologia Pro Vita Sua

JOHN HENRY NEWMAN
A moving and inspiring account of a Christian's spiritual journey **£5.99**

AVAILABILITY

All books are available from your local bookshop or direct from
Littlehampton Book Services Cash Sales, 14 Eldon Way, LinesideEstate, Littlehampton, West Sussex BN17 7HE. PRICES ARE SUBJECT TO CHANGE.

To order any of the books, please enclose a cheque (in £ sterling) made payable to Littlehampton Book Services, or phone your order through with credit card details (Access, Visa or Mastercard) on 0903 721596 (24 hour answering service) stating card number and expiry date. Please add £1.25 for package and postage to the total value of your order.

ESSAYS, CRITICISM AND HISTORY IN EVERYMAN

A SELECTION

The Embassy to Constantinople and Other Writings

LIUDPRAND OF CREMONA
An insider's view of political machinations in medieval Europe
£5.99

The Rights of Man

THOMAS PAINE
One of the great masterpieces of English radicalism **£4.99**

Speeches and Letters

ABRAHAM LINCOLN
A key document of the American Civil War **£4.99**

Essays

FRANCIS BACON
An excellent introduction to Bacon's incisive wit and moral outlook **£3.99**

Puritanism and Liberty: Being the Army Debates (1647-49) from the Clarke Manuscripts

A fascinating revelation of Puritan minds in action **£7.99**

History of His Own Time

BISHOP GILBERT BURNET
A highly readable contemporary account of the Glorious Revolution of 1688 **£7.99**

Biographia Literaria

SAMUEL TAYLOR COLERIDGE
A masterpiece of criticism, marrying the study of literature with philosophy **£4.99**

Essays on Literature and Art

WALTER PATER
Insights on culture and literature from a major voice of the 1890s **£3.99**

Chesterton on Dickens: Criticisms and Appreciations

A landmark in Dickens criticism, rarely surpassed **£4.99**

Essays and Poems

R. L. STEVENSON
Stevenson's hidden treasures in a new selection **£4.99**

£3.99

£4.99

SAGAS AND OLD ENGLISH LITERATURE IN EVERYMAN

A SELECTION

Egils saga
TRANSLATED BY
CHRISTINE FELL
A gripping story of Viking exploits in Iceland, Norway and Britain
£4.99

Edda
SNORRI STURLUSON
TRANSLATED BY
ANTHONY FAULKES
The first complete English translation
£5.99

The Fljotsdale Saga and The Droplaugarsons
TRANSLATED BY
ELEANOR HAWORTH
AND JEAN YOUNG
A brilliant portrayal of life and times in medieval Iceland
£3.99

The Anglo-Saxon Chronicle
TRANSLATED BY
G. N. GARMONSWAY
A fascinating record of events in ancient Britain
£4.99

Anglo-Saxon Poetry
TRANSLATED BY
S. A. J. BRADLEY
A widely acclaimed collection
£6.99

AVAILABILITY

All books are available from your local bookshop or direct from
**Littlehampton Book Services Cash Sales, 14 Eldon Way, LinesideEstate,
Littlehampton, West Sussex BN17 7HE.** PRICES ARE SUBJECT TO CHANGE.

To order any of the books, please enclose a cheque (in £ sterling) made payable to
Littlehampton Book Services, or phone your order through with credit card details (Access,
Visa or Mastercard) on 0903 721596 (24 hour answering service) stating card number and
expiry date. Please add £1.25 for package and postage to the total value of your order.

MEDIEVAL LITERATURE IN EVERYMAN

A SELECTION

Canterbury Tales

GEOFFREY CHAUCER

EDITED BY A. C. CAWLEY

The complete medieval text with translations **£3.99**

Arthurian Romances

CHRÉTIEN DE TROYES

TRANSLATED BY D. D. R. OWEN

Classic tales from the father of Arthurian romance **£5.99**

Everyman and Medieval Miracle Plays

EDITED BY A. C. CAWLEY

A fully representative selection from the major play cycles **£3.99**

Fergus of Galloway: Knight of King Arthur

TRANSLATED BY D. D. R. OWEN

Scotland's own Arthurian romance **£3.99**

The Vision of Piers Plowman

WILLIAM LANGLAND

EDITED BY A. V. C. SCHMIDT

The only complete edition of the B-version available **£4.99**

Sir Gawain and the Green Knight, Pearl, Cleanness, Patience

EDITED BY A. C. CAWLEY AND J. J. ANDERSON

Four major English medieval poems in one volume **£3.99**

Six Middle English Romances

EDITED BY MALDWYN MILLS

Tales of heroism and piety **£4.99**

Ywain and Gawain, Sir Percyvell of Gales, The Anturs of Arther

EDITED BY MALDWYN MILLS

Three Middle English romances portraying the adventures of Gawain **£5.99**

The Birth of Romance: An Anthology

TRANSLATED BY JUDITH WEISS

The first-ever English translation of these fascinating Anglo-Norman romances **£4.99**

Brut

LAWMAN

TRANSLATED BY ROSAMUND ALLEN

A major new translation of the earliest myths and history of Britain **£7.99**

The Piers Plowman Tradition

EDITED BY HELEN BARR

Four medieval poems of political and religious dissent – widely available for the first time **£5.99**

Love and Chivalry: An Anthology of Middle English Romance

EDITED BY JENNIFER FELLOWS

A unique collection of tales of courtly love and heroic deeds **£5.99**

AVAILABILITY

All books are available from your local bookshop or direct from
Littlehampton Book Services Cash Sales, 14 Eldon Way, LinesideEstate, Littlehampton, West Sussex BN17 7HE. PRICES ARE SUBJECT TO CHANGE.

To order any of the books, please enclose a cheque (in £ sterling) made payable to Littlehampton Book Services, or phone your order through with credit card details (Access, Visa or Mastercard) on 0903 721596 (24 hour answering service) stating card number and expiry date. Please add £1.25 for package and postage to the total value of your order.